# THE STU
## COMPA

**Terry O'Brien** is an academician by vocation and a passionate quiz enthusiast by avocation. His leit-motif is the igniting of quizzing instinct and an aptitude to develop the 3 Rs of learning: Read. Record. Recall. He is a Trainer's Trainer and a motivational speaker. He has written several books. His flair for writing and speaking comes naturally to him.

# THE STUDENTS' COMPANION

TERRY O'BRIEN

**RUPA**

Published by
Rupa Publications India Pvt. Ltd 2013
7/16, Ansari Road, Daryaganj
New Delhi 110002

*Sales centres:*
Allahabad Bengaluru Chennai
Hyderabad Jaipur Kathmandu
Kolkata Mumbai

ISBN: 978-81-291-1995-7

Fourth impression 2015

10 9 8 7 6 5 4

The moral right of the author has been asserted.

Typeset by Innovative Processors, New Delhi

Printed at Shree Maitrey Printech Pvt. Ltd., Noida

# CONTENTS

# PREFACE

*A little knowledge is a dangerous thing*
*Drink deep or taste not the Peirian spring*

*–Alexander Pope*

Here comes a book as a 'Companion' to equip one with fundamentals of the overall landscape of knowledge.

This is a ready reference handbook for students of all levels, professionals and those who pursue learning and information with a passion.

Happy reading!

Terry O'Brien

# PART ONE

# WORD POWER TODAY

We live in an age of constant oral and written expressions. In a time when our knowledge is increasing with breathless speed, particularly in specialised areas, it is important that we understand each other by having a better comprehension of some "old" words, "new" words, most of which are "borrowed" but always with every possible effort to present the "true" origins and current usages of those words. This is what *Word Power Today* is all about.

## INTERNET ABBREVIATIONS

**BISLY** But I Still Love You

**ITSFWI** If The Shoe Fits, Wear It!

**BFF** Best friends, forever!

**WIBAMU** Well, I'll be a Monkey's Uncle!

**BTAIM** Be That As It May

**TTYL** Talk To You Later

**IIRC** If I Recall Correctly...

**AFAIK** As Far as I Know

**WRT** With Respect To

**NSFW** Not Safe for Workplace Viewing (warning that there is sexual or repulsive content)

**NWT** New With Tags

**OTOH** On the Other Hand

**AFK** Away from Keyboard

**ASL** Age/Sex/Location?

**TPTB** The Powers that Be

**JMHO** Just My Humble Opinion

**IMHO** In My Humble Opinion

**OATUS** On a Totally Unrelated Subject

**PMFJI** Pardon Me for Jumping In

**SFSG** So Far, So Good

**TC** Take Care!

**BTHOM** Beats the Hell Out of Me

**SGTM** Sounds Good to Me!

**O RLY** Oh, Really (sarcasm)

**OP** The Original Poster (who started this discussion thread)

**WB** Welcome Back

**IDK** I Don't Know

**LBW** Love and best wishes

**OOAK** One of a Kind

**MEGO** My Eyes Glaze Over

**IBTL** In Before the Lock!

**BBIAB** Be Back in a Bit

**SASA** Short and Sweet Reply

**YMMV** Your Mileage May Vary

**MTFBWY** May the Force Be With You

**NIMBY** Not in My Back Yard

**MT** Mistell (mistaken chat message, please disregard)

**AMAIR** As Much as I Recall

**KISS** Keep It Short and Simple

## INTERNET ETIQUETTE

- NETHICS: Ethics on the Net
- BRB: Be Right Back
- The "Golden Rule" of Netiquette is: Remember the human
- "Lurk before you leap" in cyberspace: It's important to get the lay of the land before jumping in
- "Flaming" is: Sending derogatory email or "verbally" attacking someone in a chat
- A "newbie": They are new to the internet or the chat room
- "You have pm": They have sent you a "private message" or email
- "Internet troll": Someone who participates in a message board or chat with intentions of disrupting it in some way
- ACK : Acknowledged
- HTH: "Hope this helps" "Happy to help"
- SCREAM: Write in all capital letters
- HAND: Have a nice day

## DANCE WORDS

Dance seems to be a lot like ice cream flavours...it's so hard to choose just one. If you are thinking of trying out a new dance style, there may be a few you haven't even considered.

BALLET: Ballet uses music and dance to tell stories. Ballet dancers have the ability to transport an audience to another world.

JAZZ Many jazz dancers mix different styles into their dancing, incorporating their own expression. Jazz dancing often uses bold, dramatic body movements, including body isolations and contractions.

TAP: Tap dancers use their feet like drums to create rhythmic patterns and timely beats.

HIP-HOP: Hip-hop is a dance style, usually danced to hip-hop music, that evolved from the hip-hop culture. Hip-hop includes various moves such as breaking, popping, locking and krumping, and even house dance.

MODERN DANCE: Modern dance was created as a rebellion against classical ballet, emphasising creativity in choreography and performance.

SWING DANCE: Swing dance is a lively dance style in which couples swing, spin and jump together. Swing dancing is a general term that means dancing to swing music, or music that "swings".

CONTRA DANCE: Contra dance is a form of American folk dance in which the dancers form two parallel lines and perform a sequence of dance movements with different partners down the length of the line.

COUNTRY AND WESTERN DANCE: Country and western dance includes several dance forms, usually danced to country-western music.

FLAMENCO DANCE: Flamenco dance is an expressive dance form that mixes percussive footwork with intricate hand, arm and body movements. Flamenco is a Spanish art consisting of three forms: Cante, the song, Baile, the dance, and Guitarra, guitar playing.

LATIN DANCE: Latin dance is a fast-paced, often sensual, partner dance characterised by sexy hip movements. However, hip movements are not intentional in any of the Latin dances. The hip motion is a natural consequence of changing weight from one foot to the other.

FOLK DANCE : Folk dance refers to a variety of dances developed by groups or communities, as opposed to being made up by a choreographer.

SALSA: Salsa is a Latin dance form with origins from the Cuban Son-Salsa is normally a partner dance, although there are forms such as a line dance form "Salsa suelta", where the dancers dance individually and a round dance form "Rueda de Casino" where multiple couples exchange partners in a circle. Salsa can be improvised or performed with a set routine.

## WORDS DENOTING NUMBERS

A faculty of academics

A stand of arms

A conflagration of arsonists

A park of artillery

A belt of asteroids

A culture of bacteria

A poverty of pipers

A festival of balloons

A shower of bastards

A bevy of beauties

A flotilla of boats

A cluster of bombs

A blush of boys

A shuffle of bureaucrats

A flock of bustards

A draught of butlers

A rabble of butterflies

A rainbow of butterflies

A coalition of cheetahs

An intrusion of cockroaches

A roll of coins

A cluster of computers

A convocation of eagles

A clashing of economists

A pain of ex-wives

An impatience of wives

A caste of flowerpots

A giggle of girls

A cloud of gnats

A pantheon of gods

A wisdom of grandparents

A cloud of grasshoppers

A cluster of grasshoppers

An arsenal of guns

A battery of guns

A bloat of hippopotamuses

A crash of hippopotamuses

An argumentation of historians

A charm of hummingbirds

A shimmer of hummingbirds

A multiply of husbands

An unhappiness of husbands

A wealth of information

A cache of jewels

A mob of kangaroos

A huddle of lawyers

A colony of lepers

A lounge of lizards

A number of mathematicians

A riches of matrons

A gallimaufry of noises

A superfluity of nuns

A rope of onions

An illusion of painters

A ponder of philosophers

A poverty of pipers

A kindness of ravens

A descent of relatives

A confraternity of smokers

## Words denoting numbers (*contd.*)

A quarrel of sparrows

A disguising of tailors

A pool of typists

A spawn of umbrellas

A mob of wallabies of wives

An impatience of wives

A trip of wildfowl

A plump of wildfowl

A coven of witches

A bond of women

A clew of worms

A swarm of sycophants

A leaning of left-wingers

An absolution of priests

A press of journalists

A consideration of judges

A patience of saints

A crash of computers

An irritation of mobile/cell phones

An anorexia of supermodels

A smirk of estate agents

An attitude of teenagers

A decline of men

An ascension of women

An idiocy of reality television contestants

A clinch of lovers

A loneliness of long-distance runners

## *Non-animal group words*

A company of actors

A host of angels

A claque of hired applauders

A sheaf of arrows

A troupe of artiste

A field of athletes

A hand of bananas

A batch of bread

A rooks of building

A sheaf of corn

A bale of cotton

A shock or fell of hair

A truss of hay

A hamlet of houses in a village

A panel of jurymen

A bevy of ladies

A rouleau of money

A rope of pearls

An anthology of poems

A posse of police to quell a mob

A pencil of rays

A nest of shelves

## *Non-animal group words* (contd.)

A board of directors

A chest of drawers

A clutch of eggs

A bunting of flags

A bouquet of flowers

A crate of fruits

A tuft of grass

A caffle or gang or cluster of stars

A set of tools

A clump of trees

A stack of wood

A skein of woolen threads

A gang of workmen

## ANIMALS – NOUNS OF ASSEMBLY

a herd of antelope

a shrewdness of apes

a pack or herd of asses

a nest of ants

a cete of badgers

a sleuth of bears (sloth)

a stud of mares

a swarm or grist of bees

a chattering of choughs

a covert of coots

a murder of crows

a litter of cubs

a herd of deer

a paddling of ducks (in water)

a team of ducks (in flight)

a gang of elk

a fesnyng of ferrets

a shoal, draught or haul of fishes

a swarm of flies

a flock or flight of birds

a sedge or siege of bitterns

a sounder of boars

a brace or leash of bucks

a herd of buffaloes

a drove or herd of cattle

a clowder of cats

a brood or peep of chicken

a labour of moles

a troop of monkeys

a barren of mules

a watch of nightingales

a parliament of owls

a yoke, drove or team of oxen

a covey of partridges

a muster of peacocks

a nye or nide of pheasants

a flock or flight of pigeons

a wing or congregation of plovers

## Animals – nouns of assembly *(contd.)*

a skulke of foxes
a gaggle of geese (on ground)
a skein of geese (in flight)
a herd or tribe or trip of goats
a charm of goldfinches
a covey of grouse
a colony of gulls (breeding)
a down or husk of hares
a cast of hawks
a brood of hens
a sedge or siege of herons
a shoal of herrings
a pack or mute of hounds
a swarm of insects
a troop of kangaroos
a kindle of kittens
an exaltation of larks
a leap of leopards
a pride of lions

a school of propoises
a litter of pups
a bevy of quails
a nest of rabbits
crash of rhinoceroses
a building or clamour of rooks
a herd or pod of seals
a flock of sheep
a host of sparrows
a murmuration of starlings
a flight of swallows
a herd or bevy of swans
a sounder or drift of swine
a knot of toads
a rafter of turkeys
a school or pd of whales
a pod of whiting
a pack, rout or herd of wolves
a fall of woodcock

# WORDS DENOTING PLACES

| | |
|---|---|
| A house or shelter of a Kirghis | kabitka |
| A house or shelter of an American Indian | wigwam, tepee |
| A house or shelter of an Arab | dowar |
| A house or shelter of a Swiss peasant | chalet |
| A place where birds are kept | aviary |
| A place where bees are kept | apiary |
| A place where fishes are kept | aquarium |
| A place where rabbits are kept | hutch |
| A place where pigs are kept | sty |

## Words denoting places (*contd.*)

| | |
|---|---|
| A place for keeping or breeding insect's | insectariums |
| A house or shelter of an Eskimo | igloo |
| A house or shelter of a gipsy | caravan |
| A Zulu village | kraal |
| A house or shelter for a dog | kennel |
| A house or shelter for a horse | stable |
| A house or shelter for a cow | pen, byre |
| A house or box in which live pigeons or doves | dovecot |
| A dwelling-place of an animal underground | burrow |
| A home of a lion | den |
| A squirrel's home | drey |
| A resting place of a wild animal | lair |
| A house or bed of a hare | form |
| A nest of a bird of prey | eyrie, aerie |
| A place where medicines are compounded | dispensary |
| A place for the treatment of sick people | hospital |
| A residence for monks or priests | monastery |
| A residence for nuns | convent |
| A place where milk is converted into butter and cheese | dairy |
| A place where bread and cakes are made | bakery |
| A place where animals are slaughtered for the market | abattoir |
| A factory for manufacturing beer | brewery |
| A place where spirituous liquors are produced | distillery |
| A place where clothes are washed and ironed | laundry |
| A place for housing cars | garage |
| A place for housing aeroplanes | hanger |
| A place where travellers may obtain lodging and refreshment | hotel, inn |
| A place where people may obtain food and refreshment | restaurant |
| A variety show performed in a restaurant | cabaret |

## Words denoting places (*contd.*)

| | |
|---|---|
| A kitchen of a ship | caboose, galley |
| A house for the residence of students | hostel |
| A place where books are kept | library |
| A place where Government records are kept | archives |
| A place where any manufacture is carried on | factory |
| A place where scientific experiments are conducted | laboratory |
| A place where house refuse is reduced to ashes | incinerator |
| A place where athletic exercises are performed | gymnasium |
| A place or room for the collection of dried plants | herbarium |
| A place where treasures of art, curiosities, etc.are preserved or exhibited | museum |
| A place where treasures, stores, ammunition are hidden | cache |
| A place for storing grain | granary |
| A place where goods are stored | depot |
| An upper room or storey immediately under the roof | garret |
| A place where leather is tanned | tannery |
| A building for the lodging and accommodation of soldiers | barracks |
| A place where soldiers are quartered | cantonment |
| A place where money is coined | mint |
| A place where astronomical observations are taken | observatory |
| A place where fruit trees are grown | orchard |
| A place where orphans are housed | orphanage |
| An institution for the reformation of young offenders | reformatory |
| A square courtyard bounded by buildings | quadrangle |
| A wide road lined with trees on both sides | avenue, boulevard |
| A street open only at one end | cul-de-sac |
| A Muslim place of worship | mosque |
| A place where water is collected and stored | reservoir |
| A place frequented for reasons of pleasure or health | resort |

## Words denoting places (*contd.*)

| | |
|---|---|
| A place with gambling tables, etc. | casino |
| A nursery where children of parents are cared for while their parents are at work | crèche |
| An enclosure adjoining a race-course where horses are kept before racing | paddock |
| A covered stall at a fair, horse races, etc. | booth |
| A place where plates, dishes, pots and other cooking utensils are washed up | scullery |
| A place where ships are repaired or built | dock |
| A place where ships are loaded and unloaded | quay |
| The sleeping-rooms in a college or public institution | dormitory |
| A refreshment hall in monasteries and convents | refectory |
| A school for infants and young children | kindergarten |
| A room or building for the preservation of sculpture | glyptotheca |
| A place where animals are kept alive, and live as nearly as possible as in their natural state | vivarium |
| A receptable for storing coal | bunker, scuttle |
| A small box in which tea is kept | caddy |
| A large cask for holding wine or beer | butt, hogshead |
| An underground place for storing wine or other provisions | cellar |
| A portable case for holding papers, drawings, etc. | portfolio |
| An ornamental glass bottle for holding wine or other alcoholic drinks | decanter |
| A small bottle for holding sauces or condiment for the table | cruet |
| A case in which the blade of swords are kept | sheath, scabbard |
| A basket in which a fisherman puts his fish | creel |
| A lady's handbag or workbag | reticule |
| A large jug or pitcher for holding water for the washbasin | ewer |

## TRADES AND PROFESSIONS

| | |
|---|---|
| One who is a falconer | accipitrary |
| One who is an expert in statistics | actuary |
| One who is a travelling salesman | bagman |
| One who collects rags and bones | bunter |
| One who is a fortune teller and uses cards | cartomancer |
| One who is a pedlar (of cheap goods) | duffer |
| One who attends to the diseases of the eye | oculist |
| One who tests eyesight and sells spectacles | optician |
| One who attends to sick people and prescribes medicines | physician |
| One who compounds or sells drugs | druggist, pharmacist |
| One who attends to the teeth | dentist |
| One skilled in the care of hands and feet | chiropodist |
| One who treats diseases by rubbing the muscles | masseur |
| A physician who assists women at child-birth | obstetrician, accoucheur |
| One who drives a motor-car | chauffeur |
| One who manages or attends to an engine | engineer |
| One who is in-charge of a ship | captain |
| The commander of a fleet | admiral |
| One who carves in stone | sculptor |
| One who cuts precious stones | lapidary, lapidist |
| One who writes for the newspapers | correspondent, journalist, reporter |
| One who sets type for books, newspapers etc. | compositor |
| One who plans | draughtsman |
| One who deals in flowers | florist |
| One who deals in fruits | fruiterer |
| One who deals in cattle | drover |
| One who sells fruits, vegetables, etc., from a barrow | costermonger |
| One who makes eyes in needles used for sewing | eyes |

## Trades and professions (*contd.*)

| | |
|---|---|
| One who is a hair dresser | friseur |
| One who is a midwife | grace wife |
| One who is a brick layer's labourer | hod |
| One who is a young male assistant | jack |
| One who gathers and sells garlic | maderer |
| One who deals in iron and hardware | ironmonger |
| One who deals in medicinal herbs | herbalist |
| One who deals in fish | fishmonger |
| One who deals in furs | furrier |
| One who works in brass | brazier |
| One who sets glass in lead, esp. mending water pipes | plumber |
| One who attends to the fire of a steam engine | stoker |
| One who makes barrels, tubs, etc. | cooper |
| One employed as a labourer to do excavating work | navvy |
| One who makes and sells ladies hats | milliner |
| One who sells small articles such as ribbons, laces, thread | haberdasher |
| One who deals in clothes and other fabrics | draper |
| One who deals in silks, cotton, woolen, and linen goods | mercer |
| A professional rider in horse races | jockey |
| One who shoes horses | farrier |
| One who looks after horses at an inn | ostler, hostler |
| One who studies rocks and soils | geologist |
| One who studies the past through objects left behind | archaeologist |
| One who studies the stars | astronomer |
| One who foretells things by the stars | astrologer |
| One who flies an aeroplane | pilot |
| One who works in a coal-mine | collier |
| One who converts raw hide into leather | tanner |
| One who makes or deals in cutting instruments, e.g.knives | cutler |

## Trades and professions (*contd.*)

| | |
|---|---|
| One who cleans the street | scavenger |
| One who is (woman) employed to clean inside buildings | charwoman |
| One who sells sweets and pastries | confectioner |
| One who induces or entraps men to serve in the army or navy | crimp |
| One who is an auctioneer | out crier |
| One who is a thief | puggard |
| One who interprets dreams | redar |
| One who prepares the body for burial | streaker |
| One who is a dyer | tinctor |
| One who is a weaver | wabster |
| One collects the bets and pays out to the winner in a gambling club | croupier |
| One who takes care of a building | janitor |
| One who sells fowls, ducks, turkeys, etc. | poulterer |
| One who pays out money at a bank | cashier, teller |
| One who makes and sells cushions and covers for chairs, motor-car seats etc. | upholsterer |
| One who lends money at exorbitant interest | usurer |
| One who draws maps | cartographer |
| One who collects postage stamps | philatelist |
| One who performs tricks by sleight of hand | conjuror, prestidigitator, juggler |
| One who walks on ropes | funambulist |
| One who performs daring gymnastic feats | acrobat |
| One who pastures cattle for the market | grazier |
| One who travels from place to place selling miscellaneous articles | huckster, pedlar, chapman, hawker |
| One who makes pots, cups, etc. | potter |

## Trades and professions (*contd.*)

| | |
|---|---|
| One who goes from place to place mending pots, pans etc. | tinker |
| One who mends shoes | shoemaker, cobbler |
| One who travels from place to place selling religious articles | colporteur |
| One who watches over students taking an examination | invigilator |
| One who is incharge of a museum | curator |
| One who is in charge of giving assistance to the hospital welfare officer | almoner |
| One who is incharge of a library | librarian |
| One who is head of college | principal |
| One who is head of a town council or corporation | mayor |
| One who lends money and keeps goods as security | pawnbroker |
| One who draws up contracts and also lends money on interest | scrivener |
| One who builds ships | shipwright |
| One who loads and unloads ships | stevedore |
| One who makes wheels for carriages and carts | wheelwright |
| One who sells articles at public sales | auctioneer |
| One who is a tradesman who manages funerals | undertaker |
| One skilled in the treatment of diseases of animals | veterinarian |
| One who writes shorthand | stenographer |
| One who writes poetry | poet |
| One who writes novels | novelist |
| One who writes books | author |
| One who compiles a dictionary | lexicographer |
| One who sells paper, ink, pens and writing materials | stationer |
| One who preserves the skins of animals and mounts them so as to resemble the living animals | taxidermist |
| One versed in the science of human races, their varieties and origin | ethnologist |
| One who studies the evolution of mankind | anthropologist |

## Trades and professions (*contd.*)

| | |
|---|---|
| One who studies the working of the human mind | psychologist |
| One who makes or sells candles | chandler |
| One who works or deals in feathers for apparel | plumassier |
| One who is the treasurer of a college or university | bursar |
| An officer in charge of the stores, provisions and accounts on a ship | purser |

## TYPES OF PEOPLE

| | |
|---|---|
| One who is difficult to please | Fastidious |
| One who has no sympathy | Callous |
| One who easily believes | Credulous |
| One who can easily be cheated | Gullible |
| One who believes in fate | Fatalist |
| One who believes in offering equal opportunity to women in every sphere | Feminist |
| One who abstains from alcohol | Teetotaller |
| One who is wild and extravagant in opinion, particulary in religious matters | Fanatic |
| One who is indifferent to pleasure and pain | Stoic |
| One devoted to pleasure of eating and drinking | Epicurist |
| One who derives pleasure from inflicting or watching cruelty | Sadist |
| One who is given to withdrawing from others | Introvert |
| One who is not given to introspection | Extrovert |
| One who is having both the qualities of an introvert and an extrovert | Ambivert |
| One who looks on the dark side of things | Pessimist |
| One who looks on the bright side of things | Optimist |
| One who understands many languages | Polyglot |

## Types of people (*contd.*)

| | |
|---|---|
| One who does not believe in the existence of God | Atheist |
| One who doubts the existence of God | Agnostic |
| One who delights to speak about himself or thinks only of his own welfare | Egotist |
| One who devotes his life to the welfare and interest of other people | Altruist |
| One who has an irresistible desire for alcoholic drinks | Dipsomaniac |
| One who hates cigarette smoking | Misocapnic |
| One who hates mankind | Misanthrope |
| One who devotes his service or wealth for the love of mankind | Philanthropist |
| One who walks in his sleep | Somnambulist |
| One who talks in his sleep | Somniloquist |
| One who has the art of speaking in such a way that the sound seems to come from another person | Ventriloquist |
| One who can use both his hands | Ambidextrous |
| One who is a hard working person | Industrious |
| One who is a sensible and prudent person | Judicious |
| One who runs away from the law | Fugitive |
| One who takes refuge in a foreign land | Alien |
| One who has an irresistible tendency to steal | Kleptomaniac |
| One who steals books | Biblioklept |
| One who breaks images or church ornaments | Iconoclast |
| One who dies for a noble cause | Martyr |
| One who leads a solitary life | Recluse, hermit |
| One who is compelled by law to serve as a soldier | Conscript |
| One new to anything | Novice |
| One who is a lover of animals | Zoophilist |
| One who engages in any pursuit for the love of it and not for gain | Amateur |
| One who feeds on fruits | Frutarian |

## Types of people (*contd.*)

| | |
|---|---|
| One who feeds on human flesh | Cannibal |
| One who travels from place to place | Itinerant |
| One who begs for alms | Mendicant |
| One who is a critical judge of art and taste | Connoisseur |
| One who is an expert at telling stories | Raconteur |
| One who quietly listens to other peoples conversations | Eavesdropper |
| One who pretends to know a great deal about everything | Mountebank |
| One who imitates the voice and gestures of others | Mimic |
| One who accompanies as a guard to a young lady | Chaperon |
| One who collects coins | Numismatist |
| One who is opposed to intellectual progress | Obscurant |
| One who eats all kinds of food | Pantophagist |
| One who is a woman with light coloured hair | Blonde |
| One who is a woman with dark hair | Brunette |
| One who dresses up women's hair | Coiffeur |
| One who is a noisy and abusive woman | Termagant |
| One who devotes his service for of mankind | Philanthropist |
| One who is a hater of mankind | Misanthrope |
| One who becomes the favourite of a distinguished personage and serves him as a slave | Minion |
| One who sneers at the aims and beliefs of his fellow men | Cynic |
| One who pretends to be a computer genius | Cyberbunny |
| One who is extremely eager or interested | Avid |
| One who has the art of speaking in such a way that the sound seems to come from another person | Ventriloquist |
| One who delights to speak about himself | Egotist |
| One who devotes his life to the welfare and interests of other people | Altruist |
| One who runs away from justice or the law | Fugitive |

## Types of people (*contd.*)

| | |
|---|---|
| One who takes refuge in a foreign country | Refugee, alien |
| One who is banished from his home or his country | Exile |
| One who maliciously sets fire to a building | Incendiary |
| One who has a great interest in someone or something | Fan |
| One who is relaxed, sociable, tolerant, comfort-loving | Endomorph |
| One who is active, assertive, vigorous, combative | Mesomorph |
| One who is quiet, fragile, restrained, non-assertive | Ectomorph |
| One who hides in the shadows of cyberspace | Lurker |
| One who takes first steps in social media | Virgin |
| One who adopts completely new personality online | Changeling |
| One who creates anonymous profiles for fear of giving out personal information | Ghost |
| One who is ready to have an unpleasant way when necessary | Badass |
| One who has a particular condition, personal quality when they were born | Classy |
| One who suffers from the fear of bathing | Ablutophobic |
| One who suffers from the fear of books | Bibliophobic |
| One who denotes mental retardation | Moron |
| One who is a mentally deficient | Idiot, dolt, or dullard |
| One who is full of elegance and high social standing | Nob |
| One who is harmless, not hurtful | Innocuous |
| One who is habitually lazy | Indolent |
| One who journeys on foot | Pedestrian |
| One who journeys to a holy place | Pilgrim |
| One who is a leader of the people who can sway his followers by his oratory | Demagogue |
| One whose reasoning is clever yet false | Sophist |
| One who makes a display of his learning | Pedant |
| One who has special skill in judging art, music, tastes, etc. | Connoisseur |
| One who loves his country and serves it devotedly | Patriot |
| One who foretells events | Prophet |

## Types of people (*contd.*)

| | |
|---|---|
| One devoted to the pleasures of eating and drinking | Epicure |
| One given up to luxurious living | Sybarite |
| One given to sensual pleasures and bodily enjoyment | Voluptuary |
| One who pretends to be what he is not | Hypocrite, impostor |
| One who pretends to know a great deal about everything | Mountebank, charlatan, quack |
| One who imitates the voice, gestures, etc. of another | Mimic |
| One who can enable people speaking different languages to understand each other | Interpreter |
| One versed in many languages | Linguist |
| One who can use both hands | Ambidexter |
| One who entertains another | Host, hostess |
| One who easily believes | Gullible |
| One under the protection of another | Protégé, ward |
| One who searches for minerals or mining sites | Prospector |
| One who is a messenger sent in great haste | Courier |
| One who steers a boat | Coxswain |
| One who bends his body into various shapes | Acrobat |
| One who is a hater of marriage | Misogamist |
| One who is a hater of women | Misogynist |
| One who is in a low state of health, or over-anxious about his health | Valetudinarian |
| One who worries a candidate for election by interruption and awkward questions | Heckler |
| One who tries to get votes for an election candidate | Canvasser |
| One who is an authority on pronunciation | Orthoepist |
| One who is an unthankful person | Ingrate |
| One who is sent out on a mission | Emissary |
| One who collects things belonging to ancient times | Antiquary |
| One who collects coins | Numismatist |

## Types of people (*contd.*)

| | |
|---|---|
| One who has been before another in office or employment | Predecessor |
| One who takes over after another in office or employment | Successor |
| One who kills political figures | Assassin |
| One who is a partner in a crime | Accomplice |
| One who works along with another | Coadjutor |
| One living at the same time as another | Contemporary |
| One who is opposed to intellectual progress | Obscurant |
| One who eats all kinds of food | Pantophagist |
| One who has an irresistible desire for alcoholic drinks | Dipsomaniac, alcoholic |
| One who abstains from alcoholic drinks | Teetotaller |
| One who is a noisy, abusive, scolding woman | Termagant |
| One who hides away on a ship to obtain a free passage | Stowaway |
| One who shoots with bows and arrows | Archer |
| One who fishes with a rod | Angler |

## GOVERNMENT WORDS

| | |
|---|---|
| A region that is independent and has power to govern itself | autonomous |
| A parliament that consists of two separate groups of people involved in making laws | bicameral |
| A country or system in which individual states make their own laws, but a national government is responsible for areas such as defence and foreign policy | a federal |
| Relating to a government | govermental |
| Relating to an empire (the rule of one country over several other countries) | imperial |
| Ruled by its own government, rather than controlled by another country | independent |
| Involving three or more groups, especially the governments of three or more countries | multilateral |

## Government Words (*contd.*)

A state or country has people of several different
     national groups living in it                    multinational

Involving more than one political party             multiparty

Owned or controlled by the government               national

Trying to achieve political independence for a particular
     group, state or nation

A country that does not receive support from a more
     powerful country                               non-aligned

Partly or completely controlled or owned
     by the government                              parastatal

Ruling or controlling people by the use of force or
     violence, or by laws that put unreasonable limits
     on their freedom                               repressive

A nation rules itself                               sovereign

Controlling a country and its people in a very
     strict way, without allowing opposition from
     another political party                        totalitarian

Controlled by officials or politicians who have
     not been elected by the people to
     represent them                                 undemocratic

Controlled by a central government or authority     unitary

Absence of Government                               anarchy

Government of the people, for the people
     and by the people                              democracy

Government by a sovereign with uncontrolled
     authority                          autocracy, despotism

Government by the nobility                          aristocracy

Government by department of state                   bureaucracy

Government by a few                                 oligarchies

Government by the wealthy                           plutocracy

Government by priests or ecclesiastics              hagiocracy

Government by divine guidance                       theocracy

Government of the church by bishops                 episcopacy

Government by a military class                      stratocracy

## Government Words (*contd.*)

| | |
|---|---|
| Government by the worst citizens | kakistocracy |
| The right of self-government | autonomy |
| The science of government | politics |
| A radical change in government | revolution |
| To decide a political question by the direct vote of the whole electorate | referendum |
| The period between two reigns | interregnum |
| One who governs a kingdom during the infancy, absence, or disability of the sovereign | regent |
| The wife or husband of a king or queen | consort |
| An official numbering of the population | census |
| Facts and figures | statistics |
| Relating to politicals absolutism | absolutist |
| A parliament that consists of two separate groups of people involved in making laws | bicameral |

# PHOBIAS
## Modern Phobias

Modern Phobia is a weird and wonderful complaint. The list here may introduce you to some you never knew you had!

- Fear of bills-versurphobia
- Fear of brands-nomenophobia
- Fear of growing old-senecophobia
- Fear of opening email- aperepiphobia
- Fear of not having the remote control-bulliphobia
- Fear of failure- cadophobia
- Fear of going bald-calvophobia
- Fear of going grey-canusophobia
- Fear of politicians-civiliphobia
- Fear of call centres- coetusermophobia
- Fear of eye contact- donoculophobia
- Fear of your boss-duxophobia

## Modern phobias (*contd.*)

- Fear of undressing - exuerphobia
- Fear of using your mobile - frigensophobia
- Fear of the unanswerable questions - illerogophobia
- Fear of being put on hold - inanophobia
- Fear of parking - insistophobia
- Fear of fans - laudaphobia
- Fear of reality television - magnufraterphobia
- Fear of texting - verbaphobia
- Fear of using wrong words - malvocophobia
- Fear of nothing - nihiliphobia
- Fear of one's wife - uxorphobia
- Fear that everyone has a better mobile than you - obsoletophobia
- Fear of escalators - scalaphobia
- Fear of watching something on the wrong channel - pluracanophobia
- Fear of commercial television - proscriptiophobia
- Fear of junk mail - quisquiliaphobia
- Fear of dancing - saltaphobia
- Fear of watching soaps - sapophobia

### More Common Phobias

These are some interesting and unusual words. Many of them **originate** in the fields of medicine and science. Some of them, however, are the coinages of witty journalists.

| Fear of | Condition | Fear of | Condition |
|---------|-----------|---------|-----------|
| air | aerophobia | darkness | scotophobia |
| aloneness | autophobia | dawn | eosophobia |
| animals | zoophobia | death | thonatophobia |
| anything | kainophobia | depths | bathophobia |
| new | neophobia | dirt | mysophobia |
| bad men | scelerophobia | disease | cenophobia |
| barren | space | animals | zoophobia |

## More Common Phobias (*contd.*)

| | | | |
|---|---|---|---|
| blood | hematophobia | dogs | cynophobia |
| bridges | gephyrophobia | dolls | pediophobia |
| burglars | scelerophobia | eating | phagophobia |
| cats | ailurophobia | everything | pantophobia |
| change | kainophobia | failure | kakorrhaphiophobia |
| choking | anginophobia | doctors | iatrophobia |
| cold | psychrophobia | floods | antlophobia |
| contamination | mysophobia | fog | homichlophobia |
| corpses | necrophobia | frogs | batrachophobia |
| crossing streets | dromophobia | forest | hylophobia |
| dampness | hygrophobia | ghosts | phasmophobia |
| height | acrophobia | girls | parthenophobia |
| high objects | batophobia | writing | graphophobia |
| injury | traumatophobia | knife | aichmophobia |
| insects | acarophobia | lice | pediculophobia |
| robber | harpaxophobia | lightning | astraphobia |
| scratches | amychophobia | marriage | gamophobia |
| sin | hamartophobia | medicine | pharmacophobia |
| sleep | hypnophobia | money | chrematophobia |
| snake | ophidiophobia | name | onomatophobia |
| speaking | laliophobia | odour | osmophobia |
| strangers | xenophobia | open spaces | agoraphobia |
| string | linophobia | work | ponophobia |
| touched | aphephobia | pain | algophobia |
| thunder | astraphobia | railroad or train | siderodromophobia |
| time | chronophobia | jealousy | zelophobia |
| travel | hodophobia | responsibility | hypengyophobia |
| vehicle | amaxophobia | heat | thermophobia |
| walking | basiphobia | ridicule | categelophobia |
| women | gynophobia | river | potamophobia |

## PORMANTEAU WORDS

A word formed by merging the sounds and meanings of two different words

- Advertainment      advertisement + entertainment
- Advertorial      advertisement + editorial
- Affluenza      affluence + influenza
- Because      by + cause
- Bionic      biology + electronic
- Bit      binary + digit
- Blog      web+blog
- Brunch      breakfast+ lunch
- Camcorder      camera+ recorder
- Cellophane      cellulose + diaphane
- Chillaxing      chilling+ relaxing
- Chingilish      Chinese+ English
- Cineplex      cinema-complex
- Diabesity      diabetes+obesity
- Dumbfound      dumb+comfound
- Econocrat      economist+bureaucrat
- Edutainment      education+entertainment
- Email      electronic+mail
- Emoticon      emotion+icon
- Fantabulous      fantastic+fabulous
- Fanzine      fan+magazine
- Fortnight      fourteen+nights
- Franglish      French+English
- Freeware      free+software
- Gainsay      against+say
- Globish      global+English
- Glitz      glamour+ritz
- Goodbye      God+be(with)+ye
- Hassle      haggle+tussle
- Hinglish      Hindi+English
- Infomercial      information+communication
- Infotainment      information+entertainment

## Pormanteau words (*contd.*)

- Intercom          internal+communication
- Internet          international+network
- Japlish           Japanese+ English
- Knowledgebase      knowledge+database
- Lox               liquid+oxygen
- Moblog            mobile+weblog
- Modem             modulator+demodulator
- Motel             motor+hotel
- Motorcade          motor+cavalcade
- Multiplex          multiple+complex
- Netiquette         internet+etiquette
- Seascape          sea+landscape
- Sitcom            situation+comedy
- Smaze             smoke+haze
- Smog              smoke+fog
- Soundscape        smoke+fog
- Soundscape        sound+landscape
- Stagflation        stagnation+inflation
- Telegenic          television+photogenic
- Telex             teleprinter+monologue
- Travelogue         travel+monologue
- Tween             teen+between
- Webinar           web+seminar
- WiFi              Wireless+fidelity
- Zonkey            Zebra+donkey

# PHILE WORDS

'*Phile*':Words pertaining to the love of something.
- acrophile          a lover of mountains
- aerophilatelist      one who collects air-mail stamps
- anglophile          a lover of England and/or the English

## Phile words (*contd.*)

- bibliophile          a lover of books
- cartophily           the collecting of cigarette cards
- cumyxaphily          the collecting of match-boxes
- discophily           the collecting of gramophone records
- hippophile           a lover of horses
- peridromophily       the collecting of bus and railway tickets
- philanthrope         a lover of mankind
- stegophily           a lover of climbing buildings
- zoophilist           a lover of animals

## MISO WORDS

*MISO*-Words pertaining to the hate of something.
- misanthrope          a hater of mankind
- misocapnik           one who hates cigarette smoking
- misogamist           one who hates marriage
- misogynist           a person who hates women
- misologist           one who hates learning or knowledge

## MANIA WORDS

*Mania:* An obsession to do something.
- anthomania           a great lover of flowers
- bibliokleptomania    a mental aberration leading to the stealing of books
- dipsomania           the compulsion to drink alcohol
- pyromania            the compulsion to start fires

## OTHERS

- aesthetics           relating to the study or appreciation of beauty
- aficionado           a keen follower of a sport

## Others (*contd.*)

- alopecia — baldness
- amnesia — loss of memory
- anorexia — loss of appetite
- capnomancy — divination from smoke
- cartomancy — divination from playing cards
- cheironomy — the science of expression by means of gestures
- dyslexia — word blindness
- misandry — a morbid fear of men by women
- phonocamptics — the study of echoes
- pyrotechnics — fireworks
- rhabdomancy — divination by rods (dowsing)
- serendipity — an aptitude for making fortunate discoveries accidentally
- syndrome — a set of symptoms

## POTPOURRI

adulterate - to make impure by adding bogus ingredients.

debase - same as adulterate.

inoculate - inject an immunizing agent into.

nebulous - cloudy, hazy, confused.

exorbitant - excessive, inordinate, going beyond usual or proper bounds.

esoteric - understood by a select few. secret; mysterious.

disparity - essentially different, unequal.

addendum - something that is added. as in to the back of a book.

fetid - having an offensive stench.

fastidious - hard to please, over nice.

lambasting - whacking or pounding.

insipid - dull, flavourless

impeccable - without fault or blemish, perfect.

tenure - The holding of something, as in property, office, etc.

transpire - emit, exhale or perspire, happen occur.

predisposition - innate tendency.

innate - existing in one from birth.

## Potpourri (*contd.*)

pernicious - highly destructive.

perplexity - problem, puzzled, make confused.

simpatico - congenial.

conjugate - formed in a pair, coupled. inflection of verbs

effigy - a life size dummy or sculpture of a person.

inflammatory - serving to inflame. excite highly, make violent, aggravate.

paleolithic - pertaining to old stone age.

demitasse - small cup of black coffee.

demeanor - behaviour

ironclad - armoured

iridescent - glittering with changeable colours like a rainbow.

infirm - not in good health.

ingenuous - candid naive, free from guile.

sans - without.

ubiquitous - existing everywhere.

canny - wary, prudent.

cantankerous - perverse in disposition, ill natured.

persecute - harass, make suffer for divergent principals.

persnickety - excessively meticulous.

appease - satisfy an appetite or demand.

verbose -wordy.

reverent - respectful; devout.

irreverent - disrespectful.

paradigm - a list of the inflected forms of a word.

inflect - turn from a direct course; bend.

guile - cunning.

cursory - hasty and superficial a glance.

fortuitous - coming by chance, accidental.

uncanny - weird.

candour - sincerity.

## Potpourri (*contd.*)

proverbial - well known.

axiom - universal proposition. easily proved.

protuberant - bulging out.

diabolic - devilish.

sequester - put aside.

ornery - of ugly disposition, hard to manage.

myopic - near sightedness.

ad hoc - relating exclusively to the subject in question.

judicious - exercising sound judgment; prudent.

consortium - society, association.

caveat - a warning, let the buyer beware.

peruse - read attentively.

smug - self satisfied.

sanctum - a private retreat.

quasi - seemingly or almost, not wholly genuine.

innocuous - harmless.

reticent - silent or reserved.

abate - beat down, diminish, lessen.

abash - make ashamed dispirited.

interim - an intervening time. the meantime.

amicable - friendly, peaceful.

amiable - pleasing, loving, friendly.

confabulate - converse.

conundrum - riddle or hard question.

qualm - sudden sensation of nausea, twinge of conscience.

compunction - same as qualm. slight regret or prick of conscience.

quarrel - dispute.

preamble - a preface, opening remarks.

precarious - uncertain, insecure.

incessant - continuing without interruption.

## Potpourri (*contd.*)

umbrage - resentment.

deplorable - lamentable, calamitous.

calamity - disaster, a great misfortune.

lamentable - regrettable.

specious - apparently, deceptive.

vicarious - substituting for, or feeling in place of, another.

symbiotic - living together of two different species harmoniously.

pabulum - food, insipid thoughts.

sycophant - a servile flatterer.

sybarite - a self indulgent, luxury loving person.

obsequious - fawning, servile, deferential.

defunct - dead.

deference - submission to the judgement of another, respectful.

coquette - a flirt.

copious - abundant, plentiful.

disparage - discredit.

impious - profane, disrespectful, impiety.

impecunious - without money, poor.

regimental - being under strict and uniform control.

regalia - emblems, insignia or personal finery.

myrmidon - one who obeys or follows without question or scruple.

impetuous - impulse, incentive.

apropos - to the purpose, in reference to. adv.

effrontery - barefaced, impropriety, shamelesness, impudence

chutzpa - effrontery, gall.

impudence - gall, offensively forward in behavior, insolent, saucy.

protean - readily assuming many shapes.

protege - a person protected or aided by another.

enamoured - inflame with love, captivate.

oblique - slanting, indirectly aimed or expressed.

opaque - cloudy.

## Potpourri (*contd.*)

propriety - fitness, rightness, correct behaviour, decorum.

decorum - the standards of conduct approved by society, propriety.

prosaic - unromantic, commonplace.

decorous - well behaved, proper.

auspice - flavouring influence; protection. a favourable circumstance.

preclude - impede, prevent.

diminutive - very small or tiny, a small thing or person.

lexicon - a dictionary, special vocabulary.

imminent - likely to occur soon; impending.

eminent - high in rank, office, worth; conspicuous, noteworthy.

gambit - any apparent sacrifice in expectation of later gain.

gam - school of whales.

extrapolate - project on the basis of known data; surmise.

permutation - any possible arrangement of any units in a group.

percipient - perceiving.

parnassus - a centre of or inspiration for poetic or artistic work.

gallivant - seek pleasure frivolously; gad about.

gad - ramble about idly. gadabout, gadder-travels aimlessly.

goad - a sharp stick for driving cattle; to urge.

frivolous - not seriously intended. trivial. silly or giddy.

quagmire - area of muddy ground, marsh. difficult position or
situation.

pukka - genuine, first rate.

ardent - fervent in feeling, intense, passionate. arduous - wearisome.

daunting - intimidating, dicouraging.

germane - closely allied, relevent.

relegate - send away or out of the way, consign, relegation.

tenacious - persistant in an opinion or view, stubborn.

tumultuous - violently disturbing, highly exciting.

pulchritude - beauty.

kudos - praise, glory.

## Potpourri (*contd.*)

inundate - flood, deluge, overwhelm.

sagacious - wise. sagacity.

fusiform - spindle shaped, i.e. streamlined.

macabre - gruesome, dance of death.

godspeed - a wish for success and prosperity.

syllabus - compendium, an abstract.

sylph - imaginery being, a slender woman.

infallible - free from fallacy, trustworthy.

inexorable - not to be persuaded or moved; unrelenting.

arcane - secret.

jettison - throw goods overboard to lighten a ship.

amatory - pertaining to lovemaking.

extenuate - make smaller in degree of appearance.

## PERTAINING TO MARRIAGE

| | |
|---|---|
| One who has only one wife or husband at a time | monogamist |
| One who marries a second wife or husband while the legal spouse is alive | bigamist |
| A man who has more than one wife at a time | polygynist |
| A woman who has more than one husband at a time | polyandrist |
| A hater of marriage | misogamist |
| One vowed to a single or unmarried life | celibate |
| Legal dissolution of the marriage of husband and wife | divorce |
| Payment of money allowed to a wife on legal separation from her husband | alimony |
| A man whose wife is dead | widower |
| A woman whose husband is dead | widow |
| The property which a new wife brings to her husband | dowry |
| Double income, no kids | dinks |
| Alimony paid in a live-in relationship | palimony |

## Pertaining to marriage (*contd.*)

| | |
|---|---|
| One engaged to be married | fiancé, fiancée |
| Engaged to be married | betrothed, affianced |
| A bride's outfit | trousseau |
| Proclamation of intended marriage | banns |
| To rub away with a lover in order to get married secretly | elope |

## SCIENCES AND ARTS

| | |
|---|---|
| An institution for education in the arts and sciences | polytechnic |
| The study of all heavenly bodies and the earth in relation to them | astronomy |
| The art of tilling the soil | agriculture |
| The art of cultivating and managing gardens | horticulture |
| The science of land management | agronomics |
| The science of family descent | genealogy |
| The study of ancient buildings and prehistoric remains | archaeology |
| The study of ancient writings | paleography |
| The art of beautiful handwriting | calligraphy |
| The art of making maps and charts | cartography |
| The art of metal working | metallurgy |
| The study of coins | numismatics |
| The science of numbers | mathematics |
| The science of measuring | mensuration |
| The art of measuring land | surveying |
| The science of triangles | trigonometry |
| The art of preserving skins | taxidermy |
| The art of making fireworks | pyrotechnic |
| The science of colours | chromatics |
| The art of elegant speech or writing | rhetoric |
| The art of effective speaking or oral reading | elocution |
| The art of telling the future by the study of the stars | astrology |

## Sciences and arts (*contd.*)

| | |
|---|---|
| The study of mankind | anthropology |
| The science which deals with the varieties of the human race | ethnology |
| The science of the structure of the human body | anatomy |
| The science which deals with the way in which the human body works | physiology |
| The scientific study of industrial arts | technology |
| The study of the human mind | psychology |
| The study of the human face | physiognomy |
| The study of physical life or living matter | biology |
| The study of plants | botany |
| The natural history of animals | zoology |
| The study of rocks and soils | geology |
| The study of birds | ornithology |
| The study of eggs | otology |
| The study of mountains | otology |
| The study of languages | philology |
| The study of the origin and history of words | etymology |
| The study of stars | astronomy |
| The study of lakes or of pond life | limnology |

## SCIENCES AND STUDIES

Over the past century, the range and scope of scientific endeavours has expanded exponentially, so that practically any field of study has a name associated with it. Most of these terms end in 'ology', from the Greek *logos*, meaning 'word'.

| Word | Definition |
|---|---|
| acarology | study of mites |
| accidence | grammar book; science of inflections in grammar |
| aceology | therapeutics |

## Sciences and studies (*contd.*)

| Word | Definition |
| --- | --- |
| acology | study of medical remedies |
| acoustics | science of sound |
| adenology | study of glands |
| aedoeology | science of generative organs |
| aerobiology | study of airborne organisms |
| aerodonetics | science or study of gliding |
| aerodynamics | dynamics of gases; science of movement in a flow of air or gas |
| aerolithology | study of aerolites; meteorites |
| aerology | study of the atmosphere |
| aeronautics | study of navigation through air or space |
| aerophilately | collecting of air-mail stamps |
| aerostatics | science of air pressure; art of ballooning |
| agonistics | art and theory of prize-fighting |
| agriology | the comparative study of primitive peoples |
| agrobiology | study of plant nutrition; soil yields |
| agrology | study of agricultural soils |
| agronomics | study of productivity of land |
| agrostology | science or study of grasses |
| alethiology | study of truth |
| algedonics | science of pleasure and pain |
| algology | study of algae |
| anaesthesiology | study of anaesthetics |
| anaglyptics | art of carving in bas-relief |
| anagraphy | art of constructing catalogues |
| anatomy | study of the structure of the body |
| andragogy | science of teaching adults |
| anemology | study of winds |
| angelology | study of angels |
| angiology | study of blood flow and lymphatic system |
| anthropobiology | study of human biology |
| anthropology | study of human cultures |
| aphnology | science of wealth |
| apiology | study of bees |
| arachnology | study of spiders |
| archaeology | study of human material remains |
| archelogy | the study of first principles |

## Sciences and studies (*contd.*)

| Word | Definition |
| --- | --- |
| archology | science of the origins of government |
| arctophily | study of teddy bears |
| areology | study of Mars |
| aretaics | the science of virtue |
| aristology | the science or art of dining |
| arthrology | study of joints |
| astacology | the science of crayfish |
| astheniology | study of diseases of weakening and aging |
| astrogeology | study of extraterrestrial geology |
| astrology | study of influence of stars on people |
| astrometeorology | study of effect of stars on climate |
| astronomy | study of celestial bodies |
| astrophysics | study of behaviour of interstellar matter |
| astroseismology | study of star oscillations |
| atmology | the science of aqueous vapour |
| audiology | study of hearing |
| autecology | study of ecology of one species |
| autology | scientific study of oneself |
| auxology | science of growth |
| avionics | the science of electronic devices for aircraft |
| axiology | the science of the ultimate nature of values |
| bacteriology | study of bacteria |
| balneology | the science of the therapeutic use of baths |
| barodynamics | science of the support and mechanics of bridges |
| barology | study of gravitation |
| batology | the study of brambles |
| bibliology | study of books |
| bibliotics | study of documents to determine authenticity |
| bioecology | study of interaction of life in the environment |
| biology | study of life |
| biometrics | study of biological measurement |
| bionomics | study of organisms interacting in their environments |
| botany | study of plants |
| bromatology | study of food |
| brontology | scientific study of thunder |
| bryology | the study of mosses and liverworts |
| cacogenics | study of racial degeneration |

## Sciences and studies (*contd.*)

| Word | Definition |
| --- | --- |
| caliology | study of bird's nests |
| calorifics | study of heat |
| cambistry | science of international exchange |
| campanology | the art of bell ringing |
| carcinology | study of crabs and other crustaceans |
| cardiology | study of the heart |
| caricology | study of sedges |
| carpology | study of fruit |
| cartography | the science of making maps and globes |
| cartophily | the hobby of collecting cigarette cards |
| castrametation | the art of designing a camp |
| catacoustics | science of echoes or reflected sounds |
| catalactics | science of commercial exchange |
| catechectics | the art of teaching by question and answer |
| cetology | study of whales and dolphins |
| chalcography | the art of engraving on copper or brass |
| chalcotriptics | art of taking rubbings from ornamental brasses |
| chaology | the study of chaos or chaos theory |
| characterology | study of development of character |
| chemistry | study of properties of substances |
| chirocosmetics | beautifying the hands; art of manicure |
| chirography | study of handwriting or penmanship |
| chirology | study of the hands |
| chiropody | medical science of feet |
| chorology | science of the geographic description of anything |
| chrematistics | the study of wealth; political economy |
| chronobiology | study of biological rhythms |
| chrysology | study of precious metals |
| ciselure | the art of chasing metal |
| climatology | study of climate |
| clinology | study of aging or individual decline after maturity |
| codicology | study of manuscripts |
| coleopterology | study of beetles and weevils |
| cometology | study of comets |
| conchology | study of shells |
| coprology | study of pornography |
| cosmetology | study of cosmetics |

## Sciences and studies (*contd.*)

| Word | Definition |
| --- | --- |
| cosmology | study of the universe |
| craniology | study of the skull |
| criminology | study of crime; criminals |
| cryobiology | study of life under cold conditions |
| cryptology | study of codes |
| cryptozoology | study of animals for whose existence there is no conclusive proof |
| ctetology | study of the inheritance of acquired characteristics |
| cynology | scientific study of dogs |
| cytology | study of living cells |
| dactyliology | study of rings |
| dactylography | the study of fingerprints |
| dactylology | study of sign language |
| deltiology | the collection and study of picture postcards |
| demology | study of human behaviour |
| demonology | study of demons |
| dendrochronology | study of tree rings |
| dendrology | study of trees |
| deontology | the theory or study of moral obligation |
| dermatoglyphics | the study of skin patterns and fingerprints |
| dermatology | study of skin |
| desmology | study of ligaments |
| diabology | study of devils |
| diagraphics | art of making diagrams or drawings |
| dialectology | study of dialects |
| dioptrics | study of light refraction |
| diplomatics | science of deciphering ancient writings and texts |
| diplomatology | study of diplomats |
| docimology | the art of assaying |
| dosiology | the study of doses |
| dramaturgy | art of producing and staging dramatic works |
| dysgenics | the study of racial degeneration |
| dysteleology | study of purposeless organs |
| ecclesiology | study of church affairs |
| eccrinology | study of excretion |
| ecology | study of environment |
| economics | study of material wealth |

## Sciences and studies (*contd.*)

| Word | Definition |
| --- | --- |
| edaphology | study of soils |
| Egyptology | study of ancient Egypt |
| ekistics | study of human settlement |
| electrochemistry | study of relations between electricity and chemicals |
| electrology | study of electricity |
| electrostatics | study of static electricity |
| embryology | study of embryos |
| emetology | study of vomiting |
| emmenology | the study of menstruation |
| endemiology | study of local diseases |
| endocrinology | study of glands |
| enigmatology | study of enigmas |
| entomology | study of insects |
| entozoology | study of parasites that live inside larger organisms |
| enzymology | study of enzymes |
| ephebiatrics | branch of medicine dealing with adolescence |
| epidemiology | study of diseases; epidemics |
| epileptology | study of epilepsy |
| epistemology | study of grounds of knowledge |
| eremology | study of deserts |
| ergology | study of effects of work on humans |
| ergonomics | study of people at work |
| escapology | study of freeing oneself from constraints |
| eschatology | study of death; final matters |
| ethnogeny | study of origins of races or ethnic groups |
| ethnology | study of cultures |
| ethnomethodology | study of everyday communication |
| ethnomusicology | study of comparative musical systems |
| ethology | study of natural or biological character |
| ethonomics | study of economic and ethical principles of a society |
| etiology | the science of causes; especially of disease |
| etymology | study of origins of words |
| euthenics | science concerned with improving living conditions |
| exobiology | study of extraterrestrial life |
| floristry | the art of cultivating and selling flowers |
| fluviology | study of watercourses |
| folkloristics | study of folklore and fables |

## Sciences and studies (*contd.*)

| Word | Definition |
| --- | --- |
| futurology | study of future |
| garbology | study of garbage |
| gastroenterology | study of stomach; intestines |
| gastronomy | study of fine dining |
| gemmology | study of gems and jewels |
| genealogy | study of descent of families |
| genesiology | study of reproduction and heredity |
| genethlialogy | the art of casting horoscopes |
| geochemistry | study of chemistry of the earth's crust |
| geochronology | study of measuring geological time |
| geogeny | science of the formation of the earth's crust |
| geogony | study of formation of the earth |
| geography | study of surface of the earth and its inhabitants |
| geology | study of earth's crust |
| geomorphogeny | study of the origins of land forms |
| geoponics | study of agriculture |
| geotechnics | study of increasing habitability of the earth |
| geratology | study of decadence and decay |
| gerocomy | study of old age |
| gerontology | study of the elderly; aging |
| gigantology | study of giants |
| glaciology | study of ice ages and glaciation |
| glossology | study of language; study of the tongue |
| glyptography | the art of engraving on gems |
| glyptology | study of gem engravings |
| gnomonics | the art of measuring time using sundials |
| gnosiology | study of knowledge; philosophy of knowledge |
| gnotobiology | study of life in germ-free conditions |
| graminology | study of grasses |
| grammatology | study of systems of writing |
| graphemics | study of systems of representing speech in writing |
| graphology | study of handwriting |
| gromatics | science of surveying |
| gynaecology | study of women's physiology |
| gyrostatics | the study of rotating bodies |
| haemataulics | study of movement of blood through blood vessels |
| hagiology | study of saints |

## Sciences and studies (*contd.*)

| Word | Definition |
| --- | --- |
| halieutics | study of fishing |
| hamartiology | study of sin |
| harmonics | study of musical acoustics |
| hedonics | part of ethics or psychology dealing with pleasure |
| helcology | study of ulcers |
| heliology | science of the sun |
| helioseismology | study of sun's interior by observing its surface oscillations |
| helminthology | study of worms |
| hematology | study of blood |
| heortology | study of religious feasts |
| hepatology | study of liver |
| heraldry | study of coats of arms |
| heresiology | study of heresies |
| herpetology | study of reptiles and amphibians |
| hierology | science of sacred matters |
| hippiatrics | study of diseases of horses |
| hippology | the study of horses |
| histology | study of the tissues of organisms |
| histopathology | study of changes in tissue due to disease |
| historiography | study of writing history |
| historiology | study of history |
| homiletics | the art of preaching |
| hoplology | the study of weapons |
| horography | art of constructing sundials or clocks |
| horology | science of time measurement |
| horticulture | study of gardening |
| hydrobiology | study of aquatic organisms |
| hydrodynamics | study of movement in liquids |
| hydrogeology | study of ground water |
| hydrography | study of investigating bodies of water |
| hydrokinetics | study of motion of fluids |
| hydrology | study of water resources |
| hydrometeorology | study of atmospheric moisture |
| hydropathy | study of treating diseases with water |
| hyetology | science of rainfall |
| hygiastics | science of health and hygiene |

## Sciences and studies (*contd.*)

| Word | Definition |
| --- | --- |
| hygienics | study of sanitation; health |
| hygiology | hygienics; study of cleanliness |
| hygrology | study of humidity |
| hygrometry | science of humidity |
| hymnography | study of writing hymns |
| hymnology | study of hymns |
| hypnology | study of sleep; study of hypnosis |
| hypsography | science of measuring heights |
| iamatology | study of remedies |
| iatrology | treatise or text on medical topics; study of medicine |
| iatromathematics | archaic practice of medicine in conjunction with astrology |
| ichnography | art of drawing ground plans; a ground plan |
| ichnology | science of fossilized footprints |
| ichthyology | study of fish |
| iconography | study of drawing symbols |
| iconology | study of icons; symbols |
| ideogeny | study of origins of ideas |
| ideology | science of ideas; system of ideas used to justify behaviour |
| idiomology | study of idiom, jargon or dialect |
| idiopsychology | psychology of one's own mind |
| immunogenetics | study of genetic characteristics of immunity |
| immunology | study of immunity |
| immunopathology | study of immunity to disease |
| insectology | study of insects |
| irenology | the study of peace |
| iridology | study of the iris; diagnosis of disease based on the iris of the eye |
| kalology | study of beauty |
| karyology | study of cell nuclei |
| kidology | study of kidding |
| kinematics | study of motion |
| kinesics | study of gestural communication |
| kinesiology | study of human movement and posture |
| kinetics | study of forces producing or changing motion |
| koniology | study of atmospheric pollutants and dust |

## Sciences and studies (*contd.*)

| Word | Definition |
| --- | --- |
| ktenology | science of putting people to death |
| kymatology | study of wave motion |
| labeorphily | collection and study of beer bottle labels |
| larithmics | study of population statistics |
| laryngology | study of larynx |
| lepidopterology | study of butterflies and moths |
| leprology | study of leprosy |
| lexicology | study of words and their meanings |
| lexigraphy | art of definition of words |
| lichenology | study of lichens |
| limacology | study of slugs |
| limnobiology | study of freshwater ecosystems |
| limnology | study of bodies of fresh water |
| linguistics | study of language |
| lithology | study of rocks |
| liturgiology | study of liturgical forms and church rituals |
| loimology | study of plagues and epidemics |
| loxodromy | study of sailing along rhumb-lines |
| magirics | art of cookery |
| magnanerie | art of raising silkworms |
| magnetics | study of magnetism |
| malacology | study of molluscs |
| malariology | study of malaria |
| mammalogy | study of mammals |
| manège | the art of horsemanship |
| Mariology | study of the Virgin Mary |
| martyrology | study of martyrs |
| mastology | study of mammals |
| mathematics | study of magnitude, number, and forms |
| mazology | mammalogy; study of mammals |
| mechanics | study of action of force on bodies |
| meconology | study of or treatise concerning opium |
| melittology | study of bees |
| mereology | study of part-whole relationships |
| mesology | ecology |
| metallogeny | study of the origin and distribution of metal deposits |
| metallography | study of the structure and constitution of metals |

## Sciences and studies (*contd.*)

| Word | Definition |
| --- | --- |
| metallurgy | study of alloying and treating metals |
| metaphysics | study of principles of nature and thought |
| metapolitics | study of politics in theory or abstract |
| metapsychology | study of nature of the mind |
| meteoritics | the study of meteors |
| meteorology | study of weather |
| metrics | study of versification |
| metrology | science of weights and measures |
| microanatomy | study of microscopic tissues |
| microbiology | study of microscopic organisms |
| microclimatology | study of local climates |
| micrology | study or discussion of trivialities |
| micropalaeontology | study of microscopic fossils |
| microphytology | study of very small plant life |
| microscopy | study of minute objects |
| mineralogy | study of minerals |
| molinology | study of mills and milling |
| momilogy | study of mummies |
| morphology | study of forms and the development of structures |
| muscology | the study of mosses |
| museology | the study of museums |
| musicology | study of music |
| mycology | study of funguses |
| myology | study of muscles |
| myrmecology | study of ants |
| mythology | study of myths; fables; tales |
| naology | study of church or temple architecture |
| nasology | study of the nose |
| nautics | art of navigation |
| nematology | the study of nematodes |
| neonatology | study of newborn babies |
| neossology | study of nestling birds |
| nephology | study of clouds |
| nephrology | study of the kidneys |
| neurobiology | study of anatomy of the nervous system |
| neurology | study of nervous system |
| neuropsychology | study of relation between brain and behaviour |

## Sciences and studies (*contd.*)

| Word | Definition |
| --- | --- |
| neurypnology | study of hypnotism |
| neutrosophy | study of the origin and nature of philosophical neutralities |
| nidology | study of nests |
| nomology | the science of the laws; especially of the mind |
| noology | science of the intellect |
| nosology | study of diseases |
| nostology | study of senility |
| notaphily | collecting of bank-notes and cheques |
| numerology | study of numbers |
| numismatics | study of coins |
| nymphology | study of nymphs |
| obstetrics | study of midwifery |
| oceanography | study of oceans |
| oceanology | study of oceans |
| odology | science of the hypothetical mystical force of od |
| odontology | study of teeth |
| oenology | study of wines |
| oikology | science of housekeeping |
| olfactology | study of the sense of smell |
| ombrology | study of rain |
| oncology | study of tumours |
| oneirology | study of dreams |
| onomasiology | study of nomenclature |
| onomastics | study of proper names |
| ontology | science of pure being; the nature of things |
| oology | study of eggs |
| ophiology | study of snakes |
| ophthalmology | study of eye diseases |
| optics | study of light |
| optology | study of sight |
| optometry | science of examining the eyes |
| orchidology | study of orchids |
| ornithology | study of birds |
| orology | study of mountains |
| orthoepy | study of correct pronunciation |
| orthography | study of spelling |

## Sciences and studies (*contd.*)

| Word | Definition |
| --- | --- |
| orthopterology | study of cockroaches |
| oryctology | mineralogy or paleontology |
| osmics | scientific study of smells |
| osmology | study of smells and olfactory processes |
| osphresiology | study of the sense of smell |
| osteology | study of bones |
| otology | study of the ear |
| otorhinolaryngology | study of ear, nose and throat |
| paedology | study of children |
| paedotrophy | art of rearing children |
| paidonosology | study of children's diseases; pediatrics |
| palaeoanthropology | study of early humans |
| palaeobiology | study of fossil plants and animals |
| palaeoclimatology | study of ancient climates |
| palaeolimnology | study of ancient fish |
| palaeolimnology | study of ancient lakes |
| palaeontology | study of fossils |
| palaeopedology | study of early soils |
| paleobotany | study of ancient plants |
| paleo-osteology | study of ancient bones |
| palynology | study of pollen |
| papyrology | study of paper |
| parapsychology | study of unexplained mental phenomena |
| parasitology | study of parasites |
| paroemiology | study of proverbs |
| parthenology | study of virgins |
| pataphysics | the science of imaginary solutions |
| pathology | study of disease |
| patrology | study of early Christianity |
| pedagogics | study of teaching |
| pedology | study of soils |
| pelology | study of mud |
| penology | study of crime and punishment |
| periodontics | study of gums |
| peristerophily | pigeon-collecting |
| pestology | science of pests |
| petrology | study of rocks |

## Sciences and studies (*contd.*)

| Word | Definition |
| --- | --- |
| pharmacognosy | study of drugs of animal and plant origin |
| pharmacology | study of drugs |
| pharology | study of lighthouses |
| pharyngology | study of the throat |
| phenology | study of organisms as affected by climate |
| phenomenology | study of phenomena |
| philately | study of postage stamps |
| philematology | the act or study of kissing |
| phillumeny | collecting of matchbox labels |
| philology | study of ancient texts; historical linguistics |
| philosophy | science of knowledge or wisdom |
| phoniatrics | study and correction of speech defects |
| phonology | study of speech sounds |
| photobiology | study of effects of light on organisms |
| phraseology | study of phrases |
| phrenology | study of bumps on the head |
| phycology | study of algae and seaweeds |
| physics | study of properties of matter and energy |
| physiology | study of processes of life |
| phytology | study of plants; botany |
| piscatology | study of fishes |
| pisteology | science or study of faith |
| planetology | study of planets |
| plutology | political economy; study of wealth |
| pneumatics | study of mechanics of gases |
| podiatry | study and treatment of disorders of the foot; chiropody |
| podology | study of the feet |
| polemology | study of war |
| pomology | study of fruit-growing |
| posology | science of quantity or dosage |
| potamology | study of rivers |
| praxeology | study of practical or efficient activity; science of efficient action |
| primatology | study of primates |
| proctology | study of rectum |
| prosody | study of versification |

## Sciences and studies (*contd.*)

| Word | Definition |
| --- | --- |
| protistology | study of protists |
| proxemics | study of man's need for personal space |
| psalligraphy | the art of paper-cutting to make pictures |
| psephology | study of election results and voting trends |
| pseudology | art or science of lying |
| pseudoptics | study of optical illusions |
| psychobiology | study of biology of the mind |
| psychogenetics | study of internal or mental states |
| psychognosy | study of mentality, personality or character |
| psychology | study of mind |
| psychopathology | study of mental illness |
| psychophysics | study of link between mental and physical processes |
| pteridology | study of ferns |
| pterylology | study of distribution of feathers on birds |
| pyretology | study of fevers |
| pyrgology | study of towers |
| pyroballogy | study of artillery |
| pyrography | study of woodburning |
| quinology | study of quinine |
| raciology | study of racial differences |
| radiology | study of X-rays and their medical applications |
| reflexology | study of reflexes |
| rhabdology | knowledge or learning concerning divining rods |
| rhabdology | art of calculating using numbering rods |
| rheology | science of the deformation or flow of matter |
| rheumatology | study of rheumatism |
| rhinology | study of the nose |
| rhochrematics | science of inventory management and the movement of products |
| runology | study of runes |
| sarcology | study of fleshy parts of the body |
| satanology | study of the devil |
| scatology | study of excrement or obscene literature |
| schematonics | art of using gesture to express tones |
| sciagraphy | art of shading |
| scripophily | collection of bond and share certificates |
| sedimentology | study of sediment |

## Sciences and studies (*contd.*)

| Word | Definition |
| --- | --- |
| seismology | study of earthquakes |
| selenodesy | study of the shape and features of the moon |
| selenology | study of the moon |
| semantics | study of meaning |
| semantology | science of meanings of words |
| semasiology | study of meaning; semantics |
| semiology | study of signs and signals |
| semiotics | study of signs and symbols |
| serology | study of serums |
| sexology | study of sexual behaviour |
| siderography | art of engraving on steel |
| sigillography | study of seals |
| significs | science of meaning |
| silvics | study of tree's life |
| sindonology | study of the shroud of Turin |
| Sinology | study of China |
| sitology | dietetics |
| sociobiology | study of biological basis of human behaviour |
| sociology | study of society |
| somatology | science of the properties of matter |
| sophiology | science of ideas |
| soteriology | study of theological salvation |
| spectrology | study of ghosts |
| spectroscopy | study of spectra |
| speleology | study and exploration of caves |
| spermology | study of seeds |
| sphagnology | study of peat moss |
| sphragistics | study of seals and signets |
| sphygmology | study of the pulse |
| splanchnology | study of the entrails or viscera |
| spongology | study of sponges |
| stasiology | study of political parties |
| statics | study of bodies and forces in equilibrium |
| stemmatology | study of relationships between texts |
| stoichiology | science of elements of animal tissues |
| stomatology | study of the mouth |
| storiology | study of folk tales |

## Sciences and studies (*contd.*)

| Word | Definition |
| --- | --- |
| stratigraphy | study of geological layers or strata |
| stratography | art of leading an army |
| stylometry | studying literature by means of statistical analysis |
| suicidology | study of suicide |
| symbology | study of symbols |
| symptomatology | study of symptoms of illness |
| synecology | study of ecological communities |
| synectics | study of processes of invention |
| syntax | study of sentence structure |
| syphilology | study of syphilis |
| systematology | study of systems |
| taxidermy | art of curing and stuffing animals |
| tectonics | science of structure of objects, buildings and landforms |
| tegestology | study and collecting of beer mats |
| teleology | study of final causes; analysis in terms of purpose |
| telmatology | study of swamps |
| teratology | study of monsters, freaks, abnormal growths or malformations |
| teuthology | study of cephalopods |
| textology | study of the production of texts |
| thalassography | science of the sea |
| thanatology | study of death and its customs |
| thaumatology | study of miracles |
| theology | study of religion; religious doctrine |
| theriatrics | veterinary medicine |
| theriogenology | study of animals' reproductive systems |
| thermodynamics | study of relation of heat to motion |
| thermokinematics | study of motion of heat |
| thermology | study of heat |
| therology | study of wild mammals |
| thremmatology | science of breeding domestic animals and plants |
| threpsology | science of nutrition |
| tidology | study of tides |
| timbrology | study of postage stamps |
| tocology | obstetrics; midwifery |
| tonetics | study of pronunciation |

## Sciences and studies (*contd.*)

| Word | Definition |
| --- | --- |
| topology | study of places and their natural features |
| toponymics | study of place-names |
| toreutics | study of artistic work in metal |
| toxicology | study of poisons |
| toxophily | love of archery; archery; study of archery |
| traumatology | study of wounds and their effects |
| tribology | study of friction and wear between surfaces |
| trichology | study of hair and its disorders |
| trophology | study of nutrition |
| tsiganology | study of gypsies |
| turnery | art of turning in a lathe |
| typhlology | study of blindness and the blind |
| typography | art of printing or using type |
| typology | study of types of things |
| ufology | study of alien spacecraft |
| uranography | descriptive astronomy and mapping |
| uranology | study of the heavens; astronomy |
| urbanology | study of cities |
| urenology | study of rust molds |
| urology | study of urine; urinary tract |
| venereology | study of venereal disease |
| vermeology | study of worms |
| vexillology | study of flags |
| victimology | study of victims |
| vinology | scientific study of vines and winemaking |
| virology | study of viruses |
| vitrics | glassy materials; glassware; study of glassware |
| volcanology | study of volcanoes |
| vulcanology | study of volcanoes |
| xylography | art of engraving on wood |
| xylology | study of wood |
| zenography | study of the planet Jupiter |
| zoiatrics | veterinary surgery |
| zooarchaeology | study of animal remains of archaeological sites |
| zoochemistry | chemistry of animals |
| zoogeography | study of geographic distribution of animals |
| zoogeology | study of fossil animal remains |

## Sciences and studies (*contd.*)

| Word | Definition |
| --- | --- |
| zoology | study of animals |
| zoonomy | animal physiology |
| zoonosology | study of animal diseases |
| zoopathology | study of animal diseases |
| zoophysics | physics of animal bodies |
| zoophysiology | study of physiology of animals |
| zoophytology | study of plant-like animals |
| zoosemiotics | study of animal communication |
| zootaxy | science of classifying animals |
| zootechnics | science of breeding animals |
| zygology | science of joining and fastening |
| zymology | science of fermentation |
| zymurgy | branch of chemistry dealing with brewing and distilling |

## MEDICAL

| | |
| --- | --- |
| A disease affecting many persons at the same place and time | epidemic |
| A disease widely epidemic | pandemic |
| A disease confined to a particular district or place | endemic |
| A disease affecting widely scattered groups of people | sporadic |
| A substance which destroys or weakens germs | antiseptic |
| A substance used by dentists to deaden the gum and nerve | cocaine |
| A substance used in surgery for unconsciousness | chloroform |
| Any medicine which produces insensibility | anesthetic |
| A medicine which alleviates pain | anodyne |
| The mark or scar left after a wound is healed | cicatrice, cicatrix |
| A powder or paste (usually sweet-smelling) used for cleaning the teeth | toothpaste, dentrifrice |
| A medicine to counteract poison | antidote |
| An instrument used by physicians for listening to the action of the heart and lungs | stethoscope |
| Free or exempt from infection | immune |
| To place apart to prevent from infecting others | isolate |

## Medical (*contd.*)

| | |
|---|---|
| A medicine for producing sleep | narcotic, opiate |
| A medicine to cause vomiting | emetic |
| Confinement to one place to avoid spread of infection | quarantine |
| To cut off a part of the body to avoid infection | amputate |
| A cure for all diseases | panacea |
| One who is recovering from illness | convalescent |
| Gradual recovery from illness | convalescence |
| A vehicle for conveying sick or injured people to the hospital | ambulance |
| Want or poorness of blood | anaemic |
| Affecting the lungs | pulmonary |
| A substance to keep down bad smells | deodorant |
| To be able to tell the nature of a disease by its symptoms | diagnose |
| A forecast of the result of a disease or illness | prognosis |
| To disinfect by smoke | fumigate |
| The science of diseases of the human body | pathology |
| The mosquito which transmits filarial | culex |
| The mosquito which transmits malaria | anopheles |
| The mosquito which transmits yellow fever | stegomyia |

## ITIS

This is the 'itis' know-how of medicine.

| | | | |
|---|---|---|---|
| otisis | ear | dermatitis | skin |
| neuritis | nerves | arthritis | joints |
| carditis | heart | conjunctivitis | eye |
| bronchitis | lungs | cystitis | bladder |
| nephritis | kidneys | tonsillitis | throat |
| colotis | intestines | meningitis | brain |
| rhinitis | nose | osteomyelitis | bones |
| gastritis | stomach | thrombophlebitis | blood vessels |
| hepatitis | liver | peritonitis | abdomen |
| myelitis | spine | | |

## WORDS CONNECTED WITH NATURE STUDY

| | |
|---|---:|
| At home equally on land or in water | amphibious |
| Living or going in flocks or herds | gregarious |
| The dormant condition in which plants and animals pass the winter | hibernation |
| Trees which lose their leaves annually | deciduous |
| A cud-chewing animal, e.g.the cow | ruminant |
| A gnawing animal, e.g.the rat | rodent |
| A four-footed animal | quadruped |
| Animals which carry their young in a pouch, e.g. kangaroo | marsupials |
| Soil composed largely of decayed vegetable matter | humas |
| Soil washed down and carried away by rivers | alluvium |
| A preparation for killing insect's | insecticide |
| A plant or animal growing on another | parasite |
| Lasting for a single year or season | annual |
| Lasting for two years | biennial |
| Living for many years | perennial |
| That part of the seed which develops into the plant | embryo, germ |
| The part of the embryo which forms the root | radical |
| The part of the embryo which forms the stem | plumule |
| The process by which the young plant begins to grow | germination |
| The process by which plants give off excess water through their leaves | transpiration |
| The process by which plants manufacture food | assimilation |
| The process by means of which plants and animals breathe | respiration |
| The process by which plants take up mineral salts in solution through their roots | absorption |
| Tiny openings on the under-surface of leaves through which the plant breathes | stomata |
| The green coloring matter in the leaves of plants | chlorophyll |
| A slimy substance between the wood and bark of a stem | cambium |

## Words connected with nature study (*contd.*)

| | |
|---|---|
| Two leaf-like appendages at the base of some leaves | stipules |
| A spiral shoot of a plant which itself twirls round another body for support | tendril |
| The process by which pollen dust is transferred from the stamen to the pistil | pollination |
| The entrance of the pollen grains into the ovules in the ovary | fertilization |
| An instrument for making holes in the soil for seeds or seedlings | dibble |
| One who studies plants and animal life | naturalist |
| The parts of an animal killed for food which are rejected or considered waste | offal |
| Rock from which metal is extracted | ore |
| The track of a wild animal | spoor |
| The meat of deer | venison |
| The flesh of sheep | mutton |
| A cluster of flowers on a branch | inflorescence |
| The seed leaves of the embryo | cotyledon |
| Plants with one seed-leaf, e.g. corn | monocotyledonus |
| Plants with two seed-leaves, e.g. lime | dicotyledonous |
| A thick underground stem | rhizome |
| Animals with backbone | vertebrates |
| Animals without backbone | invertebrates |
| The inside of a nut | kernel |
| The central or innermost part of a fruit | core |
| The animals of a certain region | fauna |
| The plants and vegetation of a certain region | flora |
| The last stage through which an insect passes before it becomes a perfect insect | chrysalis |
| Absence of rain for long time | drought |
| To supply land with water by artificial means | irrigate |
| The feelers of an insect | antennae |
| The dead skin cast off by a snake | slough |

## OPPOSITES

| | |
|---|---|
| Writing that is easy to read | legible |
| Writing that is difficult to decipher | illegible |
| Able to read | literate |
| Unable to read | illiterate |
| Fit for food | edible |
| Unfit for human consumption | inedible |
| Fit to be chosen or selected | eligible |
| Not having the qualities of being chosen | ineligible |
| Loud enough to be heard | inaudible |
| Born of married parents | legitimate |
| Born of unmarried parents | illegitimate |

## OTHERS

| | |
|---|---|
| To move from one country to another | migrate |
| One who leaves his country to settle in another | emigrant |
| One who comes into a foreign country to settle there | immigrant |
| To send back a person to his own country | repatriate |
| To banish from one's country | expatriate |
| Love of one's country | patriotism |
| Goods brought into a country | imports |
| Goods carried out of a country | exports |
| A list or table of duties payable on exports or imports | tariff |
| A list of goods dispatched with quantity and price to the purchaser | invoice |
| One to whom goods are dispatched | consignee |

## NEGATIVES

| | |
|---|---|
| That which cannot be pierced or penetrated | impenetrable |
| That which cannot be taken by assault | impregnable |

## Negatives (*contd*)

| | |
|---|---|
| That which cannot be passed | impassable |
| That which cannot be conquered | invincible |
| That which cannot be wounded or injured | invulnerable |
| That which cannot be lessened | irreducible |
| That which cannot be repaired or remedied | irreparable |
| That which cannot be made good in case of loss | irreplaceable |
| That which cannot be imitated | inimitable |
| That which cannot be rubbed out or blotted out | ineffaceable, indelible |
| Incapable of making errors | infallible |
| Incapable of being destroyed | indestructible |
| Incapable of being redeemed from evil, i.e. beyond correction | incorrigible |
| Incapable of being burnt | incombustible |
| That which cannot be avoided or prevented | inevitable |
| That which cannot be made plain or understood | inexplicable |
| Enduring for all times | imperishable |
| Not admitting the passage or entrances of water etc. | impervious |
| Not endowed with animal life | inanimate |
| Absolutely necessary, cannot be dispensed with | indispensable |
| Not to the point | irrelevant |
| Unable to die | immortal |
| That which cannot be moved | immovable |
| That which cannot be heard | inaudible |
| That which cannot be seen | invisible |

## MILITARY WORDS

| | |
|---|---|
| An unprovoked attack by an enemy | aggression |
| Nations carrying on warfare | belligerents |
| Compulsory enrolment as soldiers or sailors | conscription |

## Military words (*contd.*)

| | |
|---|---|
| The killed or wounded in battle | casualties |
| A number of ships travelling together under escort for the sake of safety | convoy |
| Smuggling of goods or engaging in prohibited traffic | contraband |
| The act or practice of spying | espionage |
| To remove from one place to another to avoid the destruction | evacuate |
| An order prohibiting ships to leave the ports | embargo |
| To make troops, ships etc. ready for war service | mobilize |
| To enter a country as an enemy | invade |
| Taking neither side in the struggle | neutral |
| A foreigner in a belligerent country | alien |
| To keep citizens in confinement | intern |
| Shells, bombs, military stores | ammunition |
| Heavy guns, artillery and army stores | ordnance |
| A knife fixed on to the end of a gun | bayonet |
| A promise given by a prisoner not to try to escape if given temporary release | parole |
| Lone strips of cloth bound round the legs of a soldier from the ankle to the knee | puttees |
| Music for awakening soldiers in the morning | reveille |
| A place where naval or military weapons are made or stored | arsenal |
| An apparatus which opens like an umbrella to enable A person to drop safely from an aircraft | parachute |
| A shower of bullets | volley |
| The firing of many guns at the same time to mark an occasion | salvo |
| Horse-soldiers | cavalry |
| Foot-soldiers | infantry |
| A number of firearms being discharged continuously | fusillade |
| To make an examination or preliminary survey of enemy territory or military objective | reconnoiter |

## Military words (*contd.*)

An agreement to stop fighting — armistice
To surrender to an enemy on agreed terms — capitulate
To reduce to nothing — annihilate
A general pardon of offenders — amnesty
The main division of an army — battalion
To surround a place with the intention of capturing it — besiege
A soldier recently enlisted for service — recruit
A soldier's holiday — leave, furlough
Official reports on the progress of the war — bulletin
The art of conducting negotiations between nations — diplomacy
A body of soldiers stationed in a fortress to defend it — garrison
A fortified place defended by soldiers, canons, etc. — garrison
A broad belt worn across the shoulder and chest.
With pockets for carrying ammunition — bandolier
A person who is forced by law to become a soldier — conscript
An irregular warfare conducted by scattered or
   independent bands — guerilla war
Movement of ships or troops in order to secure an
   advantage over the enemy — manoeuvre
To seize for military use — commandeer
To release from the army — demobilize
To camp in the open air without tents or covering — bivouac
A place where soldiers can buy drinks and other refreshments
   canteen

## LITERARY WORDS

A book in which the events of each day are recorded — diary
A book containing the words of a language with their
   definitions, in alphabetical order — dictionary
A book of names and addresses — directory

## Literary words (*contd.*)

| | |
|---|---|
| A book of accounts showing debits and credits | ledger |
| A book containing information on all branches of knowledge | encyclopedia |
| A book with blank pages for putting autographs, pictures stamps, etc. | album |
| A list of books in a library | catalogue, bibliography |
| A list of explanations or rare, technical or obsolete words | glossary |
| A written account, memorable experiences of one's life | memoirs |
| The trade mark of the maker seen on paper | watermark |
| One who pretends to have a great deal of knowledge | wiseacre |
| A brief summary of a book | epitome |
| An extract or selection from a book of writing | excerpt |
| The heading or short description of a newspaper article, chapter of a book etc. | caption |
| A statement which is accepted as true without proof | axiom |
| A list of the headings of the business to be transacted at a meeting | agenda |
| Language which is confused and unintelligible | jargon |
| A declaration of plans and promises put forward by a Candidate for election, a political party or a sovereign | manifesto |
| To remove the offensive portions of a book | expuragate |
| Still in use (of books published long ago) | extant |
| A picture facing the title of a book | frontispiece |
| The exclusive right of an author or his heirs to publish or sell copies of his writings | copyright |
| An error or misprint in printing, or writing | erratum |
| An exact copy of handwriting, printing, or of a picture | facsimile |
| A principle or standard by which anything is or can be Judged | criterion |
| Delivered (A speech delivered) without previous preparation | extempore, impromptu |

## Literary words (*contd.*)

| | |
|---|---|
| A short speech by a player at the beginning of a play | prologue |
| A short speech by a player at the end of a play | epilogue |
| Passing off another author's work as one's own | plagiarism |
| A writing or speech in praise of a person | eulogy, encomium |
| A person's own handwriting | autograph |
| A record of one's life written by himself | autobiography |
| The history of the life of a person | biography |
| A humorous play, having a happy ending | comedy |
| A play with a sad or tragic end | tragedy |
| A mournful song (or poem) for the dead | dirge |
| A poem of lamentation, especially for the dead | elegy |
| A conversation between two persons | dialogue |
| Speaking to oneself | soliloquy |
| Study by night | lucubration |
| A succession of the same initial letters in passage | alliteration |
| A note to help the memory | memorandum |
| A list of articles and their description | inventory |
| The concluding part of a speech | peroration |
| A noisy or vehement speech intended to excite passions | harangue |
| To make expressive gestures or motions while speaking | gesticulate |
| Language that is very much used | hackneyed |
| To pronounce words distinctly | enunciate |
| One who writes plays | dramatist, playwright |
| A poem in which the first letters of each line, taken in order, form a name or a sentence | acrostic |

## MISCELLANEOUS

| | |
|---|---|
| Fluent in two languages | bilingual |
| Lasting only for a day | ephemeral |
| Word for word | verbatim |

## Miscellaneous (*contd.*)

| | |
|---|---|
| To change to stone | petrify |
| To reduce to powder | pulverize |
| Wasteful in spending | extravagant |
| To learn by heart | memories |
| (Travelling) under a name other than one's own | incognito |
| Capable to being drawn out | malleable, ductile |
| Consisting of several kinds | miscellaneous |
| The exclusive right to buy or sell a commodity | monopoly |
| Unable to pay one's debts | insolvent |
| The outfit of a new-born baby | layette |
| Easily broken | fragile |
| Capable of being reduced to powder | friable |
| Capable of being separated or torn asunder | discerptible |
| Close at hand | imminent |
| Serving for money | mercenary |
| Irresistible craving for alcoholic drinks | dipsomania |
| Excessive devotion to the female sex | gyneolatry |
| A fence or railing of stakes, or iron,etc. | Palisade |
| A job for which one is paid, but which has few or no duties attached to it | sinecure |
| An appendix to a will | codicil |
| Correct spelling | orthography |
| Bad spelling | cacography |
| A line of people waiting for something | queue |
| Steps to enable one to get over a fence | stile |
| Loss of memory | amnesia |
| Loss of voice | aphonia, aphony |
| A seat on the back of an elephant | howdah |
| To turn a train etc. on a side track | shunting |
| The liquid which comes out from a sewerage tank | effluent |

## Miscellaneous *(contd.)*

| | |
|---|---|
| To separate the husks from the grain | winnow |
| A bar or pair of bars for confining cattle in a stall | stanchion |
| The likeness or representation of a person, especially on coins or medals | effigy |
| A forsaken or neglected child who has no home | waif |
| An iron ring placed at the end of a staff to prevent it from splitting | ferrule |
| Living on flesh | carnivorous |
| Living on grass | herbivorous, graminivorous |
| Living on fish | piscivorous |
| Feeding on both animal and vegetable food. i.e. eating all kinds of food | omnivorous |
| A chairman's hammer | gavel |
| A stick used by a music conductor, or by a policeman | baton |
| The yellow part of an egg | yolk |
| The white of an egg | albumen |
| The stripes on the sleeves of policeman and non commissioned officers in the services to denote their rank | chevron |
| A bridge carrying a road or railway across a river or valley | viaduct |
| A mixture of metals, especially when an inferior metal is Mixed with one of richer value | alloy |
| A rich covering over a throne or bed or carried over some dignitary in a procession | canopy |
| To lay a ship on its sides in order to clean it | careen |
| Home-sickness or a sentimental longing for the past | nostalgia |
| A list of the various items of food to be served at a meal | menu |
| Directions for preparing certain dishes, sweetmeats, pastries etc. | recipe |
| The part of milk from which cheese is made | casein |
| Able to adapt oneself readily to many situations | versatile |
| Goods thrown overboard in order to make a ship lighter | jetsam |

## Miscellaneous (*contd.*)

| | |
|---|---|
| Goods found floating after a shipwreck | flotsam |
| A rally of Boy Scouts or a joyful gathering of youth | jamboree |
| A set of bells so arranged that tunes of songs or hymns can be played on them | carillon |
| A picture of a person or thing drawn in such a highly exaggerated manner as to cause laughter | caricature |
| A name taken on by a person but which is not his real name alias | pseudonym |
| A picture or pattern produced by putting together small pieces of coloured glass, marble or stone | mosaic |
| A leather for sharpening razors | strop |
| A leather travelling-bag carried in the hand | valise |
| A list showing the order in which a number of persons have to perform certain duties | roster |
| One of a pair of baskets slung over the back of a donkey | pannier |
| A thing worn by some persons as a charm against, evil, withcraft, sickness etc. | amulet |
| The bony framework of a car | chassis |
| A covering of canvas to shade windows and doors from the sun | awning |
| To put to one's own use the money of another with which one is entrusted | embezzle |
| To be over particular about spending of money | parsimonious |
| The space which for safety is left unfilled in a cask or vessel before it is sealed | ullage |
| A hollow space in a wall for a statue | niche |
| To compensate for loss or damage | indemnify |
| To bring a person before a court of law to answer a charge | arraign |
| An enclosure for prisoners in a courthouse | dock |
| The whole rim (or one of the segments of the rim) of a wheel | felloe |

# PART TWO

# OUR WORLD

## THE WORLD WE LIVE IN

**Solar System**
- Solar System is the family of the sun
- It has eight known **planets** which orbit around it.
- Natural **satellites** accompany the planets
- **Asteroids** are several thousand minor planets
- There are **also** a large number of **comets**.
- **Planets** are the bodies revolving around the sun (at the same time rotating on their own axis).

**There are eight known planets:**

*Mercury*
- This planet is closest to the sun.
- It rotates on its own axis in 58.65 days
- Takes 88 days to complete one revolution around the sun.
- It is the fastest planet in our solar system.

*Venus*
- The brightest object in the sky after the sun and the moon.
- Also the hottest planet in our solar system.
- It rotates backwards (unlike other planets) on its axis.

*Earth*
- It is the only planet that has inhabitation.

*Mars*
- The fourth planet from the sun
- It is next after the earth.
- It is also known as the red planet.
- It bears similarities with earth

- Astronomers have been speculating on the existence of some kind of life on this planet.

*Jupiter*

- The largest planet in our solar system.
- Diameter is 11 times the diameter of the earth.
- 63 satellites.

*Saturn*

- Outermost planet visible to the naked eye
- Second largest in size after Jupiter.
- Most spectacular feature of Saturn is its system of rings.

*Uranus*

- The seventh planet from the sun
- Not visible to the naked eye.
- It was discovered in 1781 by William Herschel.

*Neptune*

- Eighth in position from the sun.
- Discovered by J. G. Galle in 1846.

*Pluto*

- Discovery in 1930
- Until 2006, it was considered the ninth and smallest planet.
- August 24, 2006, the International Astronomical Union (IAU) has reclassified Pluto as a dwarf planet
- So we now have eight planets in our solar system.

**Satellites**

- The celestial bodies that revolve around the planets.

### Approximately 153 satellites in our solar system

| Planet | No. of Satellites | Planet | No. of Satellites |
|--------|------|--------|------|
| Mercury | 0 | Venus | 0 |
| Earth | 1 | Mars | 2 |
| Jupiter | 63 | Saturn | 47 |
| Uranus | 27 | Neptune | 13 |

## Moon
- Earth's natural satellite
- Nearest neighbour in space.
- Revolves around the earth while rotating on its own axis.
- About 1/6th the size of the earth.
- Takes 27 days, 7 hrs, 43 min and 11.47 secs to complete one revolution of the earth.
- Rotates on its axis in exactly the same time.
- Hence, we see only one side of the moon.

**NOTE:** The moon is the first member of our solar system to have been visited by man. July 21, 1969 - Neil Armstrong and Edwin Aldrin created history - they first set foot on the moon: 'one small step is a giant leap for mankind.'

## Asteroids
- Debris left over from the formation of the inner planets.
- Too small to retain any atmosphere of their own.
- Planetoids: Asteroids are also called 'planetoids' or small planets.
- Circle around the sun between the orbits of Mars and Jupiter.
- About 50000 known asteroids in our solar system.
- Largest is Ceres - a diameter of 1025 km.

## Meteors
- Small bodies often seen in the sky
- Shooting with great speed from one point to another and producing a trail of light.
- Shooting Stars: They may burn up or fall on earth (known as shooting stars)
- Meteorites: They form of dust or fragments (called meteorites).

## Comets
- Celestial bodies that move around the sun.
- Comet has a long tail
- Name comes from the Greek word kometes, meaning 'hair-like'.

## Major Comets

### Halley's Comet

- Named after the British astronomer, Edmund Halley
- Halley discovered it in 1705.
- Stated that the comets seen in 1531,1607 and 1683
- Were the same body which circles the sun every 76 years
- Halley's comet last appeared in 1986
- It may reappear again after 76 years.

### Comet 'Smith-Tuttle

- A huge comet heading on a collision course with earth on August 17, 2116
- First sighted in 1862 ; Re-discovered in 1992
- Note: It could kill off most forms of life with an explosion more powerful than the explosion of a million nuclear bombs put together.

## The Earth

- Placed at the third position from the sun
- Earth is the fifth largest planet in the solar system.
- Earth is an oblate spheroid (ball flattened at the poles) (almost spherical, flattened a little at the poles, and with a slight bulge at the centre (equator).
- Spinning (rotation) of the earth at a high speed has caused its mass to bulge at the equator and dip at the poles.
- Made up of a number of concentric layers of material as in the bulb of an onion.

### Components of the Earth

- Earth contains more than 100 different elements.

Important ones are:

- Oxygen                46.6%
- Silicon                27.72%
- Aluminium            8.13%
- Iron                    5.01 %

- Calcium                        3.63%
- Sodium                        2.85%
- Potassium                   2.62%
- Magnesium                 2.09%

## Spheres of the Earth

There are four distinct spheres of the earth:

- *Lithosphere*            The top crust which includes land surface and ocean floor.

- *Hydrosphere*          The water surface which includes oceans, seas, rivers and lakes.

- *Atmosphere*           The cover of air that envelops the earth's surface.

- *Biosphere*             The region where life exists.

## The Earth: Diameter:

- At the equator           12756.32 km
- At the poles             12713.54 km
- Mean diameter          12734 km
- Equatorial Radius       6377 km
- Total Surface Area      509700000 sq. km
- Total Land Area         148400000 sq. km
  (29.08%)
- Total Water Area       361300000 sq. km
  (70.92%)
- Mean Distance from    149407000 km
  the Sun
- Time for Rotation on   23 hr 56 min and 4.09 sec
  its own Axis
- Period for Revolution   365 days, 6 hrs, 9 mm and 9.54 sec
  around the Sun

## Change of Seasons

- The earth's axis is inclined at an angle of 66.5° to the plane of its orbit.

- So the earth is in different positions while revolving around the sun.
- During the first half of the year the northern hemisphere tilts towards the sun resulting in the season of summer in the region.
- During the second half of the year the southern hemisphere tilts towards the sun, and thus experiences summer and the northern hemisphere experiences winter during this period.
- The revolution causes the four seasons:
- *Spring*        The sun is directly overhead the equator during this season.
- *Summer*      The sun is directly overhead the Tropic of Cancer and the north temperate zone experiences summer.
- *Autumn*      The sun returns to the equator and the north temperate zone experiences the season of autumn.
- *Winter*        The sun is at the Tropic of Capricorn and the north temperate zone experiences winter.

**Equinoxes**

- Dates when the nights and days are equal.
- During these days the sun shines directly over the equator.
- March 21 is called *vernal equinox*
- September 23 is called *autumnal equinox*.

**Solstice**

- The time of the year when the difference between the length of days and nights is the largest it is referred to as solstice.
- Summer solstice: June 21: the North Pole tilts towards the sun that shines directly over the Tropic of Cancer.
- On or around December 22, the earth is at the opposite end of its orbit
- Winter Solstice: South Pole tilts towards the sun and the North Pole away from it.

**Eclipses**

- When the light of the sun or the moon is obscured by another body the sun or moon is said to be in eclipse.

*Lunar Eclipse*

- When the earth comes between the moon and the sun, the shadow cast by the earth on the moon results in a lunar eclipse.
- Note: *Lunar eclipse* occurs only on a full moon day but not on every full moon day.

*Solar Eclipse*

- Solar Eclipse: When the moon comes between the sun and the earth, it causes obstruction of the sun's light when viewed from the earth.
- A solar eclipse occurs on a new moon day when the moon is in line with the sun.
- Note: However, solar eclipse does not occur on every new moon day.

## Atmosphere

- Atmosphere is a gaseous cover that surrounds the earth.
- Composition of atmosphere changes as we go higher from the earth's surface.
- Up to about a height of 50 km from the earth, the atmosphere is composed of:
- Nitrogen                78.09%
- Oxygen                 20.95%
- Argon                    0.93%
- Minor gases (carbon dioxide, hydrogen, neon, helium,0.03%
- methane, xenon, krypton, etc.)

## Atmospheric layers

The atmosphere of earth is arranged into four layers:

- *Troposphere:* The layer nearest to earth's surface up to a height of about 15 km.
- *Stratosphere:* The region of uniform temperature extending from an altitude of about 15 km above the earth to about 50km.
- *Mesosphere:* The very cold region which extends from 50 to 90 km above the earth's surface.

- *Ionosphere:* Lies immediately above the mesosphere and extends from 80 to 400 km above the earth's surface. The middle layer of this region is called the thermosphere where the temperature is above 100°C. The outer limit of the atmosphere is called exosphere where the gravity of the earth is exceedingly weak.

## Winds

- When a horizontal difference in air pressure, air from high pressure areas flows to the low pressure areas, this horizontal movement of air causes formation of winds.
- The force that results due to horizontal pressure differences and drives the winds is called *pressure gradient force.*

*Types of Winds*

- *Local Winds* Some of the local winds are:
- *Some Hot winds*
- Santa Ana (Mexico)
- Brickfielder (Australia)
- Sirocco
- Leneche (Sahara)
- Harmattan (W. Africa)
- Khamsin (Egypt)
- Simoon (Sahara)
- Zonda (Paraguay)

*Some Cold Winds*

- Bora (Yugoslavia)
- Southerly Buster (Australia)
- Buran (Europe)
- Panyero (Argentina)
- Mistral (France).

*Trade Winds*

- Blow from the sub-tropical high pressure areas (about 300 North and South) towards the equatorial low pressure belt.

- The North-eastern trades in the Northern hemisphere.
- South-eastern trades in the Southern hemisphere.
- Caused by the rotation of the earth, these winds do not cross the isobars at right angles, but are deflected:
- When these winds meet at the equator and clash, they cause heavy rainfalls at the line of convergence.

*The Westerlies*

- Blow from the subtropical high pressure belts towards the sub-polar low-pressure belts.
- In the Northern hemisphere, they blow from South-West to North-East
- In the Southern hemisphere they blow from North-West to South-East.

## Land and Sea Breeze

- Formed across the coastal strip, due to pressure gradient at the sea and land.
- Cause - During day time, the land becomes more heated up as compared to sea, thus developing higher pressure at sea.
- The air from sea starts flowing towards land which has less pressure is called the *sea breeze*.
- During nights, due to heat radiation land becomes cooler than sea and develops higher pressure than sea. The air which blows from land to sea during night is called *land breeze*.

*Periodic Winds*

- The winds that change their directions due to change in seasons are called periodic winds.

Monsoons are also a type of periodic wind.

## Monsoon

- In summer, due to changing pattern of solar heating of earth, the subtropical high pressure belt and the thermal equator are displaced northwards.
- As such, the equatorial westerlies also move northwards.

- The route they take is, from the oceans to the lands as they blow over the Asian continent bringing the South-West Summer Monsoons.
- The monsoons are seasonal modifications of the general planetary wind system.
- Monsoons blow over the regions of India, Pakistan, Sri Lanka, Bangladesh, Myanmar, China, Northern Australia.

*Planetary Winds*

- The latitudinal differences in air pressure cause planetary winds.
- They blow throughout the year from one latitude to the other.

*Mountain and Valley Breeze*

- The air pressure in the valley during the day time is more than on the mountain slopes as the mountain slopes get heated up more compared to the valley floor.
- Valley breeze is due to the formation of breeze from valley to the slopes in upward direction.
- Mountain breeze is due to the air beginning to breeze from the mountain slopes, lower down to the valley floor.
- *Jet Streams* are the narrow bands of swift winds which blow from West to East in the upper troposphere near the tropopause. They get embedded into the westerlies on this course and encircle the whole globe.

There are two types of jet streams:

- Sub-tropical jet streams
- Polar Front jet streams.
- The average speed of jet stream is 350 km per hour in summers
- The speed is as high as 450 km per hour during winters.

*Tropical Winds*

- Air masses caused at the tropical regions, made up of several layers are called tropical winds.

These are subdivided into two types:

- Maritime tropical
- Continental tropical

*Polar Winds*

- The air masses, much of the type of tropical winds in the polar regions are called polar winds. They are divided into two types:
- Maritime Polar
- Continental Polar

*Warm and Cold Fronts*

- When the warmer and lighter air masses move along the colder, the warm air mass rides above the colder one. The boundary zones of convergence separating the two air masses are called *warm fronts*.
- When the cold air mass forces its way under the mass of warmer air and tends to push the warm air mass upward, then this form is called a *cold front*.

**Rocks**

- The earth's crust is formed of mineral material called rocks.
- The rocks can be grouped into three broad categories: *Igneous Rocks Sedimentary Rocks & Metamorphic Rocks*

*Igneous Rocks*

- These are formed by the solidification of molten magma from the interior of the earth.
- About 90% of the earth's crust is made of this type of rock.
- Examples are granite, basalt, volcanic rocks.

*Sedimentary Rocks*

- These are formed from the sediment deposits on the ocean beds.
- Only about 5% of the earth's crust has this.
- Also known as stratified rocks.
- This is because they are formed in horizontal layers or strata.
- Gypsum, chalk and limestone are formed by the deposits created by chemical action or chemical sedimentation.
- Peat, lignite, bituminous coal and anthracite are formed by deposits of organic matter or marine remains.
- Gravel, pebbles and shingle, sandstone and shale are formed by the deposits of sediments in water.

*Metamorphic Rocks*

- Originally these rocks were called either igneous or sedimentary.
- They metamorphose or change due to pressure, temperature or the action of water and chemicals.
- Slate, quartzite, gneiss and marble are some of these.

## The Continents

- The earth's surface is divided into seven continents
- This covers about one quarter of the total surface area.

| Name | Area (km²) | Population (2001 est.) |
|---|---|---|
| Asia | 44614000 | 3772103000 |
| Africa | 30348110 | 816524000 |
| North America | 24247039 | 454225000 |
| South America | 17858520 | 350977000 |
| Antarctica | 14245000 | — |
| Europe | 10400000 | 666498000 |
| Australia | 7692030 | 19702000 |

**Note:** *Australia with New Zealand, Tasmania, New Guinea and the Pacific Islands is also called 'Australasia'.*

**The World** – *Countries:*

- Has 193 sovereign countries (192 of them are members of UNO).
- Till the end of 1989, there were only 170 sovereign countries.
- Namibia joined as the 171st country when it achieved independence in March 1990.
- Note: The unification of North and South Yemen in May 1990 and East and West Germany in October 1990, brought the total number of sovereign countries to 169 at the end of 1990.
- With the disintegration of former USSR towards the end of 1991 (which comprised 15 union Republics) the number of the countries in the world became 183.
- Today there are 193.

# THE INDEPENDENT COUNTRIES OF THE WORLD

## (As recognised by the United Nations)

| Name and Location | Capital | Currency | Population | Area (km²) |
|---|---|---|---|---|
| • Afghanistan Asia (Central) | Kabul | Afghan afghani | 29863010 | 652090 |
| • Albania Europe (South East) | Tirana | Albanian lek | 3129678 | 28748 |
| • Algeria Africa (North Central) | Algiers | Algerian dinar | 32853800 | 2381741 |
| • Andorra Europe (South West) | Andorra la Vella | Euro | 67151 | 468 |
| • Angola Africa (South West) | Luanda | Angolan kwanza | 15941390 | 1246700 |
| • Antigua and Barbuda North America (South East) | St. John's | East Caribbean dollar | 81479 | 442 |
| • Argentina South America (South East) | Buenos Aires | Argentine peso | 38747150 | 2780400 |
| • Armenia Asia (Central West) | Yerevan | Armenian dram | 3016312 | 29800 |
| • Australia Oceana (South West) | Canberra | Australian dollar | 20155130 | 7741220 |
| • Austria Europe (South Central) | Vienna | Euro | 8189444 | 83858 |
| • Azerbaijan Asia (Central West) | Baku | Azerbaijani manat | 8410801 | 86600 |
| • Bahamas North America (South East) | Nassau | Bahamian dollar | 323063 | 13878 |
| • Bahrain Asia (South West) | Manama | Bahraini dinar | 726617 | 694 |
| • Bangladesh Asia (South Central) | Dhaka | Bangladeshi taka | 141822300 | 143998 |
| • Barbados North America (South East) | Bridgetown | Barbadian dollar | 269556 | 430 |
| • Belarus Europe (Central East) | Minsk | Belarusian ruble | 9755106 | 207600 |
| • Belgium Europe (Central West) | Brussels | Euro | 10419050 | 30528 |

## The independent countries of the world (*contd.*)

| Name and Location | Capital | Currency | Population | Area (km²) |
|---|---|---|---|---|
| • Belize North America (South East) | Belmopan | Belize dollar | 269736 | 22966 |
| • Benin Africa (North West) | Cotonou | West African CFA franc | 8438853 | 112622 |
| • Bhutan Asia (South Central) | Thimphu | Bhutanese ngultrum Indian rupee | 2162546 | 47000 |
| • Bolivia South America (Central) | La Paz | Bolivian boliviano | 9182015 | 1098581 |
| • Bosnia and Herzegovina Europe (South East) | Sarajevo | Convertible mark | 3907074 | 51197 |
| • Botswana Africa (South Central) | Gaborone | Botswana pula | 1764926 | 581730 |
| • Brazil South America (North East) | Brasília | Brazilian real | 186404900 | 8514877 |
| • Brunei Asia (South East) | Bandar Seri Begawan | Brunei dollar; Singapore dollar | 373819 | 5765 |
| • Bulgaria Europe (South East) | Sofia | Bulgarian lev | 7725965 | 110912 |
| • Burkina Faso Africa (North West) | Ouagadougou | West African CFA franc | 13227840 | 274000 |
| • Burundi Africa (Central East) | Bujumbura | Burundian franc | 7547515 | 27834 |
| • Cambodia Asia (South East) | Phnom Penh | Cambodian riel | 14071010 | 181035 |
| • Cameroon Africa (Central West) | Yaoundé | Central African CFA franc | 16321860 | 475442 |
| • Canada North America (North Central) | Ottawa | Canadian dollar | 32268240 | 9970610 |
| • Cape Verde Africa (North West) | Praia | Cape Verdean escudo | 506807 | 4033 |
| • Central African Republic Africa (Central) | Bangui | Central African CFA franc | 4037747 | 622984 |
| • Chad Africa (North Central) | N'Djamena | Central African CFA franc | 9748931 | 1284000 |
| • Chile South America (South West) | Santiago | Chilean peso | 16295100 | 756096 |

# The independent countries of the world (*contd.*)

| Name and Location | Capital | Currency | Population | Area (km²) |
|---|---|---|---|---|
| • China | | | | |
| • Asia (Central East) | Beijing | Chinese yuan | 1315844000 | 9596961 |
| • Colombia South America (North West) | Bogotá | Colombian peso | 45600240 | 1138914 |
| • Comoros Africa (South East) | Moroni | Comorian franc | 797902 | 2235 |
| • Congo, Democratic Republic of the Africa (Central) | Kinshasa | Congolese franc | 57548740 | 2344858 |
| • Congo, Republic of the Africa (Central West) | Brazzaville | Central African CFA franc | 3998904 | 342000 |
| • Costa Rica North America (South East) | San José | Costa Rican colón | 4327228 | 51100 |
| • Croatia Europe (South East) | Zagreb | Croatian kuna | 4551338 | 56538 |
| • Cuba North America (South East) | Havana | Cuban convertible peso; Cuban peso | 11269400 | 110861 |
| • Cyprus Asia (Central West) | Nicosia | Cypriot pound | 264172 | 3355 |
| • Czech Republic Europe (Central) | Prague | Czech koruna | 10219600 | 78866 |
| • Denmark Europe (North Central) | Copenhagen | Danish krone | 5430590 | 43094 |
| • Djibouti Africa (North East) | Djibouti City | Djiboutian franc | 793078 | 23200 |
| • Dominica North America (South East) | Roseau | East Caribbean dollar | 78940 | 751 |
| • Dominican Republic North America (South East) | Santo Domingo | Dominican peso | 8894907 | 48671 |
| • Ecuador South America (North West) | Quito | United States dollar | 13228420 | 283561 |
| • Egypt Africa (North East) | Cairo | Egyptian pound | 74032880 | 1001449 |
| • El Salvador North America (South East) | San Salvador | Salvadoran colón; United States Dollar | 6880951 | 21041 |
| • Equatorial Guinea Africa (Central West) | Malabo | Central African CFA franc | 503519 | 28051 |

## The independent countries of the world (*contd.*)

| Name and Location | Capital | Currency | Population | Area (km²) |
|---|---|---|---|---|
| • Eritrea Africa (North East) | Asmara | Eritrean nakfa | 4401357 | 117600 |
| • Estonia Europe (North East) | Tallinn | Estonian kroon | 1329697 | 45100 |
| • Ethiopia Africa (Central East) | Addis Ababa | Ethiopian birr | 77430700 | 1104300 |
| • Fiji Oceana (Central East) | Suva | Fijian dollar | 847706 | 18274 |
| • Finland Europe (North East) | Helsinki | Euro | 5249060 | 338145 |
| • France Europe (South West) | Paris | Euro | 60495540 | 551500 |
| • Gabon Africa (Central West) | Libreville | Central African CFA franc | 1383841 | 267668 |
| • Gambia Africa (North West) | Banjul | Gambian dalasi | 1517079 | 11295 |
| • Georgia Asia (Central West) | Tbilisi | Georgian lari | 4474404 | 69700 |
| • Germany Europe (Central) | Berlin | Euro | 82689210 | 357022 |
| • Ghana Africa (North West) | Accra | Ghanaian cedi | 22112810 | 238533 |
| • Greece Europe (South East) | Athens | Euro | 11119890 | 131957 |
| • Grenada North America (South East) | St. George's | East Caribbean dollar | 102924 | 344 |
| • Guatemala North America (South East) | Guatemala City | Guatemalan quetzal | 12599060 | 108889 |
| • Guinea Africa (North West) | Conakry | Guinean franc | 9402098 | 245857 |
| • Guinea-Bissau Africa (North West) | Bissau | West African CFA franc | 1586344 | 36125 |
| • Guyana South America (North Central) | Georgetown | Guyanese dollar | 751218 | 214969 |
| • Haiti North America (South East) | Port-au-Prince | Haitian gourde | 8527777 | 27750 |

## The independent countries of the world (*contd.*)

| Name and Location | Capital | Currency | Population | Area (km²) |
|---|---|---|---|---|
| • Honduras North America (South East) | Tegucigalpa | Honduran lempira | 7204723 | 112088 |
| • Hungary Europe (South East) | Budapest | Hungarian forint | 10097730 | 93032 |
| • Iceland Europe (North West) | Reykjavík | Icelandic króna | 294561 | 103000 |
| • India Asia (South Central) | New Delhi | Indian rupee | 1103371000 | 3287263 |
| • Indonesia Asia (South East) | Jakarta | Indonesian rupiah | 222781500 | 1904569 |
| • Iran Asia (Central West) | Tehran | Iranian rial | 69515210 | 1648195 |
| • Iraq Asia (Central West) | Baghdad | Iraqi dinar | 28807190 | 438317 |
| • Ireland Europe (North West) | Dublin | Euro | 4147901 | 70273 |
| • Israel Asia (Central West) | Jerusalem | Israeli new sheqel | 6724564 | 22145 |
| • Italy Europe (South Central) | Rome | Euro | 58092740 | 301318 |
| • Ivory Coast Africa (North West) | Abidjan | West African CFA franc | 18153870 | 322463 |
| • Jamaica North America (South East) | Kingston | Jamaican dollar | 2650713 | 10991 |
| • Japan Asia (Central East) | Tokyo | Japanese yen | 128084700 | 377873 |
| • Jordan Asia (Central West) | Amman | Jordanian dinar | 5702776 | 89342 |
| • Kazakhstan Asia (North West) | Astana | Kazakhstani tenge | 14825110 | 2724900 |
| • Kenya Africa (Central East) | Nairobi | Kenyan shilling | 34255720 | 580367 |
| • Kiribati Oceana (North East) | South Tarawa | Australian dollar; Kiribati dollar | 99350 | 726 |
| • Korea, North Asia (Central East) | Pyongyang | North Korean won | 22487660 | 120538 |

## The independent countries of the world (*contd.*)

| Name and Location | Capital | Currency | Population | Area (km²) |
|---|---|---|---|---|
| • Korea, South Asia (Central East) | Seoul | South Korean won | 48846823 | 99538 |
| • Kuwait Asia (South West) | Kuwait City | Kuwaiti dinar | 2686873 | 17818 |
| • KyrgyzstanAsia (Central) | Bishkek | Kyrgyzstani som | 5263794 | 199900 |
| • Laos Asia (South East) | Vientiane | Lao kip | 5924145 | 236800 |
| • Latvia Europe (North East) | Riga | Latvian lats | 2306988 | 64600 |
| • Lebanon Asia (Central West) | Beirut | Lebanese lira | 3576818 | 10400 |
| • Lesotho Africa (South Central) | Maseru | Lesotho loti; South African rand | 1794769 | 30355 |
| • Liberia Africa (North West) | Monrovia | Liberian dollar | 3283267 | 111369 |
| • Libya Africa (North Central) | Tripoli | Libyan dinar | 5853452 | 1759540 |
| • Liechtenstein Europe (South Central) | Vaduz | Swiss franc | 34521 | 160 |
| • Lithuania Europe (North East) | Vilnius | Lithuanian litas | 3431033 | 65300 |
| • Luxembourg Europe (Central West) | Luxembourg City | Euro | 464904 | 2586 |
| • Macedonia Europe (South East) | Skopje | Macedonian denar | 2034060 | 25713 |
| • Madagascar Africa (South East) | Antananarivo | Malagasy ariary | 18605920 | 587041 |
| • Malawi Africa (South East) | Lilongwe | Malawian kwacha | 12883940 | 118484 |
| • Malaysia Asia (South East) | Putrajaya | Malaysian ringgit | 25347370 | 329847 |
| • Maldives Asia (South Central) | Male | Maldivian rufiyaa | 329198 | 298 |
| • Mali Africa (North West) | Bamako | West African CFA franc | 13518420 | 1240192 |
| • Malta Europe (South Central) | Valletta | Maltese lira | 401630 | 316 |

# The independent countries of the world (*contd.*)

| Name and Location | Capital | Currency | Population | Area (km²) |
|---|---|---|---|---|
| • Marshall Islands Oceania (North Central) | Majuro | United States dollar | 61963 | 181 |
| • Mauritania Africa (North West) | Nouakchott | Mauritanian ouguiya | 3068742 | 1025520 |
| • Mauritius Africa (South East) | Port Louis | Mauritian rupee | 1244663 | 2040 |
| • Mexico North America (South Central) | Mexico City | Mexican peso | 107029400 | 1958201 |
| • Micronesia, Federated States of Oceana (North Central) | Palikir | Micronesian dollar; United States dollar | 110487 | 702 |
| • Moldova Europe (Central East) | Chisinau | Moldovan leu | 4205747 | 33851 |
| • Monaco Europe (South Central) | Monaco | Euro | 35253 | 1 |
| • Mongolia Asia (North East) | Ulaanbaatar | Mongolian tugrug | 2646487 | 1564116 |
| • Montenegro Europe (South East) | Podgorica | Euro | 630548 | 14026 |
| • Morocco Africa (North West) | Rabat | Moroccan dirham | 31478460 | 446550 |
| • Mozambique Africa (South East) | Maputo | Mozambican metical | 19792300 | 801590 |
| • Myanmar (Burma) Asia (South East) | Naypyidaw | Myanmar kyat | 50519490 | 676578 |
| • Namibia Africa (South West) | Windhoek | Namibian dollar; South African rand | 2031252 | 824292 |
| • Nauru Oceana (North Central) | None | Australian dollar; Nauruan dollar | 13635 | 21 |
| • Nepal Asia (South Central) | Kathmandu | Nepalese rupee | 27132630 | 147181 |
| • Netherlands, The Europe (Central West) | Amsterdam | Euro | 16299170 | 41528 |
| • New Zealand Oceana (South East) | Wellington | New Zealand dollar | 4028384 | 270534 |

## The independent countries of the world (*contd.*)

| Name and Location | Capital | Currency | Population | Area (km²) |
|---|---|---|---|---|
| • Nicaragua North America (South East) | Managua | Nicaraguan córdoba | 5486685 | 130000 |
| • Niger Africa (North West) | Niamey | West African CFA franc | 13956980 | 1267000 |
| • Nigeria Africa (North West) | Abuja | Nigerian naira | 131529700 | 923768 |
| • Norway Europe (North Central) | Oslo | Norwegian krone | 4620275 | 385155 |
| • Oman Asia (South West) | Muscat | Omani rial | 2566981 | 309500 |
| • Pakistan Europe (South Central) | Islamabad | Pakistani rupee | 157935100 | 796095 |
| • Palau Oceana (North West) | Melekeok | Palauan dollar; United States dollar | 19949 | 459 |
| • Panama North America (South East) | Panama City | Panamanian balboa; United States dollar | 3231502 | 75517 |
| • Papua New Guinea Oceana (Central) | Port Moresby | Papua New Guinean kina | 5887138 | 462840 |
| • Paraguay South America (Central) | Asunción | Paraguayan guaraní | 6158259 | 406752 |
| • Peru South America (North West) | Lima | Peruvian nuevo sol | 27968240 | 1285216 |
| • Philippines Asia (South East) | Manila | Philippine peso | 83054480 | 300000 |
| • Poland Europe (Central East) | Warsaw | Polish zloty | 38529560 | 312685 |
| • Portugal Europe (South West) | Lisbon | Euro | 10494500 | 91982 |
| • Qatar Asia (South West) | Doha | Qatari riyal | 812842 | 11000 |
| • Romania Europe (South East) | Bucharest | Romanian leu | 21711470 | 238391 |
| • Russia Asia (North West) | Moscow | Russian ruble | 143201600 | 17098242 |
| • Rwanda Africa (Central East) | Kigali | Rwandan franc | 9037690 | 26338 |
| • Saint Kitts and Nevis North America (South East) | Basseterre | East Caribbean dollar | 42696 | 261 |

# The independent countries of the world (*contd.*)

| Name and Location | Capital | Currency | Population | Area (km²) |
|---|---|---|---|---|
| • Saint Lucia North America (South East) | Castries | East Caribbean dollar | 160765 | 539 |
| • Saint Vincent and the Grenadines North America (South East) | Kingstown | East Caribbean dollar | 119051 | 388 |
| • Samoa Oceana (Central East) | Apia | Samoan tala | 184984 | 2831 |
| • San Marino Europe (South Central) | San Marino | Euro | 28117 | 61 |
| • São Tomé and Príncipe Africa (Central West) | São Tomé | São Tomé and Príncipe dobra | 156523 | 964 |
| • Saudi Arabia Asia (South West) | Riyadh | Saudi riyal | 24573100 | 2149690 |
| • Senegal Africa (North West) | Dakar | West African CFA franc | 11658170 | 196722 |
| • Serbia Europe (South East) | Belgrade | Serbian dinar | 9396411 | 88361 |
| • Seychelles Africa (Central East) | Victoria | Seychellois rupee | 80654 | 455 |
| • Sierra Leone Africa (North West) | Freetown | Sierra Leonean leone | 5525478 | 71740 |
| • Singapore Asia (South East) | Singapore | Brunei dollar; Singapore dollar | 4483900 | 699 |
| • Slovakia Europe (Central East) | Bratislava | Slovak koruna | 5400908 | 49033 |
| • Slovenia Europe (South Central) | Ljubljana | Euro | 1966814 | 20256 |
| • Solomon Islands Oceana (Central East) | Honiara | Solomon Islands dollar | 477742 | 28896 |
| • Somalia Africa (North East) | Mogadishu | Somali shilling | 8227826 | 637657 |
| • South Africa Africa (South Central) | Bloemfontein | South African rand | 47431830 | 1221037 |
| • Spain Europe (South West) | Madrid | Euro | 43064190 | 505992 |
| • Sri Lanka Asia (South Central) | Kotte | Sri Lankan rupee | 20742910 | 65610 |

## The independent countries of the world (*contd.*)

| Name and Location | Capital | Currency | Population | Area (km²) |
|---|---|---|---|---|
| • Sudan Africa (North East) | Khartoum | New Sudanese pound; Sudanese dinar | 36232950 | 2505813 |
| • Suriname South America (North Central) | Paramaribo | Surinamese dollar | 449238 | 163820 |
| • Swaziland Africa (South East) | Mbabane | Swazi lilangeni | 1032438 | 17364 |
| • Sweden Europe (North Central) | Stockholm | Swedish krona | 9041262 | 449964 |
| • Switzerland Europe (South Central) | Bern | Swiss franc | 7252331 | 41284 |
| • Syria Asia (Central West) | Damascus | Syrian pound | 19043380 | 185180 |
| • Taiwan (Republic of China) Asia (Central East) | Taipei | New Taiwan dollar | 22894384 | 35980 |
| • Tajikistan Asia (Central) | Dushanbe | Tajikistani somoni | 6506980 | 143100 |
| • Tanzania Africa (Central East) | Dar es Salaam | Tanzanian shilling | 38328810 | 945087 |
| • Thailand Asia (South East) | Bangkok | Thai baht | 64232760 | 513115 |
| • Togo Africa (North West) | Lomé | West African CFA franc | 6145004 | 56785 |
| • Tonga Africa (Central East) | Nuku'alofa | Tongan pa'anga | 102311 | 747 |
| • Trinidad and Tobago North America (South East) | Port of Spain | Trinidad and Tobago dollar | 1305236 | 5130 |
| • Tunisia Africa (North West) | Tunis | Tunisian dinar | 10102470 | 163610 |
| • Turkey Europe (Central West) | Ankara | Turkish new lira | 73192840 | 783562 |
| • Turkmenistan Asia (Central) | Ashgabat | Turkmenistani manat | 4833266 | 488100 |
| • Tuvalu Oceana (Central East) | Funafuti | Australian dollar; Tuvaluan dollar | 10441 | 26 |
| • Uganda Africa (Central East) | Kampala | Ugandan shilling | 28816230 | 241038 |

## The independent countries of the world (*contd.*)

| Name and Location | Capital | Currency | Population | Area (km²) |
|---|---|---|---|---|
| • Ukraine Europe (Central East) | Kyiv | Ukrainian hryvnia | 46480700 | 603700 |
| • United Arab Emirates Europe (South West) | Abu Dhabi | United Arab Emirates dirham | 4495823 | 83600 |
| • United Kingdom Europe (North West) | London | British pound | 59667840 | 242900 |
| • United States North America (Central) | Washington, D.C. | United States dollar | 298212900 | 9629091 |
| • Uruguay South America (South East) | Montevideo | Uruguayan peso | 3463197 | 175016 |
| • Uzbekistan Asia (Central) | Tashkent | Uzbekistani som | 26593120 | 447400 |
| • Vanuatu Oceana (Central East) | Port Vila | Vanuatu vatu | 211367 | 12189 |
| • Vatican City Europe (South Central) | Vatican City | Euro | 783 | – |
| • Venezuela South America (North West) | Caracas | Venezuelan bolívar | 26749110 | 912050 |
| • Vietnam Asia (South East) | Hanoi | Vietnamese dong | 84238230 | 331689 |
| • Yemen Asia (South West) | Sana | Yemeni rial | 20974660 | 527968 |
| • Zambia Africa (South Central) | Lusaka | Zambian kwacha | 11668460 | 752618 |
| • Zimbabwe Africa (South East) | Harare | Zimbabwean dollar | 13009530 | 390757 |

# WORLD HISTORY

## IMPORTANT BATTLES

| Battle | Period | Countries Involved |
|---|---|---|
| Hundred Years War | 1337-1453 AD | France and England. |
| War of Roses | 1455-1485 | Civil War in England between the two rival royal houses of Lancaster and York; White and red rose were their respective symbols. |
| Anglo-Spanish War | 1588 | Spanish and English fleets fought in the English Channel; Defeat of the Spanish fleet |
| Battle of Gibraltar Bay | 1607 | The Dutch defeated the Spaniards and the Portuguese. |
| Thirty Years War | 1618-1648 | A religious-cum-political war between (Conto) the Lutherans and Catholics in Germany and developed into an international war. |
| Civil War of England | 1642 -1649 | Cavaliers (King Charles's supporters) and forces of the Parliament led by Oliver Cromwell; King Charles I was executed. |
| Seven Years War | 1756- 1763 | Britain and France against Austria and Prussia; British alliance won. |
| Battle of Nile | 1798 | British arid French fleets; Britain was victorious. |
| Battle of Trafalgar | 1805 | British fleet defeated fleets of France and Spain; British fleets commanded by Admiral Nelson, who was killed in the battle. |
| Battle of Austerlitz | 1805 | Britain, Austria, Russia and Prussia on one side and France on the other; French forces were victorious. |

## Important battles (*contd.*)

| Battle | Period | Countries Involved |
|--------|--------|--------------------|
| Battle of Borodino | 1812 | France led by Napoleon and the Russia; the resulted with the defeat of Napoleon. |
| Battle of Leipzig | 1813 | Germany and the combined forces of Austria, Prussia and Russia defeated Napoleon (French forces). |
| Battle of Waterloo | 1815 | British forces led by Duke of Wellington defeated French forces led by Napoleon Bonaparte; it was Napoleon's last battle; Napoleon was abdicated and was exiled to the Island of St Helena in South Atlantic where he died in 1821. |
| First China War | 1840 | China and Britain; Chinese forces yielded. It was a Trade War known as the 'Opium War'. |
| American Civil War | 1861-1865 | Northern Vs Southern states of America for the abolition of slavery; Abraham Lincoln defeated the Southern states. |
| Russo -Japanese War | 1904- 1905 | Russia and Japan in the Sea of Japan; Russia defeated; also called the 'Battle of Port Arthur' or 'Battle of Yalu'. |
| Balkan War | 1912 | Turkey and Balkan countries (Montenegro, Serbia, Bulgaria and Greece); Turkey defeated. |
| Balkan War II | 1913 | Invasion of Serbia and Greece by Bulgaria; Bulgaria was defeated by combined forces of Serbia, Greece, Romania, Montenegro, which stripped Turkey of most of its European territories. |
| World War 1 | 1914- 1918 | Germany (with Austria, Hungary and Turkey) against Britain (with France, US, Russia, Japan, Canada, Austria and Belgium); Germany and its allies were defeated. |

## Important battles (*contd.*)

| Battle | Period | Countries Involved |
|---|---|---|
| Battle of Jutland | 1916 | During World War I, naval battle between Germany and England in which Germany was defeated. |
| World War II | 1939 -45 | Axis powers (Germany, Italy and Japan) against the Allies (Britain, USSR, US, France and several other countries); Axis powers were defeated. |
| Desert War | 1942 | Italian Army from Libya invaded Egypt in order to attack British forces. |
| Korean War | 1954 | South Korea invaded by North Korea; North Korea was forced back by UN forces. |
| Israel-Arab War | 1967 | Six-day War, shortest war in history; Arab forces led by Egypt, Syria and Jordan were defeated. |
| Pakistan-Bangladesh | 1971 | Mukti Bahini forces aided by India against Pakistani forces stationed in Bangladesh (former East Pakistan); Pakistani forces surrendered and Bangladesh came into being as a new free nation. |
| Gulf War | 1991 | US led multinational forces attacked Iraq to oust Iraqi troops from Kuwait. |
| Kargil War | 1999 | India defeated Pakistani forces at Kargil. |
| US-Afghanistan War | 2001 | US led coalition forces attacked Afghanistan to bring down the Taliban regime in Afghanistan in retaliation to the September 11 terrorist attack in the USA. |
| Gulf War II | 2003 | US led coalition forces dethroned the Iraqi President Saddam Hussein |
| Israel-Lebanon | 2006 | Hezbollah kidnaps two Israeli soldiers and kills other three. Israel responds with massive air-strikes and artillery fire on targets in Lebanon. |

# HISTORY OF EUROPE

## Some Remarkable Features

*Magna Carta* (1215AD)

- A *Charter of Rights* granted to the Englishmen by King John II.
- It laid down the important principle that England should be governed by a definite law.
- Not to be ruled by the whims or will of a despotic ruler.
- Laid the foundation stone of the rights and liberties of the English people.
- Led to the setting up of a constitutional monarchy and a parliamentary form of government in England.

*Feudalism*

- A political and economic system of medieval Europe based on the relation of lord to a vassal.
- A lord would promise to protect a smaller landowner.
- In return, the small landowner surrendered his land and became a vassal.
- Feudal lords became rich and powerful.
- Kings had to depend on them for men and money.
- Land was the basis of such a system.

*Crusades*

- The military expeditions undertaken by European Christians in the 11th, 12th and 13th centuries to reclaim the holy land of Jerusalem from the Muslims. The Muslims did the vice-versa called 'crescentade'.

*Renaissance*

- Literally means 'revival' or 'rebirth'.
- During the reign of the Roman Empire, all the manuscripts containing the wisdom of the ancient Greeks were kept in Constantinople (now Istanbul).
- In 1453, Turkish Sultan Mahomet II attacked and occupied Constantinople.

- The scholars fled taking with them the manuscripts and settled in the cities of Italy to spread learning throughout the Western Europe.
- The movement slowly spread to England in the 15th and 16th centuries.

## Some Notable Rebels for Independence

### *American War for Freedom*

- Great Britain's command over trade in the American colonies created annoyance among the settlers.
- They were utterly dissatisfied with the controls and checks imposed upon them.
- There were acts of rebellion and this hostility flared into war in 1776.
- A declaration of independence was announced from Philadelphia under the leadership of George Washington.
- The struggle ended in victory in 1783.

### *The French Revolution* (1789- 1793)

- The autocratic monarch, nobles, clergy and privileged classes brought the socio-economic order to a point of collapse.
- King Louis XVI was inefficient enough to control an empire.
- The medieval feudal society's oppression of the serf-peasants led the country to financial bankruptcy.
- Period of French philosophers like Voltaire and Montesquieu.
- This class of intellectuals were inspired to change the face of social life of France.
- They gave a call for 'Liberty, Equality and Fraternity'.
- King Louis XVI and Queen Marie Antoinette were executed.
- Napoleon Bonaparte emerged as a great warrior bringing glory to France and breaking down feudalism in Europe.

### *The Russian Revolution* (1917 - 1922)

- The Czars of Russia were the most autocratic rulers of Europe.
- Their autocracy provoked the first stage of the Russian Revolution in February 1917 overthrowing the Czar Nicholas II.

- The second stage of this Revolution in October 1917 led to the establishment of the world's first communist state of the Bolsheviks under the leadership of Lenin.
- This was perhaps the greatest revolution after the French Revolution as it was not confined to Russia alone but it affected almost all countries of the world.
- It established the ideology of Marxism and led to the independence of several countries.

## THE WORLD WARS

*World War I (1914- 1918)*

- Franco-German rivalry proved to be the main cause of World War I.
- Prominent contestants at War were the Central Powers comprising Germany, Austria-Hungary, Turkey and Bulgaria on the one hand, and the Allied Powers comprising England, France, Belgium, Serbia, which were joined by Russia and Italy in 1915 and 1917, respectively.
- The immediate cause of War emerged when Austria attacked Serbia, after one month of Prince Ferdinand's murder which drew Russia towards Serbia.
- Germany entered the war to support Austria for it had vested interests in Turkey and was committed to support Austria. France, England along with some other countries joined the war and it took the shape of the World War I.

*Results/Consequences*

- Central powers were defeated.
- About 50 lakh Allied soldiers were killed.
- 1crore and 10 lakh were wounded.
- Bulgaria, Turkey and Austria surrendered.
- Germany signed the *Armistice Treaty* on November 11, 1918 and World War I ended.
- 1919 the *Treaty of Versailles* was signed which curbed powers of the German empire, further humiliating and weakening it.

*World War II* (1939- 1945)

- The situations responsible for the Second World War were as follows:
- The unjust Treaty of Versailles
- Improper behaviour of France
- Rise of the Nazis in Germany
- Dissatisfaction of Italy with the treaty
- Japan's expansion policy
- Imperialism of England and France.
- The main contestants of this War were the Axis Powers, also called the central powers, that included Germany, Italy and Japan on the one side while on the other side were the Allied Powers that included Britain, France, Russia, US, Poland and Benelux countries.(Bi-polarization)

*Results/Consequences*

- Hitler, who was responsible for this war, was initially very successful.
- Hitler later met with strong resistance when he attacked Russia in 1941, and was forced to retreat to Berlin.
- On learning that Germany had collapsed, he committed suicide on April 30, 1945 in Berlin.
- Thereafter Germany was divided into two parts- The East Germany under the control of Russia and the West Germany under the control of England, France and America (allies).
- Russia emerged as the single biggest power in the world.
- At the same time the struggle for freedom in the colonies under European control in Asia (India, Myanmar (Burma), Sri Lanka (Ceylon), Malaysia (Malaya), Egypt, etc.) caught on.
- The British Empire thus rapidly lost its command as more and more colonies won independence.
- The UNO was then established in 1945.
- IMPORTANT: When Japan did not agree to the demands of the allied powers to surrender, the first atom bomb was dropped on Hiroshima on August 5, 1945.

- The second atom bomb was dropped on Nagasaki on August 9, 1945.
- Japan then surrendered unconditionally on August 14, 1945 and World War II ended.

## TIMELINES OF WORLD HISTORY

| | |
|---|---|
| **BC** 6000 | • Neolithic settlements at Mehrgarh, Baluchistan and in the Indus Valley |
| | • Cultivation of wheat and barley |
| | • Discovery of copper |
| 5000 | • Rise of the Sumerian civilisation between the rivers of Tigris and Euphrates, an area later named— Mesopotamia (now Iran, South-western Asia, Turkey and Iraq) |
| | • Invention of the first written language |
| | • Invention of the wheel |
| | • Neolithic settlement in Egypt |
| | • From the annual rising of the waters of the Nile river, the first calendar of 365 days was evolved consisting of 12 months of 30 days each |
| 3500 | • Discovery of bronze in Egypt. Development of pottery in the Indus Valley, potter's wheel in use |
| | • Sumeria develops cuneiform writing |
| 2700 - 2600 | • Building of the pyramids in Egypt (one of the seven wonders of the ancient world) |
| 2500 | • Building of Mohenjodaro- site of the third oldest civilisation after the Sumerian and Egyptian |
| | • Sumerians evolved a numerical system, lunar calendar developed |
| 2500 | • Settlement of Andean civilisation (South America) |
| 2300 | • The Babylonians, Egyptians and Chinese built observatories upon the flat roofs of temples and this marked the beginning of Astrology |

|          |   |
|----------|---|
|          | • The Neolithic age in northern Europe |
| 2400     | • The Aryan migrants—the tribe from the banks of the Danube and South Russia spread southwards |
|          | • Moved through central and southern Europe and into India |
|          | • Evolution of the Aryan language from which most of the European languages have developed |
| 2205-1122 | • Rise of the Chinese civilisation along the banks of the Hwang Ho—building of stone-age villages |
|          | • Traditional beginning of the Hsia dynasty in China |
| 2200     | • Indonesian settlement in the Malay Peninsula |
|          | • Iron Age—during Hittites time, a fierce nation of Aryans who had conquered the Anatolian Peninsula developed the art of refining iron |
|          | • The rise of Babylon—city in ancient Mesopotamia. King Hammurabi raised the first army of the world |
|          | • The Bronze Age reaches Europe when Britain and its neighbours are invaded |
|          | • Civilization in Japan by the Jomons who invaded country from China and Korea |
| 1500     | • Compilation of the Rig Veda, the first book and the oldest sacred scriptures of Hinduism |
|          | • Rise of the Ganges civilisation—The Aryans advanced towards India reaching Ganges and Jamuna rivers |
| 1480     | • Moses leads Israelites out of Egypt |
| 1027     | • Chou dynasty begins in China |
| 1013     | • Rise of the Israelites in Palestine |
|          | • David (101 –973) established Israelite hegemony |
| 1000     | • Egypt ceases to be a power |
|          | • Epic civilisation in India—composition of the great epics: the Ramayana and the Mahabharata |
|          | • Phoenicians developed alphabetical writing |
| 850      | • The great works of poet Homer—Illiad and Odyssey |

| 776 | • The first Olympics in the city of Olympia in Greece |
|-----|---|
| 753 | • Foundation of the City of Rome by Romulus |
| 604 | • New empire in Mesopotamia with Babylon as capital |
|     | • Birth of Lao-Tse (China) — Founder of Taoism |
| 660 | • Birth of Zarasthushtra or Zoroaster, the founder of Zoroastrianism in Medea (Iran) |
| 600 | • Zoroaster spread his teaching that became Zoroastrianism |
| 586 | • Babylonians capture Jerusalem |
| 560 | • Birth of Lord Buddha |
| 553 | • Work of Pythagoras: A Greek settled in Italy, regarded as the greatest early Greek philosopher who discovered music and determined that an octave has eight nodes. |
| 550 | • Birth of Confucianism— the third great religion which emerged from China and became its state religion |
| 509 | • Foundation of the Roman Republic when great temples baths, circuses and triumph arches were built |
| 500 | • Building of the theatre at Delphi: The first man of theatre was a Greek called Thespis who founded the modern theatre around 500 BC |
| 490 | • The battle of Marathon, Athenians defeat Persians |
| 399 | • Socrates, the Athenian philosopher condemned to death |
| 387 | • Plato, a disciple of Socrates, founded the Academy Athens and wrote 'The Republic' |
| 347 | • Death of Plato: At this time he was working on his treatise The Laws |
| 336 | • Accession of Alexander the Great at the age of 22 he proclaimed that he would become master of the world |
| 335 | • Aristotle (a disciple of Plato) founded school of Philosophy |
| 300 - 280 | • Creation of the Colossus of Rhodes (one of the seven wonders of the ancient world) an immense Statue of Helios (Apollo), the Sun god. |

279 • Pharaohs' Lighthouse at Alexandria built (one of the seven wonders of the ancient world)

264 • Ashoka becomes Emperor of India

215 • The Great Wall of China built by Shih Hunga Ti (221 206)

73 • Slaves' revolt in Rome

58 • Caesar begins conquest of Gaul

55 • Invasion of Britain by Julius Caesar

44 • Julius Caesar murdered by Brutus

4 • Birth of Jesus Christ, the founder of Christianity

**AD** 29 • Crucifixion of Jesus Christ

64 • Burning of Rome—The fire continued for six days and almost demolished Rome; the Roman emperor Nero (AD 37 - 68) is said to have been responsible for the great fire

120 • Accession of Kanishka (Afghanistan)

570 • Birth of Prophet Mohammed (Mecca) the founder of Islam

868 • The first printed book Diamond Sutra—Buddhist scripture

1138 • Civil War in England – death of Henry I, his daughter Matilda was to become successor

1139 • Stephen ruled after Henry I died—Henry 11 son of Matilda

1163 • Oxford University founded

1215 • Magna Carta signed

1337 • Hundred Years War began between England and France ended in 1453

1348 • Plague in England

1388 • Geoffrey Chaucer wrote Canterbury Tales

1400 • Welsh War of Independence

1431 • Burning of Joan of Arc at the stake

1455 • War of Roses——Britain's civil war from 1455 to 1485

| 1492 | • Christopher Columbus discovers the West Indies |
|------|--------------------------------------------------|
| 1504 | • Mona Lisa painted by Leonardo da Vinci in Paris |
| 1556 | • Creation of Akbar's empire |
| 1564 | • Birth of Shakespeare |
| 1618 | • Thirty Years War commences in Germany |
|      | • Civil War in Britain; struggle between K Charles 1 and his Parliament which demanded democratic rights for Englishmen |
| 1653 | • Charles I of England executed |
| 1666 | • A Great Fire in London lasted four days; more than 1300 houses were destroyed |
| 1688 | • Glorious Revolution in Britain |
| 1689 | • Establishment of constitutional monarchy in England |
| 1756 | • Seven Years War began between combined forces of Britain and Prussia against Austria, France and Russia |
| 1770 | • James Cook discovers New South Wales |
| 1776 | • American Declaration of Independence |
| 1783 | • Recognition of independence of the United States of America by Britain |
| 1787 | • Drafting of the American Constitution |
| 1789 | • Outbreak of the French Revolution |
|      | • Louis XVI calls the Estates General |
|      | • The fall of Bastille |
| 1792 | • France becomes a Republic |
| 1793 | • Louis XV1, King of France, was executed on January 21, 1793 |
| 1798 | • Rebellion in Ireland; Execution of Wolfe Tone (1763-98), an Irish an evolutionary, inspired by the French Revolution |
|      | • Battle of the Nile |
| 1801 | • England and Ireland unite following unsuccessful rebellion in Ireland in 1798 |

1804    • May 18, 1804, Napoleon Bonaparte takes over as Emperor of France

1805    • Battle of Austerlitz: In July 1805, Britain, Austria, Russia and Prussia form a coalition against France. Though Russian and Austrian army outnumbered Napoleon's army, the French army was victorious

1812    • Battle of Borodino: Took place between French and Russians, Napoleon invaded Russia, defeating the Russians in Borodino but his men suffered heavily after reaching Moscow

1815    • Battle of Waterloo; Napoleon was defeated and exiled

1821    • Napoleon dies in St Helena
        • Greek Nationalist Revolt: Greeks launched war of independence against Turks

1830    • Greeks gain independence

1830    • Belgian independence
        • Revolution in July in France—! 8 years reign of King Louis Philippe begins

1833    • Abolition of slavery in Britain

1836    • Battle of Alamo: Texas became a republic but nine years later joined United States

1837    • Accession of Queen Victoria (1819-1901)

1838    • First Afghan War

1840    • Opium war between Britain and China; opium was illegally traded by British and Chinese merchants
        • Antarctica discovered

1843    • First International Peace Congress held in London

1847    • First Black Republic of Liberia founded

1848    • Karl Marx writes Communist Manifesto
        • February Revolution in France against Louis Philippe European Revolutions: Italy, Sicily France, Belgium, Holland, Germany, Prussia, Hungary and Czech Republic revolt

| | |
|---|---|
| 1854 | • Crimean War (Peninsula of Russia) between Russian troops and Turkish Empire |
| | • Florence Nightingale goes to Crimea |
| 1859 | • Origin of Species published by Darwin which created a major controversy (Theory of Natural Selection) |
| 1861 | • American Civil War on the question of African slaves Slavery abolished in America |
| 1863 | • Slavery abolished in the US by a proclamation by President Abraham Lincoln |
| | • International Football Association formed |
| 1864 | • Durant found Red Cross |
| 1865 | • End of American Civil War, Abraham Lincoln, President of USA, assassinated |
| 1869 | • Suez Canal opened |
| 1870 | • Franco-Prussian War by Bismarck (Prussian PM) for Spanish Throne—Treaty of Frankfurt signed |
| 1871 | • Rugby Football Union founded in London |
| 1878 | • Cyprus ceded to Britain |
| 1881 | • First South African War—Dutch settlers in South Africa rose against the British to gain independence and the British were defeated. |
| 1882 | • Australian cricket team wins against England in the 'Ashes' |
| 1883 | • Egypt occupied by Britain |
| 1886 | • Lawn Tennis Association formed in England |
| 1889 | • Eiffel Tower built in Paris |
| 1896 | • Olympic Games revived in Athens |
| 1899 | • Second South African War between British and Dutch settlers—Union of South Africa formed |
| 1901 | • Theodore Roosevelt becomes the youngest President in the history of USA Death of Queen Victoria of England |
| 1904 | • Russo-Japanese War; Russia made peace with Japan in 1906 |

| 1905 | • Unrest in Russia—preparation for the great revolution |
|------|------|
| 1909 | • Discovery of North Pole by Commander Robert Peary Russian navy defeated by Japan |
| 1910 | • Korea occupied by Japan |
| 1911 | • China declared Republic—Revolution took place under Sun Yat Sen (1866— 1925) |
| 1912 | • Establishment of the Chinese Republic |
| 1914 | • First World War begins |
|      | • Panama Canal opens |
| 1916 | • First World War spreads—Italy joins allies (Bulgaria and Central Powers) |
|      | • Battle of Verdun (France) between France and Germany (during World War I) |
| 1917 | • United States enters the World War |
|      | • Outbreak of Russian Revolution |
| 1918 | • First World War ends—Armistice signed on November 11 |
|      | • Czech Republic and Poland become independent Czar Nicholas II (Russia) assassinated |
| 1919 | • Treaty of Versailles |
| 1920 | • League of Nations formed under Treaty of Versailles |
|      | • International Court of Justice established at the Hague, Netherlands |
| 1921 | • Formation of Irish Free State |
| 1922 | • Egypt gains independence from British rule |
| 1923 | • End of monarchy in Turkey—Mustafa Kamal becomes President |
|      | • Hitler imprisoned due to political unrest in Germany and fear of communist revolution |
| 1924 | • Lenin dies—rise of Stalin |
|      | • First Labour government established in Britain |
| 1931 | • Spanish Republic proclaimed |

| | |
|---|---|
| 1933 | • Hitler comes to power in Germany and becomes Chancellor |
| 1934 | • After the death of Von Hindenburg, Hitler becomes President of Germany |
| 1935 | • Italy invades Abyssinia |
| 1936 | • Abyssinia annexed by Italy |
| | • Civil War in Spain |
| 1938 | • Germany annexes Austria |
| 1939 | • Germany annexes Czech Republic |
| | • Second World War commences |
| 1940 | • Germany invades Denmark, Norway and the low countries |
| | • Churchill becomes Prime Minister of Britain |
| | • Fall of France—after German invasion |
| | • Battle of Britain with Germany |
| 1941 | • Germany invades Russia but is defeated |
| | • Japan attacks Pearl Harbour |
| 1942 | • The Desert War |
| | • Battle of Stalingrad |
| | • Japanese capture south-east Asian countries up to Burma |
| 1943 | • Surrender of Italy |
| 1944 | • Allied forces invade France |
| | • Liberation of Paris—General Charles de Gaulle takes over provisional government |
| 1945 | • Surrender of Germany and Japan—First atom bomb was dropped over Hiroshima, Japan (August 6, 1945) followed by the second over Nagasaki, Japan (August 9, 1945) |
| | • San Francisco Conference on the formation of the United Nations Organisation (April 25- 26); Formation of the UNO (October 24) |
| 1946 | • General Charles de Gaulle resigns |
| 1947 | • India attains independence—Partition of India |

1948
- Czech Republic forms Communist Government
- State of Israel proclaimed in Palestine (Jewish state)
  First Indo-Pak war

1949
- NATO (North Atlantic Treaty Organisation) formed; establishment of German Republic
- Mao-Tse-Tung proclaims Chinese People's Republic (Communist Government formed)

1950
- War in Korea; Tibet occupied by Chinese forces

1951
- Japanese Peace Treaty signed

1952
- King Farouq of Egypt overthrown. Accession of Queen Elizabeth II of England

1953
- Eisenhower becomes US President
- Mount Everest scaled by Edmund Hillary and Tenzing Norgay
- Death of Stalin
- Ceasefire in Korea

1954
- First Hydrogen bomb tested by the United States
- Nikita Khruschev becomes First Secretary of the Communist Party of Soviet Union

1955
- First Afro-Asian conference of heads of states held in Bandung, Indonesia

1956
- Hungarian Revolution
  Joint invasion of Egypt by Britain, France and Israel
- Nationalization of Suez Canal

1957
- Sputnik I launched by the former USSR—the first man made satellite

1958
- Coup in Iraq and monarchy abolished

1960
- Africa Year—16 African countries achieve independence
  France explodes atomic device in Sahara (Africa)

1961
- John F. Kennedy becomes the US President
- First man in space—Yuri Alekseyevich Gagarin of Russia
- Building of Berlin wall around former west Berlin to cut off communication with the former East Berlin

| 1962 | • Algeria attains independence |
|------|--------------------------------|
| 1963 | • Partial Test Ban Treaty signed in Moscow by UK, US and the former USSR |
|      | • John F. Kennedy, President of US assassinated |
| 1964 | • American president signs the Civil Rights Bill granting equal rights to Blacks |
|      | • Escalation of the Vietnam War |
|      | • Martin Luther King (Black American clergyman) awarded Nobel Peace Prize |
|      | • China explodes its first atomic device |
| 1965 | • Sir Winston Churchill dies |
|      | • First space walk March 8, 1965 by Russian cosmonaut Aleksei Arkhipovich Leonov |
|      | • Second Indo-Pak War |
|      | • Singapore becomes sovereign nation |
| 1966 | • Cultural Revolution in China |
|      | • Tashkent Declaration between India and Pakistan signed |
| 1967 | • The Six-day Arab-Israel war—Arabs defeated |
|      | • Military coup in Greece |
|      | • First human heart transplant operation conducted by Dr Christian Barnard on Louis Washkansky donor was Denise Darval |
| 1968 | • Martin Luther King assassinated Invasion of Czech Republic by Warsaw Pact countries |
|      | • South Pacific Island of Nauru and Mauritius become independent |
|      | • UN approves Nuclear Non-Proliferation Treaty |
| 1969 | • US astronauts Neil Armstrong and Edwin E. Aldrin Jr land on the moon on July 21 and Michael Collins orbits the moon in the mother ship |
|      | • Richard Nixon becomes 37th President of the US |
| 1970 | • West German-Soviet Non-Aggression Treaty signed |
|      | • Charles de Gaulle, former President of France, dies |

- Soviet Lunokhod 1 lands on the moon
- Fiji achieves Independence

1971
- Indo-Pak War (December 3- 17)
- Mujibur Rahman declares Bangladesh independent
- China admitted to UN; Taiwan expelled
- India recognises Bangladesh
- Apollo-15 launched; man's first drive on the moon

1972
- Bhutto releases Mujibur Rahrnan
- Pakistan leaves Commonwealth
- Ceylon becomes Sri Lanka Republic

1973
- Bahamas becomes independent
- Afghanistan ends monarchy and becomes a Republic
- War breaks out in West Asia between Israel, Egypt and Syria

1974
- South Vietnam Government (supported by US) surrenders to National Liberation Front Forces ending the civil war India's first nuclear blast at Pokharan in Rajasthan (Thar desert)
- Malta becomes a Republic

1975
- Mujibur Rahman assumes full power as the President; one- party rule in Bangladesh
- Margaret Thatcher elected first woman leader of the British Conservative Party
- Mozambique becomes free after nearly 500 years of Portuguese rule Angola free from Portuguese rule India enters space age with the launch of satellite 'Aryabhatta'
- India lifts Hockey World Cup at Kuala Lumpur
- Laos becomes a Republic
- Army coup in Bangladesh and Sheikh Mujibur Rahman assassinated

1976
- Mao Tse-Tung of China dies
- Jimmy Carter becomes President of the US
- India elected to UN Security Council

| | |
|---|---|
| 1977 | • Gen. Zia-ul-Haq takes over the Pakistan Government |
| | • Maj. Gen. Zia-ur-Rahman sworn in as new Bangladesh President |
| 1978 | • First test tube baby: Louise Brown born in Lancashire |
| 1979 | • Observed as International year of the Child |
| | • Iran proclaimed Islamic Republic and Ayatollah Khomeini returns to Iran after 14 years of exile |
| | • Margaret Thatcher becomes the first woman Prime Minister of Britain |
| | • China invades Vietnam |
| | • Soviet intervention in Afghanistan |
| | • Zulfikar Ali Bhutto, former Prime Minister of Pakistan, executed |
| | • Zimbabwe achieves independence. |
| | • Iran—Iraq war commences |
| | • Ronald Reagan becomes President o the US |
| | • Marshal Tito of Yugoslavia dies. |
| | • Observed as International Year of the Disabled |
| | • US Space Shuttle Columbia makes a space trip |
| | • President Sadat of Egypt and Zia-ur-Rahman of Bangladesh assassinated. |
| | • Belize becomes independent |
| | • Barbuda becomes independent |
| | • Ronald Reagan sworn in as the 40th President of the US |
| | • Egypt officially gets back Sinai peninsula after 15 years of Israeli occupation |
| | • Sheila Cameron becomes the first woman Vicar-General of the Church of England |
| | • Queen Elizabeth honours Mother Teresa with the Order of Merit (Highest British honour) |
| 1984 | • China and Britain sign agreement to return Hong Kong to Chinese control in 1997 |
| | • 23rd Olympic Games held in Los Angeles |

Egypt resumes diplomatic relations with the USSR

- Ronald Reagan re-elected President of the US
- Mikhail Gorbachev takes over as the first elected Secretary- General of the Communist Party of Russia
- Pakistan's first civilian government in eight years headed by Prime Minister Mohammed Khan Junejo sworn in; Marshal Law lifted in Pakistan
- More than 20,000 people dead as volcano erupts in Columbia
- US solar system probe, Voyager-2, discovers six new moons of the planet Uranus
- US Space Shuttle, Challenger, explodes after launching, all the seven on-board killed
- Swedish Prime Minister, Olaf Palme, killed
  Lt. Gen. H. M. Ershad elected 10th President of Bangladesh
- Benazir Bhutto returns triumphant to Pakistan from exile

1987
- West German Chancellor, Helmut Kohl, returned to power
- Mrs Margaret Thatcher wins a third consecutive term of office as PM of Britain
- Lebanese PM Rashid Karami killed in helicopter crash
- Australian PM Beb Hawke wins third terra
- David Lange re-elected PM of New Zealand

1988
- Khan Abdul Ghafar Khan passed away in Peshawar
- French President Francois Mitterrand re-elected for another term of seven years
- Pakistan President Zia ul Haque killed in a plane crash
- George Bush elected the 41st US President
- PLO Chairman Yasser Arafat declares state of Palestine with capital at Jerusalem
- Benazir Bhutto sworn in PM of Pakistan
- Ghulam Ishaq Khan elected President of Pakistan
- R. Premadasa elected President of Sri Lanka

1989
- George Bush sworn in President of the US
- PLO leader, Yasser Arafat, elected President of Palestine
- Iranian leader, Ayatollah Khomeni, dies
- Rafsanjani elected as new Iranian President
- F. W. de Klerk sworn in as the President of South Africa
- Dismantling of Berlin wall begins

1990
- Nelson Mandela freed from prison after 27 years
- Iraq invades Kuwait; cue Emir of Kuwait flees to Saudi Arabia
- Benazir Bhutto relinquishes power
- West and East Germany united
- Zimbabwean President, Robert Mugabe, re-elected
- Lithuania, Latvia, Belarus and Kazakhstan declare independence from the USSR
- Nawaz Sharif sworn in as Pakistan PM
- Lt Gen. H. M. Ershad quits as Bangladesh President

1991
- The USSR formally disintegrated into 15 republics
- Russian President Gorbachev ousted in a bloodless coup
- Begum Khaleda Zia appointed the first woman Prime Minister of Bangladesh
- Iraq refuses to withdraw from Kuwait and Gulf war begins; US-led coalition forces from 28 countries attacked Iraq; ceasefire declared after 44 days and Kuwait liberated

1992
- Yugoslavia expelled from the UNO
- Boutros Boutros Ghali assumes charge as Secretary General of the UN
- Bill Clinton of the Democrat Party elected as 42nd US President
- Bangladesh President Lt Gen. H. M. Ershad sentenced to three years' imprisonment for illegally amassing wealth

- India and UK sign treaty against terrorism
- The UN Security Council votes unanimously to establish a UN Protection Force (UNPROFOR) for civil war torn Yugoslavia
- The Earth Summit—UN Conference on Environment and Development (UNCED)—held in Rio De Janeiro, Brazil
- Prince Charles and Princess Diana of Britain announce their separation
- 25th Olympics in Barcelona, Spain (July 25 — August 9)

1993
- Bill Clinton takes over as US President (January 20)
- Sri Lankan President, Ranatunga Premadassa assassinated in a powerful bomb blast
- G-15 Summit in New Delhi, March 30
- New World Trade Treaty, April 15

1994
- Chandrika Kumartunga elected Sri Lankan President
- Plague outbreak in India
- Devastating earthquake in Maharashtra
- First Communist Government in Nepal
- Refuelling Machine malfunctioning at the Wyefa nuclear plant
- Explosion in lead/zinc mine in Guangxi, China—nearly 120 died

1995
- Britain-Ireland sign Peace Pact
- 100 years of world cinema
- Devastating earthquake in Japan and Russia
- Israeli Prime Minister, Yitzhak Rabin, assassinated

1996
- Russia becomes member of European Union on Jan. 26
- Blasts in London put an end to Irish ceasefire
- Leakage of radiation due to human error and technical failure at Dimitrovgrad nuclear research centre in Russia

1997
- After being under British sovereignty for 156 years, Hong Kong was returned to China on July 1, 1997. Henceforth,

it will be called the 'Hong Kong Special Administrative Region' (HKSAR). Civil war in Cambodia

1998   • Nuclear tests conducted by India and Pakistan

1999   • Euro, the European single currency comes into effect on January 1999, with 11 countries participating

       • Kosovo crisis deepens in April 1999 as Russia moved warships into Mediterranean

       • Danger of 'Mir'—the Russian space lab averted as Kazakhstan lets Russian cargo spacecraft 'Progress' to take off from Baikonur cosmodrome in July 1999 to make urgent food, water and oxygen deliveries to the cosmonauts in the flying lab in the orbit

       • Army takes over in Pakistan in Oct 1999 in a bloodless coup headed by Army Chief Parvez Musharraf

       • The people of East Timor rejected the autonomous plan within Indonesia and votted for independence from Indonesia

2000   • In July 2000, ousted Pakistani PM Nawaz Sharif was jailed for 14 years

       • In March, acting President of Russia, Vladimir Putin, won the presidential elections

       • Bashir Assed, son of former President Hafez Assad, became President of Syria in July 2000

2001   • On September 11, 2001 in a horrific sequence of destruction, terrorists crashed two planes into the World Trade Center at New York, USA

       • America's war against terrorism begins in Afghanistan against the ruling Taliban in October 2001

       • Taliban surrenders Kandhar, their last stronghold in Afghanistan, on Dec 7, 2001

       • An earthquake hits Gujarat in India where more than 20,000 died

       • Likud party leader Ariel Sharon wins election as Prime Minister of Israel

- Former Yugoslavian President Slobadan Milosevic to be tried on war crimes; Japanese cities of Urawa, Omiya and Yono merge to form the city of Saitama
- World's first self-contained artificial heart implanted in Robert Tools
- Attack on WTC in New York City, The Pentagon in Arlington, Virginia and rural Pennsylvania
- 'Boom Accord' on Kabul (Afghanistan) signed on Dec. 5, 2001 and Hamid Karzai made makeshift President of Afghanistan

2002
- In February, the govt of Sri Lanka signed 'Permanent Ceasefire Agreement' with the Liberation Tigers of Tamil Eelam (LTTE). The peace agreement was brokered by the Norwegian govt
- In June, Afghanistan's grand assembly—'Loya Jirga'—chose leader Hamid Karzai as President of Afghanistan
- SARS (Severe Acute Respiratory Syndrome) outbreaks in China and spreads all over world killing thousands, to be contained only during June 2003
- World Summit on sustainable development
- Introduction of Euro bank notes and coins in European Union
- Beginnings of operation Anaconda in Eastern Afghanistan;
- Launch of ENVISAT (Environmental satellite), carrying heaviest payload of 8500 kg
- Quaoar, a trans-Neptunian object, discovered orbiting Sun in Kuiper belt

2003
- In February, the Space Shuttle Columbia perished in space and finally disintegrated over Texas, about 16 minutes before its scheduled landing at the Kennedy Space Centre, USA. All its 7 onboard astronauts, which included Dr Kalpana Chawla, the first and only Indian-American in space, were died

- In July, the government of Sri Lanka announced its decision to grant citizenship to 168,141 Tamils of Indian Origins (TIOs) who were denied the same at the time of Sri Lankan independence in 1948
- In May, the White House announced the US roadmap for peace in West Asia
- Luiz Inacio Lula Da Silva becomes 37th president of Brazil
- 300th anniversary of Saint Petersburg, celebrated in Russia

2004
- India wins a historic cricket series in Pakistan
- Brain Lara becomes the first cricketer to reach the coveted score of 400 runs in a test inning against England
- The 2004 US presidential campaign between President George W. Bush and Democratic Senator John Kerry was one of the closely followed and heated cases in the recent US history, Bush defeated Kerry to start his second term as US president
- Tsunami hits South-east Asian nations around Indian Ocean; more than 283000 killed
- Joseph Deiss becomes the President of Switzerland
- NASA MER-A (Spirit) and MER-B lands on Mars (Opportunity)
- EU Expansion takes place by including 10 members, namely, Poland, Lithuania, Latvia, Estonia, Czech Republic, Slovakia, Slovenia, Hungry, Malta and Cyprus
- Brazil successfully launches its first rocket into space
- Yasser Arafat, leader of the Palestinian Authority dies in a Paris Hospital

2005
- Pakistan averages its defeat in 2004 by defeating India in India in one-dayers. Test-series drawn
- Terrorists strike London transportation system. Bombing three underground rail terminals and one bus killing more than 50 people in July a day after London was awarded to host 2012 Olympics

- An earthquake with a magnitude of 7.6 struck Pakistan-controlled Kashmir on October 8. More than 81,000 people were killed and 2.5 million left homeless. India suffered about 1,500 casualties
- George W. Bush begins his second term as 43rd President of United States
- Pope John Paul II dies and is succeeded by Pope Benedict XVI
- Terrorist attack in London
- Hurricane Katrina Strikes eastern North America

2006
- On June 12, a stampede by pilgrims in the annual Haj killed more than 350 people in Mecca, Saudi Arabia
- In March 2006, India and USA agreed on Nuclear deal that permitted the sale of US Nuclear to India despite the fact India has never signed the International Nuclear Non- proliferation Agreement
- On May 27, a 6.3 magnitude earthquake killed more than 5,700 people and destroyed 135000 homes
- On July 11, more than eight bomb blasts rocked Mumbai killing more than 200 people
- Uganda's President Yoweri Muserveni wins his second re election
- Slobodan Milosevic found dead in his cell in UN war crimes tribunal's detention centre
- Han Myeong Sook becomes first female Prime Minister of South Korea
- Ban Ki-moon is elected as the new Secretary-General of the United Nations
- Saddam Hussein, former Iraq President, is executed in Baghdad;

2007
- Bulgarian and Romania join the European Union.
- Nancy Pelosi becomes the first woman speaker of the House in US
- The 200th anniversary of the finalization of the 1807

Abolition of Slave Trade Act, which abolished the slave trade in the British Empire is marked

- The Solomon Islands shaken by a magnitude 8.1 earthquake, and hit by a subsequent tsunami
- Tornado strikes Greensburg, Kansa destroying about 90% of the town and kills around 12 people
- Nicolas Sarkozy becomes the President of the French Republic
- Gordon Brown becomes Prime Minister of the UK after the present Prime Minister Tony Blair steps down
- Political crisis begins in Pakistan after the suspension of Supreme Court Chief Justice Iftikhar Muhammad Chaudhry by Gen. Pervez Musharraf
- NASA's space shuttle Atlantis returned safely to earth on June 22, 2007 at the Edwards Air Force Base, California. Sunita Williams returns after a record 195 days stay in space
- The **financial crisis of 2007–present** is a financial crisis triggered by a liquidity shortfall in the United States banking system.
- It has resulted in the collapse of large financial institutions, the "bail out" of banks by national governments and downturns in stockmarkets around the world.
- It is considered by many economists to be the worst financial crisis since the Great Depression of the 1930s.
- It contributed to the failure of key businesses, declines in consumer wealth estimated in the trillions of U.S. dollars, substantial financial commitments incurred by governments, and a significant decline in economic activity.
- Both market-based and regulatory solutions have been implemented or are under consideration

- Significant risks remain for the world economy over the 2010–2011 periods.
- Although this economic period has at times been referred to as "the Great Recession," this same phrase has been used to refer to every recession of the several preceding decades.
- The collapse of a global housing bubble, which peaked in the U.S. in 2006, caused the values of securities tied to real estate pricing to plummet thereafter, damaging financial institutions globally
- Had an impact on global stock markets, where securities suffered large losses during late 2008 and early 2009.
- Economies worldwide slowed during this period as credit tightened and international trade declined.

## CURRENT AFFAIRS

**2011 (MMXI)** was a common year that started on a Saturday in the Gregorian calendar. It was the 2011th year of the Common Era (CE) and *Anno Domini* (AD) designations; the 11th year of the 3rd millennium and of the 21st century; and the 2nd of the 2010s.The United Nations designated 2011 as the International Year of Forests and the International Year of Chemistry.

- January 4 2011 – Tunisian street vendor Mohamed Bouazizi dies after setting himself on fire a month earlier, sparking anti-government protests in Tunisia and later other Arab nations.
- March 11 – Magnitude protests become known collectively as the Arab Spring.
- Earthquake and subsequent tsunami hit the east of Japan, killing 15,840 and leaving another 3,926 missing.
- April 29 – An estimated two billion people watch the wedding of Prince William, Duke of Cambridge and Catherine Middleton at Westminster Abbey in London.

- May 1 – U.S. President Barack Obama announces that Osama bin Laden, the founder and leader of the militant group Al-Qaeda, has been killed during an American military operation in Pakistan.
- July 7 – The world's first artificial organ transplant is achieved, using an artificial windpipe coated with stem cells.

**2012 (MMXII)** is a leap year that started on a Sunday in the Gregorian calendar, and it is the current year. It is the 2012th year of the Common Era (CE) and *Anno Domini* (AD) designations, the 12th year of the 3rd millennium and of the 21st century, and the 3rd of the 2010s.

There are a variety of popular beliefs about the year 2012. These beliefs range from the spiritually transformative to the apocalyptic, and center upon various contemporary interpretations of the Mesoamerican Long Count calendar. Scientists have disputed the apocalyptic versions.

## January

- January 20 - January 28 – The death toll of a series of co-ordinated bombing attacks in Kano, Nigeria, rises to 185. The attacks, which target police stations across the city, are blamed on the radical Islamist group Boko Haram. Eleven Islamist militants are killed in a shootout in the northeastern Nigerian city of Maiduguri.
- January 23 – The European Union formally adopts embargo against Iran in protest of that nation's continued effort to enrich uranium.

## February

- February 6 – Diamond Jubilee of Queen Elizabeth II, marking the 60th anniversary of her accession to the thrones of the United Kingdom, Canada, Australia and New Zealand, and the 60th anniversary of her becoming Head of the Commonwealth.

## SCHEDULED EVENTS: 2012

## May

- May 12 – August 12 – The 2012 World Expo is to be held in Yeosu, South Korea.

## June

- June 6 – The century's second and last solar transit of Venus occurs. The next pair are predicted to occur in 2117 and 2125.

## July

- July 27 – August 12 – 2012 Summer Olympics held in London.

## August

- August 6–20 – Mars Science Laboratory, also known as the Curiosity rover, is scheduled to land on Mars.

## December

- December 21 – The Mesoamerican Long Count calendar, notably used by the pre-Columbian Mayan civilization among others, completes a "great cycle" of thirteen *b'ak'tuns* (periods of 144,000 days each) since the mythical creation date of the calendar's current era. December 31 – The first commitment period of the Kyoto Protocol ends.

# INVENTIONS AND DISCOVERIES

## 20th century

- 1905 – Albert Einstein: theory of special relativity, explanation of Brownian motion, and photoelectric effect
- 1906 – Walther Nernst: Third law of thermodynamics
- 1909 – Fritz Haber: Haber Process
- 1911 – Ernest Rutherford: Atomic nucleus
- 1911 – Heike Kamerlingh Onnes: Superconductivity
- 1912 – Alfred Wegener: Continental drift
- 1912 – Max von Laue : x-ray diffraction
- 1913 – Henry Moseley: defined atomic number
- 1913 – Niels Bohr: Model of the atom
- 1915 – Albert Einstein: theory of general relativity – also David Hilbert
- 1915 – Karl Schwarzschild: discovery of the Schwarzschild radius leading to the identification of black holes

- 1918 – Emmy Noether: Noether's theorem – conditions under which the conservation laws are valid
- 1920 – Arthur Eddington: Stellar nucleosynthesis
- 1924 – Wolfgang Pauli: quantum Pauli exclusion principle
- 1924 – Edwin Hubble: the discovery that the Milky Way is just one of many galaxies
- 1925 – Erwin Schrödinger: Schrödinger equation (Quantum mechanics)
- 1927 – Werner Heisenberg: Uncertainty principle (Quantum mechanics)
- 1927 – Georges Lemaître: Theory of the Big Bang
- 1928 – Paul Dirac: Dirac equation (Quantum mechanics)
- 1929 – Edwin Hubble: Hubble's law of the expanding universe
- 1929 – Lars Onsager's reciprocal relations, a potential fourth law of thermodynamics
- 1934 – James Chadwick: Discovery of the neutron
- 1934 – Clive McCay: Calorie Restriction extends the maximum lifespan of another species Calorie_restriction#Research_history
- 1938 – Otto Hahn and Fritz Strassmann: Nuclear fission
- 1943 – Oswald Avery proves that DNA is the genetic material of the chromosome
- 1947 – William Shockley, John Bardeen and Walter Brattain invent the first transistor
- 1948 – Claude Elwood Shannon: 'A mathematical theory of communication' a seminal paper in Information theory.
- 1948 – Richard Feynman, Julian Schwinger, Sin-Itiro Tomonaga and Freeman Dyson: Quantum electrodynamics
- 1951 – George Otto Gey propagates first cancer cell line, HeLa
- 1952 – Jonas Salk: developed and tested first polio vaccine
- 1953 – Crick and Watson: helical structure of DNA, basis for molecular biology
- 1963 – Lawrence Morley, Fred Vine, and Drummond Matthews: Paleomagnetic stripes in ocean crust as evidence of plate tectonics (Vine-Matthews-Morley hypothesis).

- 1964 – Murray Gell-Mann and George Zweig: postulate quarks leading to the standard model
- 1964 – Arno Penzias and Robert Woodrow Wilson: detection of CMBR providing experimental evidence for the Big Bang
- 1965 – Leonard Hayflick: normal cells divide only a certain number of times: the Hayflick limit
- 1967 – Jocelyn Bell Burnell and Antony Hewish discover first pulsar
- 1984 – Kary Mullis invents the polymerase chain reaction, a key discovery in molecular biology. Andrew Wiles proves Fermats Last Theorem
- 1986 – Karl Müller and Johannes Bednorz: Discovery of High-temperature superconductivity
- 1995 – Michel Mayor and Didier Queloz definitively observe the first extrasolar planet around a main sequence star
- 1997 – Roslin Institute: Dolly the sheep was cloned.
- 1997 – CDF and DØ experiments at Fermilab: Top quark.
- 1998 – Gerson Goldhaber and Saul Perlmutter observed that the expansion of the universe is accelerating.

**21st century**
- 2001 – The first draft of the human genome is completed.
- 2001 - Telesurgery was found by Jacques Marescaux
- 2001 - Self Healing Materials by Keneth Matsumura
- 2007 - James Thomson of the University of Wisconsin reported that they had reprogrammed regular skin cells to behave just like embryonic stem cells.
- 2010 – J. Craig Venter Institute creates the first synthetic bacterial cell.

# PART FOUR

# WORLD ORGANIZATIONS

## UNITED NATIONS (UN)

- On October 24, 1945, the United Nations, an association of States was formed
- It is committed to maintain international peace and security
- Committed to co-operation in solving international political, economic, social, cultural, and humanitarian problems towards achieving this end.
- The members of this association are the sovereign states bound by a Charter (Constitution).
- It is the world's largest international organization which came into existence on October 24, 1945.
- Its reconstitution was thought to be essential because the League of Nations previously organised with the same objectives was a failure.
- Hence, the governments of China, France, United Kingdom, the former USSR, the United States of America and a majority of other states ratified the UN Charter and signed it on June 26, 1945 along with the delegates of 50 countries at San Francisco (US).
- Its first regular session was held in London in January 1946 and Trygve Lie (Norway) was elected its first Secretary General.
- Its Headquarters are located at the First Avenue, UN Plaza, New York City, USA.
- *The UN Flag* was adopted on October 20, 1947 by the UN General Assembly
- The UN flag bears the white UN emblem, superimposed on a light blue background, consisting of the global map projected from the North Pole and embraced in twin olive branches which symbolises peace.

- It can never, in any situation, be subordinated to any other flag in the world.

## Aims and Objectives

- To maintain peace and security in the world
- To work together to remove poverty, disease and illiteracy and encourage respect for each others rights of basic freedom
- To develop friendly relations among nations
- To be a centre to help nations achieve these common goals

## Membership of the UN

*Admission of Members*

- New members are admitted to the General Assembly on the recommendation of the Security Council and two-thirds of the members should vote in favour.
- Members are expelled or suspended in the same manner.

## Permanent Members of the Security Council

- There are five permanent members of the Security Council: 1. China, 2. France, 3. Russia, 4. UK and 5. US .

*Veto*

- A negative vote by a permanent member barring action by the Security Council is called a veto.
- Each permanent member enjoys the power to veto.

*Membership*

- Initially there were only 51 members when the UN Charter was signed
- The membership rose to 185 by 1994.
- The nations which were admitted to the UN in 1993 are: the Czech Republic, Slovakia, Macedonia, Monaco, Eritrea and Andorra.
- Palau, a newly independent Pacific nation which had been under the trusteeship of the USA, became a member in 1994.
- The Vatican City is not a member of the UN but is an 'observer', which means it has all rights of full membership except voting.

**Note:** It can easily become a member any time by submitting a petition. Switzerland, which was also an observer state from 1948, became a member in 2002.

- Presently the total number of member nations is 192.
- The official languages of the UN are Arabic, Chinese, English, French, Russian, and Spanish.

## Organizations of the UN

The UN has allocated different functions to its different principal bodies which include:

1. The General Assembly
2. The Security Council
3. The Economic and Social Council
4. International Court of Justice
5. Trusteeship Council
6. Secretariat

## General Assembly (GA)

- It constitutes the main deliberative body comprising all the UN members.
- Its headquarters are located in New York. Each member can send five delegates but each nation has only one vote.

*Functions of the General Assembly:*

- All other UN bodies report to the General Assembly.
- It discusses and makes recommendations on any subject covered under the UN Charter, except those with which the Security Council may be dealing.

*Meetings*

- The General Assembly meets once a year in regular sessions beginning on the third Tuesday in September and the general debate is organised over a period of two weeks.

## Security Council (SC)

- Comprising 15 members – 5 permanent (China, France, Russian

Federation, UK, and USA) and 10 non-permanent (elected for a two-year term by a two-third majority)

- It has the primary responsibility, under the Charter, for the maintenance of international peace and security.
- It is so organised as to be able to function continuously.
- Its headquarters are located in New York.
- Any nation, irrespective of its membership of the UN, can put forth its problem before the Council.
- The Security Council can recommend peaceful solutions or, if necessary, may order use of force to restore peace.

**The Economic and Social Council** (ECOSOC)

- Comprising the representatives of 54 member States elected by a two-thirds majority in the General Assembly it bears the responsibilities of co-ordinating the functions of the UN with regard to international economic, social, cultural, educational, health and related matters.
- One-third of its members are elected every year to serve for a period of three years and one-third of the members retire annually.
- Its headquarters are located in New York.

**International Court of Justice** (ICJ)

- Comprising 15 judges elected by the General Assembly and the Security Council for a term of 9 years
- Responsible to give advisory opinion on legal matters to the bodies and special agencies of the UN and considers the legal disputes brought before it.
- Its headquarters are located at the Hague (Netherlands).

**NOTE:** Justice R. S. Pathak, Chief Justice of India, was elected judge of the ICJ on April 18, 1989. He became the third Indian on whom this honour has been bestowed. The other two were Mr Justice B. N. Rao and Mr Justice Nagendra Singh.

## Trusteeship Council

- Consisting five permanent members of the Security Council plus those nations who administer Trust Territories it takes adequate steps to prepare them for self-government or independence.
- Its headquarters are located in New York.

## The Secretariat

- Responsible for coordinating and supervising the activities of the UN it is headed by a Secretary- General appointed by the General Assembly on the recommendation of the Security Council.
- Tenure is for five years
- Eligible for re-election after the term expires.

*List of the Secretary-Generals of the UN*

| | | |
|---|---|---|
| 1. | Trygve Lie | 1946- 1952 |
| 2. | Dag Hammarskjöld | 1953- 1961 |
| 3. | U Thant | 1962- 1971 |
| 4. | Dr Kurt Waldheim | 1972- 1981 |
| 5. | Javier Perez de Cuellar | 1982- 1991 (two terms) |
| 6. | Dr Boutros Boutros Ghali | 1992- 1997 |
| 7. | Kofi Annan | 1997- 2007 (two terms) |
| 8. | Ban Ki Moon | 2007 till date |

*Specialised Agencies of the UN*

The inter government agencies related to the UN by special agreements are separate autonomous organisations working with the UN and each other through the coordinating machinery of the Economic and Social Council. Such agencies are:

| S. No. | Name of Agency | Abbreviation | Year of Establ. | Head-quarters | Purposes |
|---|---|---|---|---|---|
| 1. | International Labour Organization | ILO | 1919 | Geneva | To promote social justice, improve conditions and living standards of workers and promote economic stability. |
| 2. | International Atomic Energy Agency | IAEA | 1957 | Vienna | To promote peaceful uses of atomic energy. |
| 3. | Food and Agriculture Organization | FAO | 1945 | Rome | To raise nutritional levels, living standards, production and distribution of food and agricultural products, improve living conditions of rural population. |
| 4. | United Nations Educational Scientific and Cultural Organization | UNESCO | 1946 | Paris | To promote collaboration among nations through education, science and culture in order to further justice, human rights and freedom. |
| 5. | World Health Organization | WHO | 1948 | Geneva | Attainment of highest possible level of health by all people. |

| S. No. | Name of Agency | Abbreviation | Year of Establ. | Head-quarters | Purposes |
|---|---|---|---|---|---|
| 6. | International Bank for Reconstruction and Development | IBRD | 1945 | Washington | Development of economies of members by and Development facilitating investment of foreign capital and providing loans. |
| 7. | World Meteorological Organization | WMO | 1950 | Geneva | Promoting international exchange of weather reports and other weather related services. |
| 8. | Inter-governmental Maritime Consultative Organization | IMCO | 1958 | London | Promotes cooperation on technical matters, maritime safety, navigation and encourages anti-pollution measure. |
| 9. | United Nations International Children's Emergency Fund | UNICEF | 1946 | New York | Children's welfare all over the world. |
| 10. | General Agreement on Tariffs and Trade (from 1994 it is known as World Trade Organization) | GATT(WTO) | 1948 | Geneva | Treaty setting rules for world trade to reduce tariffs and eliminate other barriers to international trade |
| 11. | United Nations Development Programme | UNDP | - | New York | Help developing countries increase wealth producing capabilities of their natural and human resources |

| S. No. | Name of Agency | Abbreviation | Year of Establ. | Head-quarters | Purposes |
|---|---|---|---|---|---|
| 12. | United Nations Environment Programme | UNEP | 1972 | Nairobi | Promotes international cooperation in matters relating to human environment |
| 13. | United Nations Population Fund | UNFPA | 1969 | New York | Promotes population related programmes |
| 14. | United Nations High Commissioner | UNHCR | 1951 | Geneva | Provides international protection to for refugees |
| 15. | United Nations Industrial Development Organization | UNIDO | 1966 | Vienna | Extends assistance to LDCs for development and modernisation of industries |
| 16. | International Development Association | IDA | 1960 | Washington | An affiliate of the World Bank which aims to help underdeveloped countries raise living standards |
| 17. | International Finance Corporation | IFC | 1956 | Washington | Promotes economic development by encouraging private enterprise in its member-countries |
| 18. | International Monetary Fund | IMF | 1945 | Washington | Promotes international monetary cooperation and expansion of international trade |

| S. No. Name of Agency | Abbreviation | Year of Establ. | Head-quarters | Purposes |
|---|---|---|---|---|
| 19. International Civil Aviation | ICAO | 1947 | Montreal | Promotes safety in international aviation Organization and establishes international standards and regulations |
| 20. Universal Postal Union | UPU | 1947 | Berne | Improves various postal services and promotes international collaboration |
| 21. International Telecommunication | ITU | 1947 | Geneva | Sets international regulations for radio, telegraph, telephone and space radio communications |
| 22. International Fund for Agricultural Development | IFAD | 1977 | Rome | Finances agricultural projects to introduce, expand and improve food production and raise nutritional levels |
| 23. United Nations Conference on Trade and Development | UNCTAD | 1964 | Geneva | Promotes international trade with a view to accelerate economic growth of developing countries |

| S. No. | Name of Agency | Abbreviation | Year of Establ. | Head-quarters | Purposes |
|--------|----------------|--------------|-----------------|---------------|----------|
| 24. | United Nations Institute for Training and Research | UNITAR | 1965 | New York | Provides high priority training and research projects to help facilitate the UN objectives of world peace and security and of economic and social progress |
| 25. | United Nations Relief and Work Agency for Palestine Refugees | UNRWA | 1949 | New York | Provides food, health services, education, and vocational training for those displaced in Arab—Israel wars |

## EUROPEAN UNION

- The idea of European integration, soon after the destruction of the World War, gave birth to European Union (EU) which evolved out of European Community (EC) on February 7, 1992
- It formally came into being on November 1, 1992.
- Its purpose was to prevent the world from such destructions in future
- EUROPE DAY-It was first proposed by the French Foreign Minister Robert Suhurnan during a speech on May 9, 1950, the date, still celebrated annually as 'Europe Day'.
- The EU family of democratic European countries are committed to work together for peace and prosperity
- No single state will replace the existing states.
- Its member states have set up common institution to which they delegate some of their sovereignty, so that the decisions on specific matters of joint interest can be made democratically at European level.
- The pooling of sovereignty is also called "European Integration".
- A number of agencies and other bodies constitute the system.
- The rule of law is fundamental to the EU decisions, and the procedures are based on the treaties, which are agreed upon by all EU members.

The EU consisted of a 12- member- bloc:

- Denmark
- France
- Austria
- Greece
- Italy
- Netherlands
- Spain
- United Kingdom.
- Finland
- Belgium
- Germany
- Republic of Ireland
- Luxembourg
- Portugal
- Sweden

Twelve new members have been added which include:

- Cyprus
- Estonia
- Latvia
- Malta
- Slovakia
- Bulgaria
- Czech Republic
- Hungary
- Lithuania
- Poland
- Slovenia
- Romania

- Turkey is in the category of membership applicant.
- Austria, Finland and Sweden joined the EU in 1995.
- Thus the total strength of the EU increased to 15.
- Note: Now the EU has consented to allow admission of more European countries of the former USSR with Hungary, Poland, the Czech Republic, Bulgaria, Slovakia and Romania being the front runners.

**The Commonwealth**

- Originally known as the British Commonwealth of Nations
- It is an association of sovereign and independent states which formally constituted the British Empire.
- Established in 1947 with no written constitution.
- However, most of the member-countries have common constitutional features
- They are bound together by common ideals and interest.

**NOTE:** Despite all diversities, all its members hold certain common principles.

- They work to influence international society for the benefit of mankind.
- The Commonwealth consists of 53 sovereign States
- Includes Canada, several West Indian islands, Australia, New Zealand, the UK, and a few small Pacific islands. Members of the Commonwealth are represented in other Commonwealth countries by diplomatic officers called 'High Commissioners'.
- Though the members of the Commonwealth are completely sovereign, but Queen Elizabeth II is their ceremonial head of state.

- As the queen lives in the UK, her constitutional functions are performed by the Governors General of these nations, who are appointed by the queen after consulting the elected head of the government.

## The Non-Aligned Movement (NAM)

- A conference of the like-minded nations was held in April 1955 in Indonesia (Bandung) which gave birth to the forum for the birth of NAM.
- The major collaborators of this organisation in the beginning were Marshal Tito- the President of former Yugoslavia; Dr Sukarno- the President of Indonesia; G. A. Nasser- the President of Egypt; Pt Jawaharlal Nehru- the first Prime Minister of India.
- But the real credit for evolving the concept of NAM goes to Pt Nehru.
- Presently the total number of its members is 118 regular members and 15 observer states.
- The basic principles that form the base of NAM are known as 'Panchsheel'.

*Principles of 'Panchsheel'*

1. Mutual respect for each other's territorial integrity and sovereignty
2. Mutual non- aggression
3. Mutual non- interference in each other's affairs
4. Equality and mutual benefit
5. Peaceful coexistence

## South Asian Association for Regional Cooperation (SAARC)

- The idea of the SAARC was first mooted in 1979 by the former Bangladesh President Zia- ur- Rahman during his Sri Lanka visit.
- It finally took shape on December 8, 1985 at Dhaka. The list of its members include: (i) Bhutan, (ii) Bangladesh, (iii) India, (iv) the Maldives, (v) Pakistan, (vi) Nepal and (vii) Sri Lanka. Its secretariat is located at Kathmandu in Nepal.

**NOTE:** In April 2007 at the 14th summit, Afghanistan became the 8th member.

## Aims and Objectives of SAARC

1. To promote the welfare of the people of South Asia
2. To improve the security environment in the region
3. To accelerate economic growth and cultural development
4. To combat terrorism

## The European Economic Community (EEC)

- To promote a common market and economic prosperity among member- countries and create a single market for free import and export among member-countries the European Economic Community (EEC) was established on March 25, 1957
- Its headquarters is at Brussels in Belgium.
- Brought into existence by the 'Treaty of Rome'
- Started functioning on January 1, 1958.
- The six states that founded the EEC and the other two Communities were known as the "inner six"
- The "outer seven" were those countries who formed the European Free Trade Association
- The six were;
- France
- West Germany
- Italy
- The three Benelux countries: Belgium, the Netherlands and Luxembourg.
- The first enlargement was in 1973, with the accession of Denmark, Ireland and the United Kingdom. Greece, Spain and Portugal joined throughout in the 1980s.
- Following the creation of the EU in 1993, it has enlarged to include a further fifteen countries by 2007.

## Caribbean Community (CARICOM)

- It was established on August 1, 1973 by the Caribbean Free Trade Association
- Aim to coordinate economic policies and development of member-states.

- It also formulates common external trade, tariff and policy and provides aids to the less developed member-countries.
- Its headquarters are located at Georgetown (Guyana).

The list of its members includes:
- Anguilla
- Antigua
- Barbados
- Belize
- Dominica
- Grenada
- Guyana
- Jamaica
- Montserrat
- St Kitts-Nevis
- St Lucia
- St Vincent
- Trinidad and Tobago.

## Organization of Petroleum Exporting Countries (OPEC)

- The international oil companies' announcement for reducing prices of Middle East Crude oil led to the formation of the OPEC on November 14, 1960.
- Its goal was to control production and pricing of crude oil.
- Its headquarters are located in Vienna.
- Membership of OPEC is open to all countries with substantial exports of crude petroleum.
- Ecuador left OPEC in September 1992
- Iran also declared to stay alone in the oil market.

Presently the list of its members include:
- Algeria
- Ecuador
- Gabon
- Indonesia

- Iran
- Iraq
- Kuwait
- Libya
- United Arab Emirates
- Nigeria
- Qatar, Saudi Arabia
- Venezuela.

**Arab League** (League of Arab States)

- Its aim is to foster unity especially among Muslim nations and maintain Arab solidarity Arab League
- It was established on March 22, 1945
- Its headquarters at Tunisia.
- After Iraq's invasion of Kuwait in August 1990, its headquarters were shifted from to Cairo.
- The list of its members include:

| | |
|---|---|
| Algeria | Bahrain |
| Djibouti | Iraq |
| Jordan | Kuwait |
| Lebanon | Libya |
| Mauritania | Morocco |
| Oman | Palestine Liberation Organization |
| Qatar, Saudi Arabia | Somalia |
| Sudan | Syria |
| Tunisia | United Arab Emirates |
| Republic of Yemen | |

**European Free Trade Association** (EFFA)

- Set up to remove all tariffs on trade of industrial goods among its members
- To aid the creation of a single West European market to help boost world trade
- Organisation was established in May 1960.

- Its headquarters are located in Geneva.
- The member- states of EFTA have free trade agreements with the EEC and there is now free trade between 16 West European countries.
- Austria, Denmark, Norway, Portugal, Sweden, Switzerland and the UK were its founder members.
- Iceland joined in 1970.
- Denmark and the UK left it in December 1972.

## Central Treaty Organization (CENTO)

- CENTO was established as a defensive organization against Russian interference in 1955 by a few West Asian countries.
- Its headquarters is at Ankara, Turkey.
- Till 1958 the organization was known as the Baghdad Pact, which started with five member nations: UK, Turkey, Iran, Pakistan and Iraq (which withdrew in 1959).
- US support came in 1958.
- Turkey, Iran and Pakistan withdrew in 1979.

## Benelux Economic Union also North Atlantic Treaty Organization

- Set for the purpose of economic unity Belgium, The Netherlands and Luxembourg.
- This organization was formed in 1958.
- Its headquarters in Brussels, Belgium.
- Its members include Belgium, The Netherlands and Luxembourg.

## North Atlantic Treaty Organization (NATO)

- Set up to maintain and develop their individual and collective capacity to resist armed attack.
- Also consult each other if any of the member nations was threatened politically a group of countries.
- NATO was organised on April 4, 1949.
- They agreed that an armed attack against any of them would be countered by combined forces.
- Its headquarters are located in Brussels (Belgium).

- Its members included initially the states of Belgium, Canada, Denmark, France, Iceland, Italy, Luxembourg, The Netherlands, Norway, Portugal, the UK and USA.
- Greece and Turkey joined in 1952
- And former West Germany and Spain in 1955 and 1982, respectively.

**The Group of 7**

- It was established in 1964 under the auspices of the UN to defend the economic and trade interests of the developing world.
- Presently it has 127 developing countries from Asia, Africa and Latin America as its members.

**South-East Asia Treaty Organization** (SEATO)

- Aim was to provide collective defence and economic cooperation in South east Asia
- SEATO was established on September 8, 1954
- Its headquarters is in Bangkok, Thailand.
- Its members include Australia, France, New Zealand, Pakistan, the Philippines, Thailand, the United Kingdom and US. Pakistan withdrew itself from the organization in 1973.

Colombo Plan

- Established in 1950
- Headquarters in Colombo
- Aim is to promote the development of newly independent Asian member- countries.
- Initially it was started as a group of seven Commonwealth nations
- Now it has 26 member countries.

**Organization of African Unity** (OAU)

- Established to promote African unity and solidarity
- Aim was also to abolish colonialism in Africa
- Also coordinate the political, economic, defence, health, scientific and cultural policies of its members.
- It was formally brought into being from May 25, 1963.
- Its headquarters are located at Addis Ababa (Ethiopia).

- It consists of all 51 independent African countries, except the white dominated states and territories of the South.

## Organisation of American States (OAS)

- Established on April 30, 1948 to foster American solidarity
- Collaboration of member countries to protect their independence, sovereignty and boundaries.
- It has its headquarters in Washington DC.
- Formed at the Ninth Conference of American States in Bogotá (Colombia).
- Presently it has a membership of about 35 nations of North and South America.

## Organisation for Economic Cooperation and Development (OECD)

- Established to seek sustained economic growth, employment, higher standards of living and monetary stability in its member nations
- Formed on September 30, 1961
- Its headquarters are in Paris.
- The Organisation for European Economic Cooperation (OEEC) became OECD in 1961 with the addition of non-European countries.
- Members of this organisation include:

| | |
|---|---|
| Australia | Austria |
| Belgium | Canada |
| Denmark | Finland |
| France | Greece |
| Iceland | Ireland |
| Italy | Japan |
| Luxembourg | The Netherlands |
| New Zealand | Norway |
| Portugal | Spain |
| Sweden | Switzerland |
| Turkey | UK |
| USA | Germany |

## Association of South-East Asian Nations (ASEAN)

- ASEAN was established on August 9, 1967
- Aim is to accelerate economic progress and maintain economic stability in South-east Asia.
- Its headquarters are located in Jakarta, Indonesia.
- ASEAN was established in Thailand along with Malaysia and the Philippines. Indonesia, Singapore and Brunei joined in 1984.
- It is headed by a Secretary-General elected on rotation in alphabetical order for a term of three years.

## Central American Common Market (CACM)

- Established in 1960
- Headquarters in Guatemala City
- Aims at Central American integration, equalisation of import duties and charges, and uniform control on foreign investment.
- Its members include: Costa Rica, LI Salvador, Guatemala, Honduras and Nicaragua.

## Amnesty International

- Established on May 28, 1961
- A worldwide organisation by Peter Benson, a British lawyer.
- It investigates violations of human rights.
- It campaigns for the release of all prisoners of conscience provided they have not used or advocated violence
- Helps fair and prompt trials for all prisoners
- Fights for abolition of torture and capital punishment.
- Headquarters in London.
- Now have more than 500000 members in 150 countries all over the world.

## Red Cross

- Mr Jean Henry Durant, a Swiss businessman, was the man behind Red Cross,
- It is a charity organisation working for the war victims.
- Established in 1863.

**NOTE:** In 1859, Mr Durant while travelling through Italy, witnessed the battle of Solferino, in which about 30,000 soldiers were wounded or killed when France tried to free Italy from Austrian domination. He organised relief work for the wounded soldiers and subsequently called for the formation of a permanent relief society for those war victims.

- As a result of his appeal an international conference was held in Geneva (Switzerland) in 1864 with the representatives of 26 nations.
- The conference led to the Geneva Convention and the emblem motto of Red Cross was adopted.
- May 8, the birthday of Mr Durant, is celebrated as 'World Red Cross' and 'Red Crescent Day'.
- Its symbol is the sign of a Red Cross on a white background.
- Its flag is the reverse of the flag of Switzerland.
- The Red Cross has marched a long way
- Still it is growing at a fast speed.

**NOTE:** In the Middle-East, a Red Crescent replaces the Red Cross, while in Iran a lion or sun is used as the symbol.

- The organization was honoured with the Noble Prize in 1917, 1944 and 1963 for its dedication to humanity.
- It has about 200 million members from 131 countries of the world.
- The International Committee of the Red Cross (ICRC) constitutes with the League of Red Cross Societies, the International Red Cross. The League of Red Cross Societies was founded in 1929.

**The French Community**

- It is an organisation like the British Commonwealth offering new institutions to the French and overseas territories based on the common idea of liberty, equality, and fraternity.
- Established in 1958.
- Members include the French Republic, Central African Republic, Republic of Congo, Gabon, Senegal, Chad, Madagascar and Djibouti.

*Interpol*

- It is an international 186- nation Police Commission consisting of 186 nations.

- Its chief responsibility is to coordinate activities of member-nations.
- Established in 1923.
- Headquarters are located in Paris which was shifted to Lyons after a terrorist bomb blast in 1986.

## World Trade Organization (WTO)

- The World Trade Organisation (WTO) was established on January 1, 1995
- It replaced the General Agreement on Tariffs and Trade (GATT).
- It came into effect with the support of at least 85 founding members, including India.
- It stands as the third economic pillar of worldwide dimensions with the World Bank and the International Monetary Fund (IMF).
- It has the powers to settle trade disputes between nations and to widen the principle of free trade to sectors such as the services and agriculture and covers more areas than GATT.

# PART FIVE

# GEOGRAPHICAL FEATURES OF INDIA

## LOCATIONAL SETTING

- India is the seventh-largest country in the world (area): This is about 2.4% of the total world area.
- Location: In the northern hemisphere between 8°4' N and 37°6' N parallels of latitude and between 68°7' E and 97°25' E meridians of longitude.
- It is a part of the Asian continent.
- Population of India- Second largest in the world.

## AREA: AN OVERVIEW

| | |
|---|---|
| Distance from north to south | 3214 km |
| Distance from east to west | 2933 km |
| Length of coastline | 7516.6 km |
| Length of land frontier | 15,200 km |
| Total geographic land area | 32,87,263 sq. km |
| Percentage of earth's surface covered by India | 2.4% |

### Boundaries

- *North* India: Separated from Tibet by the Himalayan range and Nepal..(Note-the McMahon Line: The boundary line between India and China.
- *East* Myanmar (Burma) and Bangladesh
- *West* Pakistan and the Arabian Sea
- *South* Indian Ocean and Sri Lanka-Note: Gulf of Mannar and Palk Straits separate India from Sri Lanka.

## Agriculture in india

- 65 - 70% people into agriculture
- 142.42 million hectares land under cultivation
- India produces two major types of crops: 1. *Kharif*  2. *Rabi*

| Crop Seasons | Sown in | Harvested | Major Crops |
|---|---|---|---|
| Kharif | June-July | September-October | Rice, Jowar, Bajra, Ragi, Maize, Cotton and Jute |
| Rabi | October-December | April-May | Wheat, Barley, Peas, Rapeseed, Mustard and Grams |

## Major Crops and Producers

| Type | Name | Major Producers |
|---|---|---|
| Cereals | Wheat | Uttar Pradesh, Punjab, Haryana |
| | Rice | West Bengal, Tamil Nadu |
| | Gram | Madhya Pradesh, Rajasthan, Uttar Pradesh |
| | Barley | Maharashtra, Uttar Pradesh, Rajasthan |
| | Bajra | Maharashtra, Gujarat, Rajasthan |
| Cash Crops | Sugarcane | Uttar Pradesh, Maharashtra |
| | Poppy | Uttar Pradesh, Himachal Pradesh |
| Oilseeds | Coconut | Kerala, Tamil Nadu |
| | Linseed | Madhya Pradesh, Uttar Pradesh |
| | Groundnut | Andhra Pradesh, Gujarat, Tamil Nadu |
| | Rapeseed and Mustard | Rajasthan, Uttar Pradesh |
| | Sesame | Uttar Pradesh, Rajasthan |
| | Sunflower | Maharashtra, Karnataka |
| Fibre Crops | Cotton | Maharashtra, Gujarat |
| | Jute | West Bengal, Bihar, Orissa, Assam |
| | Silk | Karnataka, Kerala |
| | Hemp | Madhya Pradesh, Uttar Pradesh |
| Plantations | Coffee | Karnataka, Kerala |
| | Rubber | Kerala, Karnataka |
| | Tea | Assam, Kerala |
| | Tobacco | Gujarat, Maharashtra, Madhya Pradesh |
| Spices | Pepper | Kerala, Karnataka, Tamil Nadu |
| | Cashew nuts | Kerala, Tamil Nadu, Andhra Pradesh |

**Major crops and producers** (*contd.*)

| Type | Name | Major Producers |
|------|------|-----------------|
| | Ginger | Kerala, Uttar Pradesh |
| | Turmeric | Andhra Pradesh, Orissa |
| | Chillies | Maharashtra, Andhra Pradesh |
| | Cloves | Kerala |
| | Saffron | Karnataka, Tamil Nadu, Jammu and Kashmir |

## INDIA'S GREEN REVOLUTION

- Launched in 1967 – 68
- Aim: Improve agricultural productivity in two phases:

1. *First Green Revolution*

Done in wheat producing states like Punjab, Haryana and western Uttar Pradesh.

2. *Second Green Revolution*

Done in West Bengal, Bihar, Orissa, Madhya Pradesh and Uttar Pradesh.

### Dairy Farming in India

*Operation Flood I* (1970 - 81)

Done to capture a share of milk market in cities.

*Operation Flood II* (1981 - 85)

Done to capture a share of milk market in almost all states.

*Operation Flood III* (1985 - 90)

Done to capture a share of milk under the Seventh Five Year Plan.

The final outcome:

India became the second largest milk producer in the world

## NATIONAL PARKS AND SANCTUARIES

- 94 national parks covering approximately 33,988 sq. km
- 501 sanctuaries covering about 1,07,310, sq. km

## Important Sanctuaries and Parks

| Name | Location | Reserve For |
| --- | --- | --- |
| Achanakmar Sanctuary | Bilaspur, Madhya Pradesh | Tiger, bear, chital, sambar, bison |
| Bandipur Sanstuary | Border of Karnataka and Tamil Nadu | Elephant, tigers, panther, sambar, deer, birds |
| Corbett National Park | Nainital, Uttaranchal | Tiger, leopards, elephants, sambar |
| Dachigam Sanctuary | Dachigam, Kashmir | Kashmiri stag |
| Gandhi Sagar Sanctuary | Mandsaur, Madhya Pradesh | Chital, sambar, chinkara, barking dear, wild birds |
| Ghana Bird Sanctuary | Bharatpur, Rajasthan | Water birds, black-buck, chital sambar |
| Gir Forest | Junagarh, Gujarat | India's biggest wildlife sanctuary famous for Gir lions |
| Kaziranga National Park | Jorhat, Assam | Rhinoceros, wild buffalo, swan, deer, hog |
| Pakhal Sanctuary | Warangal Andhra Pradesh | Tiger, panther, sambar, nilgai, chital |
| Periyar Sanctuary | Idukki, Kerala | Elephant, tiger, panther, gaur, nilgai, sambar |
| Ranthambore Tiger Project | Sawal Madhopur, Rajasthan | Tiger, leopard, sloth bear, crocodile |
| Sriska Sanctuary | Alwar, Rajasthan | Tiger, panther, sambar, nilgai, chital, chinkara |
| Sharaswathy Sanctuary | Shimoga, Karnataka | Elephant, tiger, panter, sambar, gaur, chital |
| Shikari Devi Sanctuary | Mandi, Himachal Pradesh | Black dear, musk dear, leopard, partridge |
| Sunderban Tiger Reserve | South 24 Parganas, West Bengal | Tiger, deer, wild boar, leopard |
| Sonai Rupe Sanctuary | Tezpur, Assam | Elephant, sambar, wild boar, one-horned rhinoceros |
| Tungabhadra Sanctuary | Bellary, Karnataka | Panther, chital, sloth bear, four horned antelope |
| Vedanthangal Bird Sanctuary | Tamil Nadu | Important bird sanctuary |
| Wild Ass Sanctuary | Little Rann of Kutch, Gujarat | Wild ass, wolf, nilgai, chinkara |

# TOWNS AND CITIES

## 1. Indian Cities on River Banks

| City | River | State |
| --- | --- | --- |
| Agra | Yamuna | Uttar Pradesh |
| Ahmedabad | Sabarmati | Gujarat |
| Allahabad | Confluence of the Ganges, Yamuna & Saraswati | Uttar Pradesh |
| Alwaye | Periyar | Kerala |
| Ayodhya | Sarayu | Uttar Pradesh |
| Badrinath | Gangotri | Uttarakhand |
| Bhagalpur | Ganges | Bihar |
| Buxar | Ganges | Bihar |
| Kolkata | Hooghly | West Bengal |
| Cuttack | Mahanadi | Orissa |
| Delhi | Yamuna | Delhi |
| Dibrugarh | Brahmaputra | Assam |
| Guwahati | Brahmaputra | Assam |
| Hardwar | Ganges | Uttarakhand |
| Howrah | Hooghly | West Bengal |
| Hyderabad | Musa | Andhra Pradesh |
| Jamshedpur | Subamarekha | Jharkhand |
| Kanpur | Ganges | Uttar Pradesh |
| Kota | Chambal | Rajasthan |
| Leh | Indus | Jammu & Kashmir |
| Lucknow | Gomti | Uttar Pradesh |
| Ludhiana | Sutlej | Punjab |
| Mathura | Yamuna | Uttar Pradesh |
| Moradabad | Ramganga | Uttar Pradesh |
| Monghyr (Munger) | Ganges | Bihar |
| Nashik | Godavari | Maharashtra |
| Patna | Ganges/Sone | Bihar |
| Srinagar | Jhelum | Jammu & Kashmir |
| Surat | Tapti | Gujarat |
| Tiruchirappalli | Cauvery | Tamil Nadu |
| Ujjain | Shipra | Madhya Pradesh |
| Vijayawada | Krishna | Andhra Pradesh |
| Varanasi | Ganges | Uttar Pradesh |

## 2. Important Sites and Monuments

| Monument/Site | Location | Famous For |
| --- | --- | --- |
| Ajanta Caves | Aurangabad | Buddhist cave temples |
| Amarnath's cave | Kashmir | Naturally formed ice Shivlinga |
| Anand Bhawan | Allahabad | Ancestral house of the Nehru family, now turned into a National Museum. |
| Bibi-ka-Makbara | Aurangabad | Mausoleum built by Aurangzeb in memory of his wife Rabia Durrani |
| Buland Darwaza | Fatehpur Sikri | The highest and biggest gateway of India near Agra built by Akbar to commemorate his victorious campaign in Deccan |
| Char Minar | Hyderabad | |
| Dilwara Temples | Mount Abu | Five Hindu temples built between 11th and 13th century AD |
| Elephanta Caves | Mumbai | An island in Mumbai harbour famous for rock cut temples |
| Ellora Temples | Aurangabad | Buddhist temples |
| Gandhi Sadan | Delhi | Birla house where Gandhi was assassinated |
| Gateway of India | Mumbai | Erected in 1911 on King George V's visit to India |
| Got Gumbaz | Bijapur | Largest dome in India |
| Gomteshwara | Mysore | 2000 year-old statue of a Jam sage carved out of a single stone |
| Golden Temple | Amritsar | Largest Gurudwara |
| Hawa Mahal | Jaipur | A pink castle of air |
| Jallianwala Bagh | Amritsar | Venue of the massacre of hundreds of innocent Indians by the British |
| Jantar Mantar | Delhi | Observatory built in 1724 during the days of Maharaja Jai Singh II of Ajmer |
| Jama Masjid | Delhi | Biggest mosque built by Shah Jahan |
| Kanya Kumari | Tamil Nadu | Temple of the Virgin Goddess situated at Cape Camorin |
| Kranti Maidan | Mumbai | Historical avenue where Gandhi gave the call 'Quit India' in 1942 |
| Khajuraho | Near Bhopal | Mahadeva temple |
| Meenakshi Temple | Madurai | Hindu temple |
| Qutab Minar | Delhi | Largest minaret |
| Rajghat | Delhi | Samadhi of Mahatma Gandhi on the bank of the Yamuna |

## Important Sites and Monuments (*contd.*)

| Monument/Site | Location | Famous For |
|---|---|---|
| Red Fort | Delhi | A red stone structure built by Shah Jahan on the bank of the Yamuna |
| Sabarmati | Ahmedabad | Harijan Ashram |
| Sarnath | Varanasi | Centre of Buddhist pilgrimage, the place where Gautam Buddha delivered his first sermon after enlightenment |
| Shaktisthal | Delhi | Situated on the bank of the Yamuna where Mrs Indira Gandhi was cremated |
| Shantivan | Delhi | Samadhi of Pt Jawaharlal Nehru |
| Shantiniketan | Kolkata | Famous university founded by Rabindra Nath Tagore |
| Sanchi | Madhya Pradesh | Ancient Buddhist monuments |
| Tower of Victory | Chittorgarh | Famous tower built by Rana Sangha, the king of Mewar |
| Victoria Memorial | Kolkata | Famous museum |
| Vijay Ghat | Delhi | Samadhi of Lal Bahadur Shastri |
| Vir Bhumi | Delhi | Samadhi of Rajiv Gandhi |

## 3. Hill Stations

| Station | Height (ft) | Location |
|---|---|---|
| Almora | 5,500 | Kumaon Hills, Uttaranchal |
| Cherapunji | 4,455 | Near Shillong, Meghalaya |
| Coonoor | 6,740 | Nilgiri Hills in Tamil Nadu |
| Daihousie | 7,867 | Himachal Pradesh |
| Darjeeling | 7,168 | West Bengal |
| Gulmarg | 8,850 | Jammu and Kashmir |
| Kalimpong | 4,000 | Near Darjeeling, West Bengal |
| Kasauli | 7,200 | Himachal Pradesh |
| Kodaikanal | 7,200 | Tamil Nadu |
| Kullu Valley | 3,999 | Himachal Pradesh |
| Lansdowne | 1,968 | Garhwal, Uttarakhand |
| Mahabaleshwar | 4,500 | Maharashtra |
| Mt Abu | 4,500 | Rajasthan |
| Mukteshwar | 7,500 | Uttarakhand |
| Mussoorie | 7,500 | Uttarakhand |
| Shimla | 7,000 | Himachal Pradesh |
| Nainital | 6,365 | Uttarakhand |
| Ootacamund (Ooty) | 7,500 | Tamil Nadu |

## STATES AND UNION TERRITORIES

### Facts and Features

*States*

| Features | States | Figures (2001) census |
|---|---|---|
| Largest population | Uttar Pradesh | 16,60,52,859 |
| Smallest population | Sikkim | 5,40,493 |
| Largest area | Rajasthan | 3,42,200 sq km |
| Smallest area | Goa | 3,700 sq km |
| Highest density of population | West Bengal | 904 persons/km$^2$ |
| Lowest density of population | Sikkim | 76 persons/ft$^2$ |
| Largest urban population | Maharashtra | 41019734 |
| More females (sex ratio) | Kerala | 1058 |
| Highest literacy rate | Kerala | 90.92% |
| State touching maximum number of boundaries of other states | Chhattisgarh—Orrisa, Jharkhand, Madhya Pradesh, Andhra Pradesh, Maharashtra | |

### Union Territories

| | | |
|---|---|---|
| Largest area | Andaman & Nicobar Islands | 8.2* |
| Smallest in area | Lakshadweep | 0.03* |
| Highest literacy rate | Chandigarh | 81.76% |

# PART SIX

# GLIMPSES OF INDIAN HISTORY

The history of India has been broadly divided into **three** distinct periods

* Ancient India
* Medieval India
* Modern India

The history of **modern India** has **two major periods**

1. The British Period
2. The Struggle for Freedom Period

## ANCIENT INDIA

The history of Ancient India begins with the earliest Civilisation i.e. the Indus Valley Civilisation.

**Indus Valley Civilisation** (2500-1800 BC)

*HARAPPAN/Indus Valley Civilisation* (2500BC-1750 BC)

* Appropriate name: Harappan Civilization: Harappa was the first discovered site
* river
* Period: 2500Bc-1750 BC –according to Carbon-14 dating.
* Age: Chalcolithic Age/Bronze Age; Proto-Historic Period
* Area: Spread over Sindh, Baluchistan, Punjab, Haryana, Rajasthan, Gujarat, Western U.P. & Northern Maharashtra.
* Northern most site of Indus Civilization-Ropar (Sutlej)/Punjab (earlier);Manda (Chenab/Jammu-Kashmir (now)
* Southern most site of Indus Civilization- Bhagatrav (Kim)/Gujarat (earlier) Daimabad (Pravara)/Maharashtra (Now).

- Eastern-most site of Indus Civilization-Alamgirpur (Hindon/Uttar Pradesh)
- Western most site of Indus civilization-Sutkagendor (Dashk/Makran Coast, Pakistan- Iran Border)
- Capital cities- Harappa, Mohenjodaro
- Port Cities-Lothal, Utkagendor, Allahdino, Balakot, Kuntasi.

## The Aryans and the Vedic Period

*Early Vedic Period* (1500 - 1000 BC)

- The Aryans originally inhabited the area around the Caspian Sea in the Central Asia. They were semi-nomadic and pastoral people
- They entered India in around 1500 BC in search of pastures through the passes in the Hindu Kush mountains- They first settled down in Punjab
- Then they moved eastwards and spread all over the Gangetic plains.
- They worshipped the God Sun, the water, the fire, etc.
- They were lovers of nature
- It is said that they were the real originators of the Hindu civilization.
- We know about the Aryans through the following **six religious books** which gives us their beliefs, customs and culture.

### 1. *The Vedas*

The most sacred of the Hindu scriptures divided into **four books**:

- *Rig Veda*, the oldest among the Vedas, contains 1017 hymns in the form of prayers to god and said to be the oldest book in the world
- *Sama Veda* deals with music
- *Yajur Veda* deals with sacrifices, rituals and formulae
- *Atharva Veda* deals with medicine

### 2. *The Upanishads*

- They are said to be the main sources of Indian philosophy and theology .
- There are about 108 known *Upanishads* .

### 3. *The Brahamanas*

- They tell us about the socio-political life of the Aryans including their basics of religion..

4. *The Aranyakas*

- The Forest books comprising the concluding part of the *Brahmanas* are essentially treatises on mysticism and philosophy.

5. *Manu Smriti*

- A collection of the views of the great philosopher -saint Man, the great law giver in the Aryan period.
- His book *Manu Smriti* contains the laws of inheritance, duties of kings and his subjects.

6. *The Puranas*

- The great books of scriptures
- sub-divided into 18 books
- They give religious and historical details of the Aryan civilization
- They contain the discourses on legends, rituals, traditions and moral codes.

**Later Vedic Period** (1000 - 600 BC)

- During this period the tribal settlements were replaced by strong kingdoms.
- This period traces a more advanced life style in comparison to that of the previous period.
- Big cities like Ayodhya, Indraprastha and Mathura came into existence.
- This period was also called the *Brahmanical Age*.
- It was very close to the modern form of Hinduism.

The society was divided into **four castes.**

- The caste system was first based on occupation
- Later it was based on heredity
- The major castes were:
- *Brahmins*, the supreme in status, were the priestly class. They were the most respected, virtually, adorable class.
- *Kshatriyas*, the second in command, were the military class.
- *Vaishyas*, the third one in rank and file, mainly dealt in business or trading in order to earn their livelihood.

- *Shudras*, the lowest and the most hated lot of the society whose business was none other than labour. They had to discharge the meanest of the works and services for the society.

## The Epic Age

- This Age is credited with the composition of the two great epics like *Mahabharata* and the *Ramayana*.

### The Rise of Brahmanism

- The later Vedic period made the religion so much complicated with the addition of so many rituals that resulted in the dominance of the Brahmins who became the sole representative of religion. They had the only right to perform any religious ceremonies.

### The Revolt against Brahmanism

- The rise of the Brahmins who virtually monopolised religion
- Other castes to raised their voice of protest against the Brahmanical exploitation.
- These movements were led by some of princes from the royal families of the then Magadha regions.
- These movements got mass support for they were rooted to the real path of humanity.
- The rise of the Buddhism and the Jainism was greatly responded by the people.

## Magadh Empire (6th- 4th centuryBC )

- The Magadha Empire was a major power in the regions of north India especially the areas now occupying the districts of Patna and Gaya in the state of Bihar.
- Major rulers of Magadha Empire:

1. *Haryanka Dynasty*
- Originally founded by the grandfather of Bimbisara in 566BC
- The real founders were Bimbisara himself and Ajatashatru.
- They extended their reign by annexing the neighbouring territories.

2. *Shishunaga Dynasty*
- Shishunaga usurped the Haryanka Dynasty in 413BC

- He xtended his boundaries by annexing Vatsa, Avanti and Kosala to Magadha.

3. *Nanda Dynasty*

- In fact, the first major empire with a very powerful army, often described as "the first empire- builders of India" was founded by Mahapadma.
- This dynasty had faced the invasion of Alexander, the Great.

## The Invasion of Alexander (Greek Invasion)

- In **326BC**, India had to face an invasion by Alexander, the son of Phillip of Macedonia (Greece).
- Porus, the then king of Punjab, fought against Alexander and was defeated in his battle on the banks of **Jhelum**.
- This battle was remarkable in the sense that it paved the way for a link between India and the West

## The Mauryan Empire (321-232 BC)

## Chandragupta Maurya (321-298 BC)

- After overthrowing the Nandas, Chandragupta Maurya established the rule of the Maurya Dynasty in **321BC**.
- He set up an administration with an autocratic and central-based system.
- **Kautilya** (Chanakya), the prime minister and real mentor of Chandragupta, wrote the *Arthashastra*, a treatise on statecraft.
- **Megasthenes** was a Greek Ambassador to Chandragupta's court who brought out the details of the Mauryan period in his famous anecdotes *Indica*.
- Chandragupta Maurya was the first Indian king who was called a national hero.
- He was succeeded by his son Bindusara(298-273BC)who annexed south to Mysore.

## Ashoka, the Great (273 - 232 BC)

- Ashoka, a son of Bindusara
- He suceeded his father in 273BC.
- He was regarded as one of the greatest kings of all times.

- He was the first ruler who earned a tremendous popularity among the masses by maintaining his direct contact with the people.
- He ruled for over 40 years.
- Though he acceded to the throne in 273 BC but the formal consecration took place 4 years later in 268 BC.
- During his first 13 years, he carried on the traditional policy of expansion within India and friendly relations with foreign powers.
- In the 13th year of his reign, he conquered Kalinga.

### The Kalinga War

- Ashoka's Kalinga invasion was a major turning point in his life that led to his conversion to Budhhism.
- The widespread destruction and bloodshed in the battle hurt him so much that he embraced the path of religion and thereafter he concentrated himself to the business none other than the spread of Budhhism.
- He even sent his son Mahendra and daughter Sanghmitra to the far off lands such as Sri Lanka, Java and Sumatra.
- His occupation with Buddhism brought out the decline of the great Mauryan empire.

### The Gupta Dynasty (AD 320 - 550)

- Founded by Chandragupta I in 320AD, the Gupta dynasty added a new chapter to the history of India.
- It is often called the Golden Age or the Classical Age of ancient India.
- The reason: There was absolute peace and prosperity in every field of life and foreign rule was completely reversed during this period.
- This period was also jewelled with the great personalities like Kalidasa-a great poet and dramatist, Aryabhatta, Varahmihira and Brahmagupta-the great mathematicians and astronomers, Dhanvantari- the great physician.

Some of the **important rulers of Gupta Dynasty** were:

1. Chandragupta I (AD 320 - 335)
2. Samudragupta (AD 335 ~ 376)

3. Chandragupta II*(also known as Vikramaditya)* (AD 376 - 415) During his rule, India was visited by Chinese traveller **Fahien** (AD 399 - 411)

## Harshavardhana (AD 606 - 647)

- Harshavardhana was the last Hindu king of northern India
- He established a strong empire conquering Bengal, Malwa, eastern Rajasthan and the entire Gangetic plain up to Assam.
- **Hieun Tsang** was a Chinese traveller who visited India and stayed during this period (between AD 635 - 643). He wrote a detailed account of India.
- **Banabhatta**, one of the court poets of Harshavardhana, wrote *Harshacharita*, a biography of the king.

## The Rajputs (AD 650 – 12)

- The Rajputs emerged as a powerful force in Western and Central India after Harshvardhan.
- Prithviraj Chauhan was one of the great rulers of India. He ruled over Delhi and Agra.
- He fought bravely against Muhammed Ghori, a foreign invader.
- Jai Chand Rathor was the last Rajput king who was defeated and killed by Muhammad Ghori
- Ghori thereafter took over his control over the kingdom of Delhi.

## Some Other Known Dynasties

*1. The Andhras*

- Also known as the Shathavahanas , the earliest rulers of the Deccan
- They gained independence after the death of Ashoka.
- Simukha was the founder of this dynasty.
- Some of the notable rulers of this dynasty were:
- Shathakarni I (ruled 184 - 130 BC)
- Pulumayi II (AD 130 - 145)
- Yagnashathakarni (AD 175 - 225) was the last king.

*2. The Chalukyas (6th century AD to 12th century AD)*

- They were were also called the Karnataka rulers

- They can be divided into three eras:
- The Early Western Era- the Chalukyas of Badami
- **The** Later Western Era-the Chalukyas of Kalyani
- The Eastern Chalukya Era-the Chalukyas of Vengi.

Some of the notable rulers were:

- Pulakesin I (AD 543 – 567
- Pulakesin II (AD 610 - 642)
- Vinyaditya (AD 681- 696)
- Vikramaditya II (AD 733 - 774).

3. The Rashtrakutas *(AD 735 - 973)*

- They were descendants of the nobles who governed under the Andhras.
- They overthrew the Chalukyas and ruled up to AD 973.
- But the Chalukyas under Tailapa II overthrew the last Rashtrakuta king Karka II in AD 973 again took over the throne.

4. *The Chola Dynasty*

- Founded by Rajaraja I (AD 985 - 1014).
- He ruled over Madras and parts of Karnataka with Tanjore as his capital.
- Rajendra III (1246-1279 AD) was the last king of the Chola dynasty.

5. *The Yadavas* (AD 1191 -1318)

- They ruled from Devagiri. Singhana (AD 1210 - 1247)
- Ramchandra (AD 1271 - 1309) was the other important ruler.

6. *Hindu Kingdom of Vijaynagar* (1336 – 1646 AD)

- The five sons of south Indian Sangama dynasty founded by Harihar and Bukka ..
- Krishnadeva Raja (AD 1505 - 29) was the most illustrious ruler of this dynasty rule.
- The kingdom lay in Deccan, to the south of Bahami kingdom.
- They were the saviours of the Hindu way of life and they checked the Mohammedan advance.
- The Battle of Talikota (1564 - 1565) between Muslim ruler of Deccan

and the Vijaynagar ruler Ramaraja proved to be fatal for it caused the gradual collapse of this mighty empire.

## MEDIEVAL INDIA

- The history of this period is dominated by the Muslim rulers
- Muslim period began with the invasions of Mahmud Ghazni that led to the establishment of the Sultanate of Delhi.

**The Sultanate of Delhi** (1206 - 1526)

- The conquests of Muhammad Ghori proved to be the nucleus of the rise of a new political entity in India-The Sultanate of Delhi - and the emergence of the Muslim rule in India

This period can be divided into five distinct periods:

- The Slave Dynasty (1206 - 1290)
- The Khilji Dynasty (1290 - 1320)
- The Tughlak Dynasty (1320 - 1414)
- The Sayyid Dynasty (1414 - 1451)
- The Lodhi Dynasty (1451 - 1526)

*The Slave Dynasty*

- Qutub-ud-din Aibak (1206 - 1210) was its founder
- It included the following notable rulers like:
- Shams-ud-din Iltutmish(1210-1236)
- Razia Sultan(1236-1239)-the first and the only Muslim lady ruler
- Nasir-ud-din Muhammed(1246-1266);and Balban(1266-1287.

*The Khilji Dynasty*

- Its founder was Sultan Ja1a1-ud-din Khilji (1290 - 1296)
- He brought under his sway all the Rajput kingdoms.
- A1aud-din Khilji (1296 - 1316), the nephew of Sultan Jalal-ud-din himself killed him and took over the throne in 1296.
- In 1320 Khusro Khan killed Qutub-ud-din Mubarak Shah, the successor of Ala-ud-din Khi1ji and brought the Khilji dynasty down to its finish.

*The Tughlak Dynasty*

- Founder Ghiasuddin Tughlak (1320 - 1325)
- Some other notable rulers like:
- Mohammed-bin Tughlaq (1325 - 1351) known for introducing token coins of brass and copper
- Firoz Shah Tughlak (1351 - 88).

**NOTE: Ibn Batuta,** an African traveller who visited India in 1333, was appointed as the Chief Qazi of Delhi by the Sultan.

- Timur, a Turk, invaded India in 1398 and brought the Tughlak Dynasty down to its finish.

*The Sayyid Dynasty*

- Timur's representative Khizr Khan (1414 - 1421) captured Delhi and was proclaimed the new Sultan.
- He ruled over Delhi for about 7 years.
- The last Sayyid King, Alam Shah (1443 - 1451)
- He abdicated in favour of Bahlol Lodhi.

*The Lodhi Dynasty*

- Founded by Bahlol Lodhi (1451 - 1488), one of the Afghan Sardars who established himself in Punjab after the invasion of Timur.
- The other notable rulers of this dynasty were Sikander Lodhi (1489 - 1517)
- And Ibrahim Lodhi (1517 - 1526).

**First Battle of Panipat**

- The first battle of Panipat. in 1526
- It was fought between Ibrahim Lodhi-the ruler of Delhi and Babur-the ruler of Kabul.
- This battle proved to be a turning point for it established the Mughal dynasty beginning a new chapter in Indian history.

**Decline of Delhi Sultanate**

- Causes of the decline of the Delhi sultanate were mainly five:
- Despotic and military type of governments that did not have the confidence of the people,

- Degeneration of the Delhi Sultans
- The vastness of the Sultanate that was beyond effective control
- Financial instability
- Increased number of the slaves which rose to 1,80,000 in Firoz Shah's time became a burden on the treasury and created a financial crisis.

## The Mughal Dynasty(1526-1540 and 1555-1857)

*1. Babur* (1526 - 1530)

- Babur was the founder of the Mughal empire.
- He became the emperor of Delhi in 1527 after defeating Ibrahim Lodi in the first battle of Panipat
- He also defeated the Afghans in the battle of Gorge.

*2. Humayun* (1530 - 1540)

- He was son of Babur
- He ascended the throne in 1530
- Was dethroned by an Afghan warrior Sher Shah Suri.
- He again recovered the throne of Delhi in 1555
- But died in 1556.

*3. Sher Shah Suri* (1540 - 1545)

- He took over the throne of Delhi after defeating Humayun.
- He ruled the country for a brief period.
- He is known for his brilliant administration, land revenue policy and several other measures which he initiated to improve the economy of his state.
- He issued the coin called 'Rupia'
- He built the Grand Trunk Road (GT Road) linking Peshawar to Calcutta.

*4. Akbar* (1556 -1605)

- He is the real founder of the Mughal Empire was the eldest son of Humayun.
- His father or grandfather could not consolidate the empire which Akbar did successfully.
- His attitude towards Hindus was very conciliatory.

- He was the first ruler who delinked religion from politics.

**Second Battle of Panipat** (1556)

- Fought between Hemu, the Hindu leader and Akbar's regent Bairam Khan.
- Hemu was defeated on November 5, 1556
- He was captured and later slain by Bairam Khan.
- It ended the Mughal-Afghan contest for the throne of Delhi in favour of the Mughals and enabled Akbar to reoccupy Delhi and Agra.

*Battle of Haldighati* (1576)

- Fought near Gogundo (Haldighati) between Rana Pratap Singh of Mewar and the Mughal Army led by Man Singh of Amber.
- This resulted in the defeat of Rana Pratap Singh who even after that did not submit kept his struggle against the Mughals in name of India's sovereignty.

*5. Jehangir* (1605 - 1627)

- A son of Akbar ascended the throne after his death in 1605, was known for his strict administration of justice.
- In 1605, he married Mehr-un-nisa, later came to be popularised with the title of 'Nur- e- Jahan'.

*6. Shahjahan* (1628 - 1658)

- A son of Jehangir, ascended the throne after his father's death.
- He is known for the promotion of art, culture and architechure.
- The Red Fort and Jama Masjid are some of the magnificent structures of his time.
- The Taj Mahal which he built to immortalise his love for his beloved wife (died in 1531) is still considered to be one of the great wonders of the world.
- His failing health set off the war of succession among his four sons.
- His third son, Aurangzeb, succeeded in this struggle and crowned himself as the emperor in 1658.
- Shahjahan was imprisoned by Aurangzeb and died in captivity in 1666.

### 7. *Aurangzeb* (1659 -1707)

- Ruled India for 50 years
- He was known for being the most fanatic and anti-Hindu ruler.
- He demolished several Hindu Temples and banned all religious festivals.
- He executed Guru Teg Bahadur (the 9th Guru of Sikhs) when he refused to embrace Islam.

### *Decline of Mughal Empire*

- The invasion of Nadir Shah, a Persian king, in 1739, during the reign of Mohammed Shah, was a blow to the Mughal empire.
- He set a reign of terror and plundered Delhi.
- He took away the Kohinoor diamond with him to Afghanistan.

## THE SIKHS AND THE MARATHAS

### The Sikhs

- The Sikhs emerged as a powerful community during 15<sup>th</sup> century.
- It was a repercussion of the capture and execution of Guru Teg Bahadur, the 9th guru of the Sikhs in 1675 by Aurangzeb just for his refusal to embrace Islam.
- This led to the formation of a military force 'Khalsa' in 1699 under the leadership of Guru Gobind Singh, son of Guru Teg Bahadur.
- Guru Gobind Singh, however, was murdered in 1708 by an Afghan in the Deccan.
- His militant successor, Banda Bahadur, kept his mission continued but he too was murdered.

### The Marathas

- A powerful warrior Hindu community that fought against the Muslim rule in order to save their sovereignty.
- The most notable name of the Maratha leaders was that of **Shivaji** who initiated the strategy of guerilla warfare and led his mission very successfully.
- Once he was imprisoned by Aurangzeb while visiting his court in good faith in 1665 but, however, he managed to escape and in 1674

he proclaimed himself as an independent monarch.

- He died in 1680 and was succeeded by his son Sambhaji, who was executed by Aurangzeb.
- Sambhaji was succeeded by his brother Rajaram.
- Death of Rajaram in 1700
- Rajaram's widow Tarabai carried on the movement.

## Modern India

The history of modern India is marked by a different class of invaders who came not to rule but to trade.

- The Portuguese traders were the first in line who succeeded in discovering a sea-route to India in 1498
- They were followed by the Dutch in 1595
- They were followed by the English in 1600
- And finally the French in 1664.

NOTE: They all came to India with a mission to explore new avenues of trade for them and their country but later they explored some such scope that prompted them to grab India's sovereignty that led to a struggle for power in India among those foreign traders

- Finally the British superseded all of them.
- This was the new critical phase of our history:

## The Portuguese

- Vasco-da-Gama, a Portuguese sailor, first discovered a sea-route to India via the Cape of Good Hope in 1498.
- He arrived at Calicut on May 27, 1498.
- The Portuguese soon established political power along the west coast of India.
- Vasco-da-Gama was succeeded by Captain General Alfonso de Albuquerque who conquered Goa in 1510.

## The Dutch

- The Dutch marked their entry in India in 1595
- They established the Dutch East India Company in 1602
- Their first trade centre was established in 1605 in Masulipattam

- This was followed by more factories in Pulicat (1610), Surat (1616), Bimilpatam (1641), Karikal (1645), Chinsura (1653), Kasimbazar (1658), Baranagore (1658), Patna and Balasore (both 1658) and Cochin (1663).
- Pulicat was their chief trade centre till 1690
- Thereafter it was shifted to Negapatnam.
- Battle of Bedera: The struggle for survival in India between the Dutch and the English reached its height during late 17th and the early 18th century and resulted in the collapse of the Dutch with their defeat in the battle of Bedera against the English in 1759.

**The English**

- The year 1600 witnessed the formation of English East India Company through a Charter signed by Queen Elizabeth I that granted them a permission to trade with India.
- It was remarkable in the sense that it proved to be the first step towards slavery for India.
- Captain Hawkins paid a visit to the court of Jehangir, a Mughal ruler, in 1608 but failed to secure trading rights.
- But, in 1613, Sir Thomas Roe succeeded in getting the consent of the Indian empire to establish their first factory at Surat.
- Gradually the Company established its trading centres at Bombay, Calcutta and Madras.
- The English established their settlements/factories in
- Masulipattam (1611)
- Agra
- Ahmedabad
- Baroda
- Broach (1619)
- Armagaon near Pulicat (1626)
- Hariharpur and Balasore (1633)
- Patna, Dacca, Kasimbazar in Bengal and Bihar (1835)
- Madras (1639) to establish Fort St George
- Hugli (1651), a network of settlements in Bihar, Bengal and Orissa (1658)

- Bombay (1668)
- Sutanuti (1690)
- Kalikota and Govindpur (1698).
- Sutanuti, Kalikota and Govindpur were later joined together to a new city 'Calcutta' and the factory at Sutanati was fortified in 1700 and named as 'Fort William'.
- In 1686, the English declared war against Mughal Emperor Aurangzeb which resulted in the defeat of the English and they lost all their control over their settlements and factories in India in favour of the Mughals in 1688 -1689.
- But soon after it in 1690, the surrendering British were pardoned by the Mughal Emperor and in 1691 a royal 'firman' was issued by Aurangzeb in 1691 in favour of the English granting them exemption from payment of customs duties in Bengal.
- Farrukhsiyar granted British another 'firman' in 1717 which extended the privilege to British in Gujarat and Deccan.

## The French

- The French followed the track of the British and marked their entry in India in 1664.
- They set up their centres near Madras and Chandernagore on the Hooghly to trade with India.
- They also established naval bases in the islands of Bourbon and Mauritius in the Indian Ocean.
- They flourished initially till 1706, but afterwards saw their decline till 1720.
- But thereafter the governors like Lenoir and Dumas reorganised the French after 1720
- However, during 1742 the French governor Dupelex started repulsing the English power which resulted in 'Carnatic Wars' and finally in the French defeat.

## The Danish

- In 1616, the Danish East India Company from Denmark reached Indian coasts and established their settlements in Tranqubar in Tamil Nadu (1620)

- Established at Serampore in Bengal (1676).
- However, due to rising dominence of the British they had to sell out all their settlements to the British during 1845
- Finally they withdrew from India.

## East India Company and British Rule

- As the Dutch and the French were also the contenders for occupying of power in India the East India Company had to face strong opposition as they were the main contestants for political supremacy over India.
- However, the British succeeded in destabilizing the other warring forces and very successfully expanded the functions of the Comapany into political ambition.

## Robert Clive

- Robert Clive was a very diplomatic man who successfully led the English forces to capture Arcot and other regions.
- He was instrumental in laying the foundation of the British empire in India.
- In the Carnatic Wars between the French and the English it was his policies and management that brought out the defeat of the French
- In the Battle of Wandiwash he succeeded in gaining the control over South India.

## The English conquest of Bengal

- Nawab Alivardi Khan(1740-1756), an independent ruler of Bengal, was instrumental in extending protection to the European merchants in carrying on their trade.
- As he had no son of his own, he nominated his grandson (daughter's son) Siraj-ud-Daula as his heir.
- He died in April 1756.
- In the meantime the Company constructed fortifications at Calcutta and violated the terms under which they were allowed to trade.
- Siraj-ud-Daula retaliated promptly and occupied an English factory at Kasimbazar and later captured Calcutta in June 1756.

## Black-hole Tragedy

- June 20, 1756: A large number of the English prisoners were said to have been dumped into a small chamber which had a single tiny window on a hot summer night of June 20, 1756 which resulted in the death of several English prisoners out of suffocation and wounds.
- In December 1756, **Colonel Clive** and **Admiral Watson** reached Bengal from Madras and captured Calcutta.

## Mir Jafar

- Mir Jafar was the brother-in-law of Alivardi Khan
- He played a dual role under a secret pact with Clive who took him in confidence promising him the same state of Bengal.
- Mir Jafar on the other hand had also assured his support to Siraj-ud-Daula against the English.
- His dual policy bore far reaching consequences.

## Battle of Plassey (1757)

- Under the command of Robert Clive the Company's forces waged a war against Siraj-ud-Daula's army on June 23, 1757
- He saw a defeat already conspired by Mir Jafar.
- This proved to be the first move towards territorial supremacy which made it easy for the British to conquer Bengal and later the whole country.
- As a result of this battle the Nawab was captured and executed and Mir Jafar was declared as the Nawab of Bengal.
- He ceded Zamindari rights to twenty four Parganas and got Rs 16,700,000 as compensation.
- This was the first British acquisition of Indian territory.

## Battle of Buxar (1764)

- The battle of Buxar was fought between the English forces led by Clive on the one hand and a joint army of Nawab Shuja-ud-Daula of Awadh and Shah Alam II(the Mughal Empire) on the other.
- Mir Qasim, the successor of Mir Zafar, was instrumental behind it.
- Clive's forces were victorious resulting in the capture of Bihar and Bengal.

## *The Carnatic Wars:*

### First Carnatic War (1746 - 1748)

• It was fought between the forces of the French and the British companies which resulted due to the sacking of Fort St George and expulsion of the Englishmen by the French at Carnatic.

• Dupleix was the chief official of the French Company at Pondicherry at that time.

• The British army defeated the army of the Nawab of Carnatic and that of the French.

### Second Carnatic War

• The British succeeded in consolidating themselves by taking hold of Bengal, Bihar and Orissa.

• The second battle between the French and the British took place in 1760 in which the French saw the defeated that was also the end of all the dreams and prospects for the French to rule over India under the Treaty of Paris(1763).

### The Anglo-Maratha War

• The First Anglo-Maratha war (1775- 1782) took place during the tenure of Warren Hastings, the then governor- general of India.

• The war ended with the Treaty of Salbai, 1782, and the status quo restored.

### The Mysore War

• Haider Ali ,the ruler of Mysore, was a great and powerful warrior.

• He defeated the British forces in 1769 in the first Anglo-Mysore war.

• Haider Ali took hold of almost the whole of Carnatic.

• However, in 1781, Haider Ali was defeated at Porto Novo .

• After Haider Ali, the war was carried on by Tipu Sultan.

• A peace treaty was signed thereafter.

• But in 1789 another war was launched and Tipu Sultan was defeated in 1792.

## British Rule

## Governor-generals of India and reforms

*Robert Clive* (1760-1765)

- The East India Company appointed Robert Clive as the first governor general of Bengal in 1758.
- But he remained in England from 1760 - 1765 and on his return in 1765, the emperor ceded to the Company the Diwani of Bengal, Bihar and Orissa.

*Warren Hastings* (1772 - 1785)

- Succeeded Clive in 1772 and became the first Governor-General of India.
- He is known for introducing several reforms.
- He established civil and criminal courts, and courts of appeal passed the Regulating Act 1773 that sanctioned a legalized working constitution to the Company's dominion in India.
- It envisaged a Council of Ministers headed by the Governor-General.
- The Pitt's India Act of 1784 was passed by the British Parliament to put the Company's affairs in permanent centralized control of the British Parliament.

*Lord Cornwallis* (1786 - 93)

- Succeeded Hastings in 1787.
- In order to stabilize land revenue and create a loyal and contented class of zamindars he introduced a new revenue system under the Permanent Settlement of Bengal in 1793.
- As a result, the auction of periodic zamindari rights was abolished.
- It established permanent zamindari rights to collect land revenue from the tenants and pay a fixed amount to the Government treasury every year.

*Lord Wellesley* (1798 - 1805)

- Lord Welleseley was the successor of Cornwallis
- He had be part of the last, Mysore War (1799) with Tipu Sultan

who, after regaining his lost strength, set out again on his plan of ousting the British from India.

- In this attempt he sought support of Napolean and the Persian king.
- Lord Wellesley visualized the danger and so he sought an alliance with the Nizam and the Marathas.
- Finally Tipu Sultan saw the defeat and died fighting bravely against the British
- Subsidiary alliances: Apart from war, Wellesley depended on a system of subsidiary alliances for the expansion of the British territories.
- Under this system the ruler of an aligning state was made to accept permanent stationing of a British force within his territory. He was also bound to pay subsidy for its maintenance.
- Sometimes a territory was added in lieu of payment.
- The ruler was also bound to accept a British resident.
- He was not allowed to employ a European without the approval of the British authority nor to negotiate with any Indian ruler without prior consultation of the British Governor-General.
- In a way it was the loss of their sovereignty in external affairs while the British resident got all rights to interfere in the internal administration.
- The rulers lost control over their territories.

*Lord Hastings* (1813 -1823)

- During the tenure of Lord Hastings, Nepal was defeated in 1814, resulting in Nepal ceding Garhwal and Kumaon to the British.
- In 1818, the Marathas made their last attempt to regain their independence which led to the third Anglo-Maratha and finally the Marathas were completely crushed.
- This period was remarkable for a number of reforms such as the Ryotwari Settlement which introduced a system of direct settlement between the government and the Ryots (cultivators).
- The revenue was fixed for a period not exceeding 30 years on the basis of quality of soil.

- The fifty percent of the net value of the crop was to be given to the Government.
- This period was also remarkable for a special attention to education, building of roads, bridges and canals.

*Lord William Bentinck* (1828 - 1835)

Bentinck's period was remarkable in the sense that many revolutionary social reforms:

- abolition of Sati Pratha(1829)
- suppression of Thuggee
- suppression of female infanticide
- Stopped human sacrifices were introduced.
- English was introduced as a medium of higher education on the advice of a council headed by Lord Macaulay.
- Lord Bentinck also succeeded in making a pact with Maharaja Ranjit Singh, the ruler of Punjab.
- By the Charter Act 1833, the Company ceased to be a trading company and became an administrative power.
- He also adopted some corrective measures in the civil services.
- However, it was Cornwallis who founded the British Civil Service in India.

*Raja Ram Mohun Roy*

- A great social and religious reformer from the land of Bengal who was instrumental behind many social reforms like the abolition of Sati Pratha.
- He organised a new society Brahmo Samaj in 1829 in order to create an ideal society.
- He discarded idol worship, caste system and a lot of such orthodoxies and complicated rites and rituals.

*Sir Charles Metcalfe* (1836 - 1844)

- The successor of Lord Bentinck registered his popularity for removing restrictions on the press and media.

*Lord Hardinge* (1844 - 1848)

- This period was marked by the First Sikh War (1845) fought between the Sikhs and the British resulting in the defeat of the and thereby putting the Sikhs under the British control.

*Lord Dalhousie* (1848 - 1856)

- The period of Lord Dalhousie saw the Second Sikh War (1849) with the result of the Sikhs' defeat and the annexation of the whole of Punjab to the British administration.

- Dalhousie also introduced the Doctrine of Lapse through which he got the power to take over total sovereignty of the state where the had no natural heir, as the king was not allowed to adopt anyone to inherit his kingdom.

- Some of the other major reforms of this period were the opening of the first railway lines between Bombay and Thane in 1853

- Connecting Calcutta and Agra telegraph

- Setting up of P.W.D.

- The Widow Remarriage Act (1856).

## INDIAN FREEDOM STRUGGLE

### Some of the little known revolts up to 1857

| Year | Movement / Mutiny |
| --- | --- |
| 1828 | Ahoms Revolt against the Company for non-fulfilment of pledges after the Burmese War |
| 1829 | 1st Koli Rising against dismantling of forts of independent Koli tribes |
| 1831 | Kol Rising of Chhotanagpur against the transfer of land from heads of kol tribesmen to outsiders |
| 1833 | Khasi Rising in the hilly region of Jaintia and Garo hills. The revolt was lead by Tirath Singh, the ruler of Nunklow and resented by Khasis in the region |
| 1838 | Farazi Movement under the leadership of Titu Mir, later merged into the Wahabi Movement |
| 1839 | 2nd Koli rising |

| 1844 | 3rd Koli rising |
| 1844 | Surat Salt Agitation against raised salt duty |
| 1844 | Mutiny of the 34th Native Infantry |
| 1844 | Kolhapur and Savantvadi Revolts |
| 1849 | Mutiny of the 22nd Native Infantry |
| 1850 | Mutiny of the 66th Native Infantry |
| 1852 | Mutiny of the 37th Native Infantry |
| 1855 | Santhal rebellion in the Rajmahal hills region of Bihar |
| 1857 | SEPOY MUTINY -Revolt of sepoys of 3rd Cavalry at Meerut and later mutinies in Punjab, Mathura, Lucknow, Bareilly, Shahjahanpur, Kanpur, Banaras, Jhansi, Allahabad and many other places in North India |

## First War of Independence

### The Sepoy Mutiny or the Revolt of 1857

- During the period of Viceroy Lord Canning, on March 29, 1857, Mangal Pandey, an Indian sepoy of the 34th regiment, killed two British officers on parade at Barrackpore and the Indian soldiers present on parade declined the orders to arrest Mangal Pandey. However, he was later arrested, tried and hanged.

- The news spread like wildfire to all cantonments in the country and very soon a countrywide sepoy revolt broke out from Lucknow, Ambala, Burhanpur and Meerut.

- On May 10, 1857, soldiers at Meerut refused to touch the new Enfield rifle cartridges which were said to have a greased cover made of animal fat. The soldiers along with other groups of civilians, went on a rampage, broke open jails, murdered Europeans and marched to Delhi. The appearance of the marching soldiers next morning in Delhi was a signal to the local soldiers, who in turn, also revolted, besieged the city and proclaimed the 80 year old Bahadur Shah Zafar as the Emperor of India. As this movement aroused a mass resentment against the British Empire, it was called the first struggle for freedom in India.

### Failure of the Revolt

- This initial war saw a defeat and couldn't survive due to the capture of Delhi by the British on September 20, 1857.

- Emperor Bahadur Shah was imprisoned. The British military then dealt with the rebels in each centre, by term.
- The Laxmi Bai, the Rani of Jhansi, died fighting on June 17, 1858.
- Nana Saheb refused to give in and finally escaped to Nepal in January 1859, hoping to renew the struggle.
- Kunwar Singh died in May 1858, trying to escape from the British.Tantia Tope, who successfully carried out guerrilla warfare against the British until April 1859, was betrayed by a fellow rebel and was captured by the British army and later he was put to death.
- As a result the British got fair opportunity to re-establish themselves as the authority to rule all over India.

## Major reasons for the Failure of the Mutiny

- Lack of unity among Indians and poor organisation
- Lack of complete nationalism, some of the great rulers like Scindia, Holkars, the Nizam and others actively supported the British
- Lack of coordination between sepoys, peasants, zamindars and other struggling classes
- Difference of motives for participating in the revolt

## British Rule after the Revolt

- **Government of India Act 1858** India was placed under the governance of the Crown following the proclamation called 'Magna Carta of Indian Liberty' issued by Queen Victoria on November 1, 1858.

## The Indian National Congress

- The Indian National Congress was formed in 1885 by A.O.Hume, an English retired civil servant, in association with various Indian national leaders.
- Hume's ideas were unanimously supported by all Indian leaders at the Pune Conference in December1885 where the organisation the Indian National Union was renamed as the Indian National Congress (INC).
- The first session of the Congress was held in Bombay under the presidentship of W. C. Banerjee.
- With the foundation of the Indian National Congress, the struggle for freedom in India was reflamed.

## The Moderates

- The Congress initially adopted the moderate constitutional movement through confining itself to an annual debate where political issues were discussed.
- It asked the government for the remedy of their complaints, but it had no constitutional role.
- However, some Congressmen were also members of the Legislative Assembly organised to advise the viceroy and the executive committee on the drafting of new laws.
- The cause of the Indian National Congress spread rapidly among middle-class Indians.
- The Congress launched the struggle for independence initially in small, hesitant and mild but organised manner.
- The first two decades of the Indian National Congress were marked with its moderate demands and a sense of confidence in British justice and generosity.
- It had no intention to be aggressive in attaining independence lest the British should suppress them.
- This resulted in the 'Indian Council Act' in 1892 that allowed some members to be indirectly elected by Indians but kept the official majority intact.

## Swadeshi Movement

- On August 7, 1905, the Indian National Congress adopted a resolution to boycott British goods.
- Bonfires of foreign goods were conducted on a large scale in all the major cities.

## The Partition of Bengal

- With a view to mar the political influence of the intellectual middle class, Bengal was parted from the other parts vide a royal proclamation on October 16, 1905.
- It reduced the size of the province of Bengal with a separate statehood called East Bengal.

## Muslim League

- In 1906, an all India Muslim League was set up under the leadership of Aga Khan, Nawab Salimullah of Dacca and Nawab Mohsinul-Mulk.
- It supported the partition of Bengal. This led to communal differences between Hindus and Muslims.

## The Extremists

- At the turn of the century certain changes were seen in the mood of the Congress. The most important among them was the change in the attitude of the British.
- Some of the repressive and oppressive measures of the British promoted the growth of extremism within the Congress.
- The extremist leaders such as Bipin Chandra Pal, Bal Gangadhar Tilak, and Lala Lajpat Rai persuaded the people to show courage and self-reliance in the cause of India's nationalism.
- The partition of Bengal in 1905 had already aggravated the political temper of the country.
- The Congress started getting polarised into the moderates and the extremists.
- This era of militant nationalism was prevalent inside and outside the Congress during 1906 - 1919.
- Consequently in its 1906 session the Congress made a declaration for the 'Dominion Status' and to achieve it became its first political goal.
- Resolutions on boycott, swadeshi, swaraj, and national education were also adopted.

## Surat Session-Split in Congress (1907)

- During 1907 session at Surat the Indian National Congress split into two groups-the extremists and the moderates.
- Lokmanya Tilak, Lala Lajpat Rai and Bipin Chandra Pal were the leaders of the extremists while the moderates were led by Gopal Krishna Gokhale.

## Minto-Morley Reforms

- During the period of Lord Minto's governorship a Minto-Morley Reform was introduced which envisaged a separate electorate for Muslims. The government thereby intended to create a rift between the Hindus and Muslims which weakened the struggle for freedom.

## Home Rule Movement (1915 -16)

- Annie Besant, inspired by the Irish rebellion, started a Home Rule Movement in India in September 1916.
- The movement spread rapidly all over India.
- Bal Gangadhar Tilak extended his complete support to this movement. He joined forces with Dr Besant .He also persuaded the Muslim League to support the programme as well.

## Lucknow Pact (1916)

- It was a major step towards re-union of Hindu-Muslim relationship.
- The Congress and Muslim League jointly held sessions at Lucknow which created an anti-British feelings among the Muslims.
- It was a setback to the British authorities for they had planned to weaken the struggle by creating a strong rift between the two communities.
- Hence, in 1916, a British policy was announced whereby associations of Indians were increased and gradual development of local self-government introduced.

## Movements during World War I

- The Congress reunited in support of the British during World War I but soon after the war it felt disappointed for the Britain imposed restrictions on all the Indian political activities.
- The Congress put its demand for *poorna swaraj* ("complete independence") under the leadership of Mahatma Gandhi.
- It waged periodic campaigns of non-violent civil disobedience. The agitating leaders were imprisoned several times.
- Later Britain made some concessions in the 1930s.

## August Declaration of 1917

- During World War I, the British claimed that they stood for the protection of democracy around the world.

It persuaded the agitating Indians to demand for democracy for their country.

- Montague, the Secretary of State for Indian Affairs, made his Declaration before the House of Commons on August 20, 1917.
- This was called as August Declaration in which he said that to satisfy the local demands, his government was interested in giving more representation to the natives in India.
- New reforms would be introduced in the country to meet this objective.
- The control over the Indian government would be transferred gradually to the Indian people.

## The Gandhian Era

- The period from 1918-1947 was dominated by Mahatma Gandhi whose leadership changed whole concept of the struggle for freedom with his ideals of *non-violent Satyagraha.*

## Montague - Chelmsford Reforms

- Lord Montague came to India and stayed for six months.
- During this period he held meetings with different government and non-government people.
- Finally, in cooperation with Governor-General Lord Chelmsford, Montague presented a report on the constitutional reforms for India in 1918.
- The report was discussed and approved by the British Parliament and then became the Government of India Act of 1919.
- This act is commonly known as the Montague - Chelmsford Reforms.

## Rowlatt Act 1919

- A sedition committee was appointed during the period of Lord Chelmsford, the then viceroy of India.
- This committee sanctioned for the Rowlatt Act, 1919 providing unbridled powers to the government to arrest and imprison suspects without trial.

- Gandhiji started his fight against this Act giving a call for *Satyagraha*
- A number of agitating leaders like Kitchlu and Dr Satyapal were put behind the bars causing great unrest all over India.

**The Massacre of Jallianwala Bagh**

- In order to decide the future plan of action a public meeting was held on April 13, 1919 in Jallianwala Bagh in Amritsar.
- Gandhiji was scheduled to address the meeting.
- A large number of people including women and children had assembled.
- Before the meeting could start General 0'Dyer, the Lt Governor of Punjab ordered indiscriminate heavy firing on the crowd and hundreds of people were brutally killed on the spot whereas more than 1200 people were wounded
- It proved to be a turning point in the Indo-British relations provided a new strength to the struggle for freedom.

**Khilafat Movement** (1920)

- The safety and welfare of Turkey was threatened by the British during the first World War weakening the position of the Sultan of Turkey and the Caliph.
- As the Caliph was looked upon to be the religious head of the Muslim, the two brothers Mohammed Ali and Shaukat Ali launched an Anti-British movement in 1920 calling it the *Khilafat Movement*.
- Maulana Abul Kalam Azad also led the movement and Gandhiji also extended his support to it.
- It again paved the way for Hindu-Muslim unity.

**Non-cooperation Movement** (1920)

- The new social awakening for the Hindu-Muslim gave a tremendous energy to the freedom struggle.
- Gandhiji launched his non-violent, non-cooperation movement envisaging the surrender of titles, resignation from nominated offices, refusal to attend government work, boycott of foreign goods, etc.
- This was the first mass-movement that brought the whole of India at one platform. Almost all working class of society such as peasants,

teachers, students, women, and merchants came forward voluntarily to extend their support to the Movement.

• It acquired a real mass base as it gained momentum and spread across the length and breadth of the country.

• The Congress also got a facelift with this Movement gaining its recognition as an organisation for action instead of a mere deliberative assembly. The development of national unity and willingness of people to make sacrifices for the cause of national independence also emerged from this Movement.

**Movements in 1921 and 1922** Some of the major events during these two years were:

• Educational boycott and boycott of law courts (January to March 1921)

• 'Operation Tilak Swaraj Fund' organized all over India (April to June 1921)

• Boycott of foreign clothes and subsequent picketing of shops selling them (July to September 1921)

• Many local movements including the Kisan movement (November 1921 to February 1922).

**Chauri-Chaura Incident** (1922)

• The Congress decided to launch a Civil Disobedience Movement in December 1921 under the leadership of Gandhi.

• Before Gandhi could launch the movement, an agitated mob at Chauri Chaura near Gorakhpur, clashed with the police and set the police-station in flame. 22 policemen were killed during the clash.

• Gandhi felt hurt and called off the Movement on February 12, 1922.

**Swaraj Party** (1922)

• Gandhi decided to call off the agitation.

• The Indian masses were disheartened and some of the leaders like Motilal Nehru, C. R. Das and N. C. Kelkar organised a Swaraj Party which emphasised the need for Indian's entry into the legislative councils by contesting elections.

**Simon Commission** (1927)

- A Commission headed by Simon was appointed by the British Government in November 1927.
- Its purpose was to review and report as to what extent a representative government could be introduced in India.
- All the members of this Commission were Europeans so the Indian leaders decided to boycott the Commission
- In order to show their protest they hold demonstrations raising slogans 'Simon go back'.
- While leading a demonstration at Lahore, Lala Lajpat Rai was severely beaten in a police lathi charge. It caused his death.

**Lahore Session** (1929)

- During its Lahore Session in December 1929 the Indian National Congress declared Poorna Swaraj (Complete Independence) to be the goal of the national movement.

**Civil Disobedience Movement** (1930)

- In order to achieve the goal of Poorn Swaraj Gandhi launched another Civil Disobedience Movement in 1930.
- In the first phase he began with serving ultimatum to the authorities which included only the common grievances of the people of India. There he didn't include the demand for complete independence.
- Out of the 11 points there were **two demands of the peasant**
- the abolition of salt tax to eradicate the government's salt monopoly
- the reduction in the land revenue by percentage
- three demands of the middle class
- the coastal shipping to be reserved for Indians
- adequate protection to the domestic textile industry of India
- checking the deteriorating rupee-sterling exchange ratio; the rest such as the modifications in the working of the Central Intelligence Departments, release of political prisoners, complete prohibition of intoxicants, 50 per cent reduction in military expenditure, 50 per cent cut in civil administration expenditure, and changes in the

Arms Act, thus allowing citizens to bear arms for self-protection were the common grivances.

## Dandi March (1930)

- In order to break the Salt Law Gandhi started his Dandi March known as *Salt Satyagraha* from his Ashram at Sabarmati on 12 March, 1930.
- This Movement got tremendous response sparking off a widespread sense of patriotism.
- Even the Indian soldiers were also sensitised.
- It provoked the British government begin repressive measures such as mass arrests, lathi-charge and other measures to create havoc among public.
- Nearly 100000 Indians were imprisoned with a view to weaken the Movement.

## Political Scenario of India and the World War II

- Just before World War II broke out, the Congress declared its unwillingness to associate itself with the British government.
- It also clearly informed the government that India should not be pushed to war without the consent of the Indian people.
- The British government also made no clear statement concerning its war and peace aims as applicable to India.
- The British Prime Minister stated that the British were in the war to ensure the safety of democratic world and uphold the right of every nation to self-determination.
- On September 3, 1939, Britain declared war against Germany. The Governor General of India, Lord Linlithgow, began dispatching Indian troops to the battlefield, without consulting Indian leaders.
- The Governor General also declared emergency in India under the provision of Article 93 of the Governance of India Act 1935 in order to curb internal disorder.
- The Congress asked the British government first to ensure democratic set up for India if its fight with Germany was intended to maintain and extends democracy there.

- On October 10, 1939, the Congress increased pressure to make India free soon after the war.
- The Viceroy, on October 17, 1939, through an official statement, declared his Government's promise to issue dominion status to India and to reconsider the Act of 1935 after the war.

## Demand for Pakistan (1940)

- The Muslim League made its demand for a separate Muslim nation during its Lahore Session in March 1940.
- Mr Jinnah was its leader..
- The Congress had to face suppressive measures for not extending its support to the British government during World War II.
- By that time the freedom struggle had got mass support which compelled Britain to grant independence to India in 1947 following the War.
- The predominantly Hindu Congress reluctantly accepted the division of India.
- A new separate Muslim nation named as Pakistan was created.

## Cripps Mission

The important points made by the Cripps Mission were as follows:

- General elections in the provinces would be arranged as soon as the war ended.
- A new Indian dominion, associated with the United Kingdom, would be created.
- Those provinces not joining the dominion could form their own separate union.
- Minorities were to be protected.
- However, both the Congress and the Muslim League rejected these proposals.
- Jinnah opposed the plan, as it did not concede Pakistan.

## Quit India Movement (1942 -1945)

- On August 8, 1942, the Congress passed a resolution for the 'Quit India' Movement.
- It was resolved to ask the British to quit India.

- Gandhiji gave a call for 'Do or die' to his countrymen.
- Gandhi was imprisoned where he undertook a 21-day fast which worsened his condition.
- However, he survived and completed the 2l-day fast.
- This was his answer to the government which had been constantly exhorting him to condemn the violence of the people in the Quit India Movement.
- Gandhi not only refused to condemn people resorting to violence but unequivocally held the government responsible for it.
- The popular response to the news of the fast was immediate and overwhelming.
- All over the country, there were demonstrations and strikes. The fast had done exactly what it had intended to. Public morale was raised, the anti-British feeling was inflamed.
- The Quit India Movement got huge response from all classes – students, women, peasants, and the other working strata of society.
- The great significance of this historic movement was that it placed the demand for independence on the immediate agenda of the national movement.
- After Quit India there could be no retreat.
- Any future negotiations with the British government could only be on the manner of transfer of power.
- Independence was no longer a matter of bargain now.

## Contribution of Azad Hind Fauj

- Subhas Chandra Bose, popularly known as 'Netaji' was an extremist by temperament.
- He was not at all convinced by the policy of the Congress to acquire freedom.
- He found his own way to get freedom for the country by organising a military force in the name of Azad Hind Fauj(Indian National Army) in 1942 in Singapore and gave a call for "Dilli Chalo".
- He started a military campaign for the independence of India.
- Indian residents of South-east Asia and Indian soldiers and officers captured by the Japanese forces in Malaya, Singapore, and Burma joined the INA in large numbers.

## Rise and Decline

- The headquarters of the INA was set up in two places- Rangoon and in Singapore.
- Recruits were sought from civilians, funds were gathered, and even a women's regiment called the Rani Jhansi regiment was formed.
- One INA battalion also accompanied the Japanese Army to the Indo-Burma front to participate in the Imphal campaign.
- But with the defeat of Japan in 1944 -1945, the INA also died out.
- Bose is believed to have been killed in an air crash on his way to Tokyo in August 1945.

## Achievements of the INA

- The achievements of the INA fell much short of its targets but it acquired a great significance in the history of India.
- It created a design of communal harmony in India.
- India's freedom struggle which was till now a territorial struggle against the ruling government became an international issue.
- The Indian Army also started thinking of independent India and showed little will to fight for the British crown.
- It also gave Congress the knowledge that its non-violent methods to gain independence may not be adequate.
- Overall, the INA helped expedite the process of Indian independence.

## Cabinet Mission Plan

- The struggle for freedom entered a decisive phase in 1945 - 1946.
- The Cabinet Mission visited India and met the representatives of different political parties.
- The Mission envisaged the establishment of a Constituent Assembly to frame the Constitution, as well as an interim government.

## Formation of the Constituent Assembly

- The Constituent Assembly met in December 1946 and Dr Rajendra Prasad was elected its President. The Muslim League did not join the Assembly.

## Mountbatten Plan

- Lord Mountbatten made his plan open to the Indian public on June 3, 1947 to break the deadlock created by the refusal of the Muslim League to join the Constituent Assembly.
- He laid down detailed principles for the partition of the country.
- Both the Congress and the Muslim League accepted the plan which resulted in the birth of Pakistan.

## Partition of India

- In accordance with the Indian Independence Act, 1947 India was partitioned on August 15, 1947 into India and Pakistan.
- Lord Mountbatten was appointed the first Governor-General of free India and Mr Muhammed Ali Jinnah, the first Governor-General of Pakistan.

## Post-Independence India

- After Lord Mountbatten, Sir C. Rajagopalachari became the first and the only Indian Governor-General of India in 1948.
- Pt Jawaharlal Nehru took over as the first Prime Minister.
- Mahatma Gandhi undertook a fast for the sake of the Muslim rights.
- On January 30, 1948 he was assassinated by Nathuram Vinayak Godse in a Birla House prayer meeting in Delhi.
- On November 26, 1949, the Constituent Assembly passed the new Constitution of India.

DAE also financially supports seven autonomous national institutes:

1. Tata Institute of Fundamental Research (TIFR), Mumbai.
2. Tata memorial Centre (TMC), Mumbai
3. Saha Institute of Nuclear Physics (SINP), Kolkata
4. Institute of Physics (IOP), Bhubaneswar
5. Harish - Chandra Research Institute (HRI), Allahabad
6. Institute of Mathematical Studies (IMS), Chennai.
7. Institute of Plasma Research (IPR), Ahmedabad.

# PART SEVEN

# THE INDIAN CONSTITUTION

- India framed its own Constitution to assert its sovereign status.
- Thus the Constituent Assembly was set up under the Cabinet Mission Plan of 1946.
- A Drafting Committee was set up.
- The Chairperson was Dr B.R. Ambedkar, the first Law Minister of India.
- Nearly two years eleven months and eighteen days was the time taken to prepare the draft:
- 16 November, 1949: the Indian Constitution was enacted, signed and adopted by the Constituent Assembly.
- 26 January, 1950 – the Constitution made India, the Republic.

**The Indian Constitution: Its Form and Features**

- The Constitution of India gives the principles of liberal democracy
- We were given a bicameral parliament: a lower house and an upper house - This was on the format of British parliament.
- Fundamental Rights and setting up the Supreme Court was based on the constitution of the USA.
- India follows a federal system of governance in which the residual powers of legislation are vested in the central government- This was based on the Canadian set-up.
- Our Constitution also contains the State list, the Union list and the Concurrent list
- This divides the jurisdiction of powers between the Central and the State governments- This system has been adopted from Australia.
- The Directive Principles of State Policy are based on the Irish Constitution.

- The Indian Constitution is flexible by nature.
- A two-third majority of the Lok Sabha and The Rajya Sabha is required for any Amendment.
- There is a provision for the addition of Schedules through Amendments.
- At present 12 Schedules are in our Constitution.
- Till date ninety four Amendments have been made in our constitution.
- The Constitution has been divided into four major parts:
  1. The Preamble,
  2. Parts I to XXII,
  3. Schedules 1-12, and
  4. Appendix.

**The Preamble. "WE THE PEOPLE OF INDIA...**
- It is the introduction of the Constitution
- It also has the ideals and the purpose of the Constitution.
- In 1976 the original Preamble was amended as per the 42nd Amendment
- Two words were added 'Secular' and 'Socialist':

**Contents of the Indian Constitution**

| | |
|---|---|
| Part I / Articles 1 - 4 | Territory of India, admission, establishment or formation new states |
| Part II/ Articles 5 - 11 | Citizenship |
| Part III/Articles 12 - 35 | Fundamental Rights |
| Part IV/Articles 36 - 51 | Directive Principles of State Policy |
| Part IV-A/Article 51 - A | Duties of a citizen of India |
| Part V/Articles 52 - 151 | Government at the Union level |
| Part VII /Articles 152 - 237 | Government at the State level |
| Part VII/ Article 238 | Repealed by 7th Amendment, 1956 |
| Part VIII/Articles 239 - 241 | Administration of Union Territories |

- Part IX/Articles 242 - 243O     The Panchayats
- Part IX-A/Art. 243P - 243ZG     The Municipalities
- Part X/ Articles 244 - 244 A     Scheduled and tribal areas
- Part XI/Articles 245 - 263     Relations between the Union and States
- Part XII/Articles 264 - 300A     Finance, property, contracts and suits
- Part XIII/Articles 301 - 307     Trade, commerce and travel within territory of India
- Part XIV/Articles 308 - 323     Services under the Union and States
- Part XV/Articles 324 - 329A     Election and Election Commission
- Part XVII / Articles 330 - 342     Special provision to certain classes SCs/STs, OBCs and Anglo-Indians
- Part XVIV / Articles 343 - 351     Official languages
- Part XVIIV / Articles 352 - 360     Emergency provisions
- Part XIX/Articles 361 - 367     Miscellaneous provisions
- Part XX/Article 368     Amendment of Constitution
- Part XXI/Articles 369 - 392     Temporary, transitional and special provisions
- Part XXIV/Articles 393-395     Short title, commencement and repeal of the Constitution

**The Schedules**
- Schedules is a very important part of the Indian Constitution.
- Eight Schedules in the original Constitution.
- 1951: The Ninth Schedule 1st Amendment of 1951
- 1992: The Twelfth Schedule added by the 74th Amendment of 1992.
- The 12 Schedules covers:
- the designations of the states and union territories
- the emoluments for high level officials
- forms of oaths

- allocation of the number of seats in the Rajya Sabha (Council of States-the upper house of Parliament) per state or territory
- provisions for the administration and control of Scheduled Areas and Scheduled Tribes
- provisions for the administration of tribal areas in Assam
- the Union (meaning Central Government), State and Concurrent (dual) Lists of responsibilities
- the official languages
- land and tenure reforms and the association of Sikkim with India.

The Schedules contain the following issues:

*First Schedule:*

I. The States

II. The Union Territories.

*Second Schedule:* Five parts of this Schedule - deal with issues:

- Part A. Provisions as to the President and the Governors of States. It deals in their eligibilities, their appointment, their salaries etc.
- Part B. Repealed
- Part C. Provisions as to the Speaker and the Deputy Speaker of the House of the People, the Chairman and the Deputy Chairman of the Council of States, the Speaker and the Deputy Speaker of the Legislative Assembly and the Chairman and the Deputy Chairman of the Legislative Council of a State.
- Part D. Provisions as to the Judges of the Supreme Court and the High Courts of India.
- Part E. Provisions as to the Comptroller and Auditor General of India.

*Third Schedule:*

- Forms of Oaths and Affirmations.

*Fourth Schedule:*

- Allocation of seats in the Council of States.

*Fifth Schedule:*

- Provisions as to the Administration and control of the Schedules Areas and Scheduled Tribes. It is divided into four sub-parts:

- Part A. General
- Part B. Administration and Control of Scheduled Areas and Scheduled Tribes.
- Part C. Scheduled Areas.
- Part D. Amendment of the Schedule.

*Sixth Schedule*: Deals with provisions· regarding administration of tribal areas in the states of Assam, Meghalaya and Mizoram.

- This Schedule in the Constitution, amended in 1988 by the Act 67 of 1988, received the assent of the President on December 16, 1988, and was applied to the states of Tripura and Mizoram w.e.f. December 16, 1988.

*Seventh Schedule:*

- Gives the detailed lists of powers and subjects to be looked after by the Union and the States.
- It includes: *(i)* Union List that comprises subjects of all-India importance like Defence, International Affairs, Railways, Post and Telegraph, Income tax, etc.
- The Parliament has the exclusive power to legislate on these subjects.
- It contains 100 subjects: *(ii)* State List contains subjects of local importance.
- The State Legislature alone legislates on these subjects.
- It contains 66 subjects: *(iii)* Concurrent List
- Contains subjects on which the Parliament and the State Legislature enjoy authority as well.
- According to the 88th amendment, service tax is to be levied, collected and appropriated by the Union and the States.

*Eighth Schedule:*

- provides a list of 22 regional languages recognised by the Constitution.
- originally there were only 14 languages in the Schedule
- the 15th language 'Sindhi' was added by the 21st amendment in 1967
- three more languages-Konkani, Manipuri and Nepali were added by the 71st amendment in 1992.

- 2003, the 92nd Amendment added 'Bodo', 'Dogri', 'Maithili', and 'Santhali'.
- Now the total languages enlisted the Constitution are:

  1. Assamese, 2. Bengali, 3. Bodo, 4. Dogri, 5. Gujarati, 6. Hindi, 7. Kannada, 8. Kashmiri, 9. Malayalam, 10. Maithali, 11. Marathi, 12. Oriya, 13. Punjabi, 14. Sanskrit, 15. Sindhi, 16. Tamil, 17: Telugu, 18. Santhali, 19. Urdu, 20. Konkani, 21. Manipuri, 22. Nepali.

*Ninth Schedule:*

- Contains 257 Acts and Regulations of the State Legislature dealing with land reforms and abolition of the zamindari system.
- Added to the Constitution in 1951 by the First Constitution (Amendment) Act.

*Tenth Schedule:*

- contains certain provisions regarding disqualification of members on grounds of defection.

*Eleventh Schedule:*

- Added to the Constitution on April 20, 1992 by the 73rd Amendment
- lists 29 subjects on which the panchayats have been given administrative control.

*Twelfth Schedule:*

- Added to the Constitution on April 20, 1992 by the 74th Amendment
- it lists 18 subjects on which the municipalities are given administrative control.

## Appendix

*Appendix I*

- The Constitution (Application to the State of Jammu and Kashmir) Order, 1954.

*Appendix II*

- Re-statement with reference to the present text of the Constitution of the exceptions and modifications subject to which the Constitution applies to the State of Jammu and Kashmir.

*Appendix III*

- Extracts from the Constitution (Forty-fourth Amendment) Act, 1978.

*Some Unique Features of Indian Constitution:*

## Citizenship

- Part II (Articles 5 – 11) of our Constitution deals with the provision for only single citizenship for the people of India.
- There is no separate citizenship of states.
- Citizenship can be acquired (Citizenship Act, 1955) by birth, descent, registration naturalisation or when Indian acquires new territories.
- One can lose it by renunciation, termination or deprivation.
- Parliament can, by law, deprive any person of his/her citizenship if it is satisfied that citizenship was acquired by fraud, false representation, or concealment of material facts.

*Dual Citizenship 2005*

- Under the provisions made in the Citizenship Act, 2003, those eligible to become citizens of India as on January 26, 1950, could apply for dual Indian citizenship.
- The government has extended dual citizenship to all those who were holding the Person of Indian Original Card (IPIOC) and who had migrated from India after the formation of the Indian Republic.
- Persons of Indian origin who were citizens of Australia, Canada, Finland, France, Greece, Ireland, Israel, Italy, the Netherlands, New Zealand, Portugal, Cyprus, Sweden, Switzerland, the United Kingdom and the United States of America were eligible to apply for dual citizenship.
- A person who has been at any time a citizen of Pakistan, Bangladesh or any other country that the government may notify in future is not entitled to dual citizenship.

## Fundamental Rights

- Part III (Articles 12 – 35) declares the provision for Fundamental Rights for the citizens of India.
- There were seven Fundamental Rights in the beginning
- its number was reduced to six:
    1. Right of Equality *(Articles 14 - 18)*
    2. Right of Freedom *(Article 19)*. It guarantees

(i) Freedom of speech and expression

(ii) Freedom to assemble peacefully and without arms

(iii) Freedom to form associations and unions

(iv) Freedom of movement throughout India

(v) Freedom to reside and settle in any part of India

(vi) Freedom to practise any profession, or to carry on any occupation, trade or business

3. Right to Freedom of Religion *(Articles 25 - 28)*

4. Cultural and Educational Rights *(Articles 29 - 30)*

5. Right Against Exploitation *(Articles 23 - 24)*

6. Right to Constitutional Remedies *(Articles 32 - 35)*

*Right to Property*

- originally used to be a Fundamental Right but has now been included in the list of legal rights.

- It was done during the rule of the Janata Party Government which brought out this change on June 20, 1978 through the 44th Amendment Act 1978 of the Indian Constitution.

**Directive Principles.**

- Part IV (Articles 36 - 51) of the Constitution deals with the Directive Principles of State policy which include:

- Provision of adequate means of livelihood to all.

- Equitable distribution of wealth among all.

- Protection of children and youth.

- Equal pay for equal work to both men and women.

- Free and compulsory education for children up to the age of 14 years.

- Prevention of cow slaughter.

- The right to work, to education, to public assistance in case of unemployment, old age, sickness and disability.

- Prohibition of liquor.

- Establishment of village panchayats.

- Protection of historical and national monuments.

- Separation of the judiciary from the Executive to secure, for all citizens, a uniform civil code.
- Promotion of international cooperation and world security.
- Free legal aid from the state to the weaker sections of society.
- State to protect natural environment, forests and wildlife.

### The 42nd Amendment Bill, 1976

- gave the Directive Principles precedence over the Fundamental Rights. This Amendment also added two more Directive Principles:
- Free legal aid from state to weaker sections.
- State to protect natural environment, forests and wildlife.

### Fundamental Rights vs Directive Principles

- Fundamental Rights constitute a limitation upon the state actions whereas Directive Principles are instruments of instruction to a government to carry out certain responsibilities.
- Directive Principles cannot be enforced in a court of law and do not create any justifiable right in favour of an individual.

### Duties of a Citizen of India

- The 42nd Amendment Bill, 1976 had added ten Fundamental Duties that include:
- To abide by the Constitution and to respect its ideals and institutions, the national flag and the National Anthem.
- To cherish and follow the noble ideas which inspired our national freedom struggle.
- To uphold and protect the sovereignty, unity and integrity of India.
- To defend the country and render national service when called upon to do so.
- To promote harmony and spirit of common brotherhood among all the people of India, transcending religious, linguistic and regional or sectional diversities; to renounce practices derogatory to the dignity of women.
- To value and preserve the rich heritage of our composite culture.
- To protect and improve the natural environment.
- To develop a scientific temper, humanism and the spirit of enquiry

and reform.

- To safeguard public property and abjure violence.
- To strive towards excellence in all spheres of individual and collective activity so that the nation constantly rises to higher levels of endeavour 'and achievement.
- To provide opportunities for free and compulsory education to his child or ward between the age of six and fourteen years. (Added by 86th Amendment Act, 2002)

## AMENDMENTS OF THE CONSTITUTION

### Procedure (Article 368)

The methods of amendment are three-according to the subject matter of the Article concerned:

- Articles that may be amended by a simple majority.
- Articles that may be amended by a two-thirds majority of both Houses of Parliament-these are comparatively important matters.
- Articles that require not only a two-thirds majority of the Parliament but also ratification by at least one-half of the State Legislatures.

It may be noted that provisions which affect the federal character of the Constitution can be amended only with the approval of the states. Further, the initiative to amend the Constitution rests only with the Centre and the states cannot initiate any amendment.

### Some Major Amendments in Indian Constitution

- *The First Amendment 1950*, to overcome certain practical difficulties related to Fundamental Rights. It made provision for special treatment of educationally and socially backward classes, and added Ninth Schedule to the Constitution.
- *The Third Amendment 1954*, it substituted entry 33 of List III (Concurrent List) of the Seventh Schedule to make it correspond to Article 369.
- *The Seventh Amendment 1956* was necessitated on account of reorganization of states on a linguistic basis and changed First and Fourth Schedules.

- *The Eighth Amendment 1960* extended special provision for reservation of seats for SCs, STs and Anglo-Indians in Lok Sabha and Legislative Assemblies for a period of 10 years from 1960 to 1970.
- *The Ninth Amendment 1960* transferred certain territories to Pakistan following September 1958 Indo-Pak Agreement.
- *The Tenth Amendment 1961* incorporated the territories of Dadra and Nagar Haveli in Indian Union.
- *The Twelfth Amendment 1962* incorporated the territories of Goa, Daman and Diu in Indian Union.
- *The Thirteenth Amendment 1962* created Nagaland as a State of the Union of India.
- *The Fourteenth Amendment 1962* incorporated former French territory of Pondicherry in Indian Union.
- *The Eighteenth Amendment 1966* was made to facilitate reorganization of Punjab into Punjab and Haryana, and also created the UT of Chandigarh.
- *The Twenty-First Amendment* 1967 included Sindhi as the 15th regional language in the Eighth Schedule.
- *The Twenty-Second Amendment* 1969 created a sub-state of Meghalaya within Assam.
- *The Twenty-Third Amendment 1970* extended the reservation of seats for SC/ST and nomination of Anglo-Indians for a further period of 10 years (upto 1980).
- *The Twenty-Sixth Amendment 1971* abolished titles & special privileges of former rulers of princely states.
- *The Twenty-Seventh Amendment 1971* provided for the establishment of the states of Manipur and Tripura; the formation of the Union Territories of Mizoram and Arunachal Pradesh.
- *The Thirty-First Amendment 1973* increased elective strength of Lok Sabha from 525 to 545. Upper limit of representatives of state became 525 from 500.
- *The Thirty-Sixth Amendment 1975* made Sikkim a state of the Indian Union.

- *The Thirty-Eighth Amendment 1975* provided that the President can make a declaration of emergency, and the promulgation of ordinances by the President, Governors and administrative heads of UTs would be final and could not be challenged in any court.
- *The Thirty-Ninth Amendment* 1975 placed beyond challenge in courts, the election to Parliament of a person holding the office of Prime Minister or Speaker and election of the President and Vice President.
- *The Forty-Second Amendment* 1976 provided supremacy of Parliament and gave primacy to Directive Principles over Fundamental Rights; added 10 Fundamental Duties and altered the Preamble.
- *The Forty-Fourth Amendment* 1978 restored the normal duration of Lok Sabha and Legislative Assemblies to 5 Years; Right to property was deleted from Part Ill; it limited the power of the govt to proclaim internal emergency.
- *The Forty-Fifth Amendment* 1980 extended reservation for SC/ST by 10 years (upto 1990).
- *The Fifty-Second Amendment* 1985 inserted the Tenth Schedule in the Constitution regarding provisions as to disqualification on the grounds of defection.
- *The Fifty-Fourth Amendment* 1986 enhanced salaries of Judges of Supreme Court and High Courts
- *The Fifty-Fifth Amendment* 1986 conferred statehood on Arunachal Pradesh.
- *The Fifty-Sixth Amendment* 1987 Hindi version of the Constitution of India was accepted for all purposes and statehood was also conferred on the UT of Goa.
- *The Fifty-Eighth Amendment* 1987 provided reservation of seats in legislatures for the four north-eastern states of Arunachal Pradesh, Meghalaya, Mizoram and Nagaland.
- *The Sixty-First Amendment* 1989 reduced voting age from 21 to 18 years for Lok Sabha and Assemblies.
- *The Sixty-Second Amendment* 1989 extended reservation of seats for SC/ST upto the year 2000.
- *The Sixty- Third Amendment* carried out in 1990 repealed the 59th

Amendment which empowered the government to impose Emergency in Punjab.

- *The Seventy-Second Amendment* 1992 (Panchayati Raj Bill) provided Gram Sabha in villages, constitution of panchayats at village and other levels, direct elections to all seats in panchayats and reservation of seats for SC/ST and fixing of Panchayat's tenure to 5 years.

- *The Seventy-Third Amendment* 1992 (Nagarpalika Bill) provided for constitution of municipalities, reservation of seats in every municipality for the SC and ST, women and the backward classes.

- *The Seventy-Fourth Amendment* 1993 inclusion of a new part IX-A relating to the Municipalities had been incorporated in the Constitution to provide, among, other things, constitution of three types of Municipalities, that is, 'Nagar Panchayats' for areas in transition from a rural area to urban area, 'Municipal Councils' for smaller urban area and 'Municipal Corporations' for larger urban areas.

- *The Seventy-Eighth Amendment* 1995 provides for some land reforms acts included in Ninth Schedule which consists of list of laws enacted by the central governments and various state governments which, inter alia, affect rights and interest in property including land.

- *The Seventy-Ninth Amendment* 2000 extended reservation for the SC/ST for further period often years, that is, upto January 25, 2010.

- *The Eightieth Amendment* 2000 Certain changes were made to tax distribution provided under Articles 269, 270 and 272 of the constitution.

- The *Eighty-First Amendment* 2000 The unfulfilled vacancies/seats of a year, which were reserved for SC/ST candidates, for being filled up in that year in accordance with any provision for reservations made under Article 16 of the Constitution, shall be considered as a separate class of vacancies to be filled up in any succeeding year or years, and such class of vacancies shall not be considered together with vacancies of the year in which they were filled up for determining the ceiling of fifty per cent reservation against total number of vacancies of that year.

- *The Eighty-Fourth Amendment* 2002 The number of representatives in the Lok Sabha and State Assemblies to freeze to current levels for the next 25 years (till 2026).

- *The Eighty-Fifth Amendment* 2002 provided for consequential seniority in case of promotion (with retrospective effect from June 17, 1995) by virtue of the rule of reservation for government servants belonging to SCs/STs.

- *The Eighty-sixth Amendment* 2002 The Act deals with the insertion of a new Article 21A after article 21. The new Article 21A deals with Right to Education. "The state shall provide free and compulsory education to all children from the age of 6 to 14 years in such a manner as the state may, by law, determine.';

- *The Eighty-Eighth Amendment* 2003 provides for the insertion of a new Article 268A. Service tax levied by Union and collected and appropriated by the Union and the States. Amendment of article 270 Amendment of Seventh Schedule.

- *The Eighty-Ninth Amendment* 2003 provides for the amendment of Article 338. There shall be a National Commission for the SCs/STs.

- *The Ninety-First Amendment* 2003 amended the anti-defection laws and provided for amendment of Article 75. The total number of Ministers, including the Prime Minister, in the Council of Ministers shall not exceed fifteen per cent of the total number of members of the House of the people.

- *The Ninety-Second Amendment* 2003 provided for the amendment of Eighth Schedule by adding four new regional languages (Bodo, Maithili, Santhali and Dogri) thus extending the list to 22 languages.

- *The Ninety-Third Amendment* 2005 (came into effect on 20th Jan, 2006) provided' for special provision, by law, for the advancement of any socially and educationally backward classes of citizens or for the SCs/STs in so far as such special provisions relate to their admission to educational institutions including private educational institutions.

- *The Ninety-Fourth Amendment* 2006 provides for the exclusion of Bihar from the proviso to Clause (I) of Article 164 of the constitution which provides that there shall be a Minister in charge of tribal welfare who may in addition be in charge of the welfare of the scheduled castes and backward classes in Bihar, Madhya Pradesh and Orrisa. It also proposes to extend the provisions of Clause (I) of Article 164 to the newly found states of Chattisgarh and Jharkhand.

## STRUCTURE OF THE UNION GOVERNMENT

### The President

- The President of India is the supreme constitutional body of the Indian parliamentary system of governance.
- He/She represents the nation but does not rule it.
- The real power vests with the council of ministers.
- The President is elected by an electoral college consisting of the elected members of the Parliament (both Houses), and the elected members of the State Legislature.

**Qualifications** The Constitution lays the following criteria for one to become the President of India:

- must be a citizen of India.
- must not be less than 35 years of age.
- must be qualified to be an elected member of the Lok Sabha but shall not be a sitting member.
- must not be holding any office of profit under the Government of India or any other governments.

**Tenure** Elected for five years but is eligible for immediate re-election and can serve any number of terms.

**Emoluments** Rs 1,50,000 per month as per the new pay scale revised by the UPA Government announced in September 2008. This new scale is to be effective from January 2007.

**Powers:** The Constitution declares that the President of India bears the following powers:

- *Executive and Administrative Powers.* Appoints the senior officials of the state including the Prime Minister. All Union Territories are under the President of India.

- *Legislative Powers.* (a) Appoints 12 members to the Rajya Sabha and two Anglo-Indian members to the Lok Sabha; (b) Dissolves the House of People; (c) Assents or withholds his/her assent to any Bill passed by the Parliament; (d) Issues ordinances.
- *Financial Powers.* (a) Causes the budget to be laid before the Parliament; (b) Sanctions introduction of money bills; (c) Apportions revenue between the Centre and the States.
- *Judicial Powers.* Empowered to grant pardons, reprieve, remit the sentences, or suspend, remit or commute punishments.
- *Emergency Powers.* Article 352 empowers the President to proclaim an emergency and take under his direct charge the administration of any State.

**NOTE:**

- The President cannot be questioned by any court for any of the action taken by him/her in the discharge of his/her duties.
- No criminal proceedings can be launched against him/her.
- He/She may be removed from office for violation of the Constitution by impeachment *(Article 61)*.

**Vice-President**

**Election**

- The Vice-President is elected by members of an electoral college consisting of the members of both Houses of Parliament.
- However, his election is different from that of the President as the state legislatures have no part in it.

**Tenure:** Five years and is eligible for immediate re-election.

**Functions.**

The Constitution allocates the following functions for the Vice President:

- Acts as ex-officio Chairman of the Rajya Sabha.
- Officiates as President in case of death, resignation or removal of the latter.
- Functions as the President when the President is unable to discharge his functions due to illness, absence or any other cause.

**Emoluments**

- Vice-President is entitled to a salary of Rs 1.25 lac per month as per the new structure announced by the UPA Government to be effective from January 1, 2007 and other benefits in his capacity as the Chairman of Rajya Sabha.
- On retirement the Vice-President gets a monthly pension of Rs 20,000.

**The Prime Minister**

- The Prime Minister of India heads the Council of Ministers.
- He/She is the leader of the party that enjoys a majority in the Lok Sabha.
- He/She is appointed by the President.

**Tenure**

- The tenure for the Prime Minister is five years.
- But he/she holds the office with the consent of the President till a new Lok Sabha is formed.

**Resignation**

- If the government is defeated in the Lok Sabha (not in Rajya Sabha), the cabinet as well as the Prime Minister have to resign.

**Emoluments**

- The Prime Minister is entitled to get the salary and allowances the same as that of the Member of Parliament.
- In addition, he/she gets a sumptuary allowance of Rs 15,000 per month, free residence, free travel and medical facilities.

**Council of Ministers**

- In order to run the government the Constitution makes a provision for a council of ministers headed by the Prime Minister.
- It is a policy-making body and the government in the real sense.
- The President invites the leader of the political party having clear majority in House to form the government.
- The President appoints the Prime Minister
- The President appoints the other ministers and in consultation with the Prime Minister.

- Any person who is not a member of the legislature, can also be appointed as Prime Minister or a minister in the House, but he cannot continue in that capacity for more than six months unless he secures a seat in either House of Parliament.

## The Parliament

- The Parliament known as the lower house i.e. the Lok Sabha is the Union legislature of India which constitutes:
- The President of India
- The Council of States (Rajya Sabha)
- The House of People (Lok Sabha)
- The Lok Sabha consists of the members elected by direct election from territorial constituencies in various states and union territories and two members nominated (Anglo Indian) by the President.
- The total strength of the Lok Sabha is 554 (530 represent states and 20 represent Union Territories and four members are nominated by the President from the Ango-Indian community only if the President thinks this community is not adequately represented in the House.

## Speaker

- The Speaker elected by the members presides over the Lok Sabha.
- The Speaker of the House elects a Deputy Speaker, who discharges the duties of the Speaker in his absence.

## Emoluments

- The salaries and allowances payable to the Members of Parliament are determined by the Parliament itself.
- Their basic salary is Rs 12000 per month and allowances are Rs 16,500 per month.
- The allowances include Rs 10,000 per month as constituency allowance
- Rs 14,000 as office expense per month
- They also get a daily allowance of Rs 400.
- On retirement, they get pension of Rs 1,400 per month.

## Functions of the Parliament

*Ordinary bills*

- All bills, except money bills, are introduced in either House of Parliament.
- A bill, after debate, is passed by a majority vote and sent to the other House.
- In case, certain amendments are suggested in the other House, it is sent back to the House which originated the bill for reconsideration.
- The bill is regarded as passed by both the Houses if the original House accepts the amendments of the other House.
- It is then presented to the President for his assent:
- If the President gives his assent to the bill, it then becomes an Act.
- If the President withholds his assent, the bill is nullified.
- If the President neither gives his assent nor withholds his assent, he may return it to the Parliament for reconsideration.
- If, however, the Houses pass the bill again after reconsideration, the President is bound to give his assent.

## Money Bills

- A money bill can originate only in the Lok Sabha on the recommendation of the President.
- After it has been passed by the Lok Sabha, it is sent to the Rajya Sabha.
- The Rajya Sabha is given 14 days to make its recommendation.
- If it fails to do so within 14 days, the bill is considered as passed by both Houses.
- If the Rajya Sabha returns the bill with its ·recommendation, it is up to the Lok Sabha to accept or reject the recommendations.
- Even if the Lok Sabha rejects the recommendations of the Rajya Sabha, the bill is considered to have been passed.

## Joint Sitting of Parliament

- A joint session of both Houses is convened by the President to consider a particular bill in case.
- a bill is passed by one House and is rejected by the other.

- the amendments made by the other House are not acceptable to the House where the bill originated, and
- a bill remains pending (unpassed) in a House for more than six months from the date of its receipt from the House where it originated.

## Rajya Sabha

- Known as the upper house is the Council of States comprising the representatives from the states and members nominated by the President, who have distinguished themselves in literature, arts, science or social service.
- Strength of the Rajya Sabha is presently 250 members (238 members representing the States and Union Territories who come through election and 12 members who are nominated by the President).
- The **Vice-President** of India is the ex-officio **Chairman** and the Deputy Chairman is elected from the members of the Rajya Sabha.

## Tenure

- The Rajya Sabha is a permanent body, not subject to dissolution. One third of its members retire after every two years. Thus, every member enjoys a six-year tenure.

## Functions

- The Constitutional functions of the Rajya Sabha include that it shares with the Lok Sabha the power of amending the Constitution. It can originate any bill (except a money bill); refer the charge of impeachment against the President. The elected members of the Rajya Sabha take part in the election of the President and the Vice-President.

## Emoluments

- The members of the Council of Ministers are entitled to get the salaries and allowances same as that of the other Members of the Parliament. In addition they get a sumptuary allowance.

## Supreme Court

- In order to provide legal base to the Governance the Constitution provides for a unified judiciary the Supreme Court being the apex of this judicial system.

## Composition
- The Supreme Court consists of one Chief Justice and 25 other judges.
- The Chief Justice is appointed by the President
- The other judges are appointed by the President in consultation with the Chief Justice.

## Seat
- The Supreme Court normally sits in New Delhi.
- However, it can hold its meetings anywhere in India.
- The decision in this regard is taken by the Chief Justice of India in consultation with the President.

## Qualification
- Any citizen who has been a judge of a High Court for 5 years or an eminent jurist or who has been a practising advocate of High Court for a period of 10 years, can be nominated as a Supreme Court judge.

## Functions
- It decides disputes between the Union Government and the states
- It hears certain appeals in civil and criminal cases from the High Courts
- The President can refer any question of law or fact of sufficient importance to the Supreme Court for its opinion
- It can issue directions or writs for the enforcement of any of the Fundamental Rights referred by the Constitution.

## Tenure
- Judges of the Supreme Court can hold office up to the age of 65 years.

## Remuneration
- Chief Justice of India-Rs 33,000 per month
- Judges of the Supreme Court-Rs 30,000 per month

## Retirement
- The Chief Justice and other judges are entitled to a pension of Rs 60,000 and Rs 54,000 per annum, respectively. After retirement a judge of the Supreme Court shall not plead or act in any court before any authority in India.

## Removal of a Judge

- A judge of the Supreme Court can only be removed from office by an order of the President, after an address by each House of Parliament, supported by a majority of the total membership of the Houses and by a majority of not less than two-thirds of the members present and voting. He can be removed only on the grounds of: (i) Proven misbehaviour, and (ii) Incapacity to act as a judge [Article 124(4)].

## The State Executive

In order to run the governance the Constitution provides for a State Executive comprising:

- The Governor
- The Chief Minister
- The Council of Ministers

## The Governor

- The Governor is the nominal executive head of the state and is appointed by the President of India for a term of 5 years.
- He holds the office with the consent of the President.

## Remuneration

- The Governor is entitled to get Rs 1.10 Lac per month as per the pay- hike announced by the UPA Cabinet in September 2008.
- In addition he is entitled to free residence, medical facilities and certain other allowances The new Scale is to be effective from January 2007.

**Powers:** The Constitution allocates the following powers for the Governor:

- Executive Powers
- Legislative Powers
- Financial Powers
- Judicial Powers
- Discretionary Powers

## President vs Governor

- The Governor has no power to appoint judges of the State High

Courts but he is entitled to be consulted by the President.

• Unlike the President, he has no emergency powers.

## The State Legislature

## The Chief Minister

• The leader of the party that enjoys a majority in the Legislative Assembly is invited by the Governor to become the Chief Minister and form the government.

• A person, who is not a member of the State Legislature, can also be appointed as the Chief Minister but he/she is required to get himself/herself elected as a member from any House within six months of his appointment.

• The Chief Minister recommends the names of ministers together with proposed portfolios for them to the Governor, who then appoints them.

**Tenure.** The term for the state legislature is 5 years.

**Removal of Chief Minister.** The Chief Minister of a state can be removed from his/her office if

• His/her government is defeated in the state assembly

• or after his/her defeat in the State Assembly, the Chief Minister refuses to resign

• or he/her fails to get himself/herself elected to the State Assembly within six months of his appointment, in case he was not already a member

• or the President proclaims emergency in the state on account of failure on the part of the stage government to carry on the administration in accordance with the provision of the Constitution.

## The Council of Ministers

## The Formation of Council of Ministers

• As per the Constitution, every state must have a Council of Ministers to aid and advise the Governor in exercising his executive functions (apart from those functions in which he shall act at his discretion).

- Once the Governor appoints a Chief Minister, as per the Constitution, the Chief Minister finalises the list of his Ministers, which is customarily permitted by the Governor.
- Thus, the Ministry is created in the state and a formal Council of Minister takes precise shape.
- The Council of Ministers is permanently interconnected to the State Legislature and it functions as an executive arm of the State Legislature. Constitutionally, all ministers have to be members of either House of Stage Legislature.

## The Emoluments

- Before a Minister enters his office, the Governor administers the oaths of office and of secrecy to him according to the forms set out for the purpose in the Third Schedule.
- The salaries and allowances of ministers are as the Legislature of the state specifies.

## The Responsibilities of the Council of Ministers.

- The Council of Ministers are collectively responsible to the Legislature Assembly of the State.
- The ministry can remain in office till it commands the confidence of the Lower House.
- A minister who, for any period of six consecutive months, is not a member of the Legislature of the state shall, at the expiration of that period, cease to be a minister.

## The State Legislature

- It consists of the Governor and one or two houses, as the case may be.
- If the state has only one House, it is known as Legislative Assembly.
- The other is the Legislative Council.
- The states having one House are called unicameral
- The states having two Houses are called bicameral.

## Bicameral States

- At present only five states have a bicameral legislature, i.e. Bihar, Jammu and Kashmir, Karnataka, Maharashtra and Uttar Pradesh.

- All other states have only one house.

## Legislative Council (Vidhan Parishad)

- It is also called as the Upper House.

### Strength

- The total strength does not exceed one-third of the strength of the Legislative Assembly, subject to a minimum of 40 members.
- The strength varies as per population of the state concerned.

**Tenure.** Six years with one-third of the members retiring every two years.

### Election

- One-third of the members of a Legislative Council are elected by local bodies,
- one-third by the Legislative Assembly
- one-twelfth by university graduates of at least three years standing
- similar proportion by teachers
- plus one-sixth are nominated by the Governor.

## Legislative Assembly (Vidhan Sabha)

- It is called as the Lower House.

### Strength

- Legislative Assembly consists of not more than 525 members and not less than 60 members.
- However, the legislative assembly of Sikkim has only 32 members.

**Tenure.** Its tenure is fixed for 5 years.

### Election

- Its Members are chosen by direct election from the territorial constituencies of the state.
- The Council of Ministers is collectively responsible to the Assembly. The Chief Minister is the leader of the House.

## The Political System of India

- India is a federal state.
- It has a parliamentary system of government with a commitment

to hold regular, free and fair elections that determine the composition of the government, the membership of the two Houses of Parliament, the Legislative Assemblies of the State and Union Territories and also the Presidency and Vice Presidency.

- The decline of the Congress (I) since the late 1980s has brought an end to the dominance of a single-party system that had long characterised India's politics.

- Under the old system, conflict within the Congress was often a more important political dynamic than conflict between the Congress and the Opposition. The Congress had set the political agenda and the Opposition responded.

- A new party system, in which the Congress (I) is merely one of several major collaboraters of the system, was in place by 1989.

- A multi-party system has evolved in India.

## General Elections in India

- As the term for the Parliament is five years, a general election is held usually every five year in order to elect the new government.

- The Election Commission is responsible to hold and supervise the process of election.

## POLITICAL PARTIES IN INDIA

- Indian constitution provides a healthy party system in order to maintain its democratic set up, there are presently a number of political parties – some of them are the national parties and some are regional parties.

- These parties support their candidates to fight election in order to ensure their participation in the governance.

- Till 1975 Indian political arena was dominated by the Congress Party but thereafter with the birth of the Janata Party.

- Indian political scenario got a tremendous transformation and a multi-party system emerged which grew fully matured in 1996 with the government of National Democratic Alliance (NDA) under the leadership of Mr Atal Bihari Vajpayee.

- Presently there is the government of United Progressive Alliance

(UPA) under the leadership of Dr Manmohan Singh.

## Panchayati Raj System in Independent India

*Balwantrai Mehta Committee*

- After the independence, "Community Development Programme" was started in 1952, as it was not attached to the people, it proved to be a failure.
- A team headed by Balwantrai Mehta tried to find out the cause for the failure of this programme and came up with the inference that there should be an organisation at the village level, which would select the true beneficiaries and implement various government programmes and schemes.
- This organisation would act as the representative of all villagers and would ensure the development of the village as well as participation of villagers.
- Balwantrai Mehta tried to achieve local self-government through· panchayats.
- This concept of local self-government was the right step towards decentralisation of power and governance and also to keep up the concept of power to people.
- In this process, for the first time the State of Rajasthan adopted the three leveled structure of panchayati raj-Village Level, Intermediate Level and District Level.

*Ashok Mehta Committee*

- In 1977 the Ashok Mehta Committee was set up to review the working of panchayats.
- The committee found out that panchayati raj is the soul of democracy and therefore it should be empowered with more authority.
- Those panchayats which formed after 1977 are known as Second Generation Panchayats.
- In West Bengal, Panchayats became more effective after accepting the suggestions made in this report.

- During the decade of 1990s, it was realised that without constitutional power, self-government can't be fruitful.
- Thus the Central Government passed the 73rd Constitutional Amendment Act in 1992, which became effective from April 20, 1993 (from the date of publication in the Gazette of India).

*What are the Concepts behind Panchayati Raj?*

- The basic concept of Panchayati Raj is that the villagers should think, decide and act in their own socio-economic interests.
- Thus, the Panchayati Raj Act is related to village self-governance, where the people in the form of an organisation will think, decide and act for their collective interest.
- Self-government allows us to decide about ourselves without hampering others interest.
- The villagers' collective interest on one side and societal and national interest on the other are complementary.
- Where panchayats end their activities the state govt takes them up.

## Structure of Panchayati Raj

### District Level = Zila Parishad
↓

| | |
|---|---|
| People's Government | Development Administration |
| President, Vice President | Chief Secretary |
| Elected Members and | Depute Secretaries |
| Ex-Officio Members | Chief Accountant Officer |
| | Chief Planning Officer |

### Block Level = Panchayat Samiti/Block Panchayat/Taluk Panchayat

| | |
|---|---|
| Chairman | Block Development Officer |
| Ex-Officio Members | Standing Committee |

### Village Level = Mandal Panchayat / Gram Panchayat

| | |
|---|---|
| President | Secretary |
| Vice President | Village Level Workers |
| Elected members | |

### Gramsabha

College of Eligible voters

*Source:* Geoge Kurain (1998) Empowering Conditions in the Decentralisation Process – An Analysis of Dynamics, Factors and Actors in Panchayati Raj Institutions from West Bengal and Karnataka, India Center for Policy research and Advocacy, Bhubaneshwar, p124

## Zonal Councils

The five Zonal Councils are:

- Northern Zone-comprising the state of Haryana, Punjab, Rajasthan, Jammu and Kashmir, Himachal Pradesh, and the National Capital Region of Delhi.

- Eastern Zone-comprising Bihar, Jharkhand, West Bengal, Orissa, Assam, Manipur, Tripura, Nagaland, Arunachal Pradesh, Mizoram and Meghalaya.

- Central Zone-comprising the states of Uttar Pradesh, Uttaranchal, Madhya Pradesh and Chhattisgarh.

- Western Zone-comprising Gujarat, Maharashtra and Goa.

- Southern Zone-consisting of Andhra Pradesh, Tamil Nadu, Karnataka and Kerala.

## Functions

- Zonal councils acts as a consultative body to discuss matters of common interest of the member states. It recommends the member states on the issues of (a) Social Planning; (b) Inter-state Transport; (c) Economic Planning; (d) Border dispute; (e) Matters concerning minorities, etc.

## Indian Election/Political System

- The word candidate comes from the Latin 'candidatus' meaning 'one clad in white' and most, till this day carry on with this white.

- 'Ballot' and 'bullet' are both derived from words for 'balls'. The Greeks dropped a white ball when they favoured a candidate, and a black when they were against. The term 'blackballed' comes from this too.

- Designed by Electronics Corporation of India Ltd and Bharat Electronics Ltd, Electronic Voting Machines were first used in

Kerala. The highest number of candidates that an electronic voting machine can support is 64. If the number exceeds this, the manual ballot is used.

- In the Modaurichi assembly constituency in Tamil Nadu, 1033 candidates fought for a single seat in 1996. The ballot paper was in the form of a booklet!

- The Congress in 1988 did not win a single seat in Uttar Pradesh.

- Mayawati's BSP and U.S Republican Party both have the same electoral symbol-the elephant.

- The lowest voter turnout in a polling station is three. It happened in Bomdila district in Arunachal Pradesh.

- Elections in 1950s were carried out using different ballot boxes for each candidate, rather than voting on ballot paper. Different coloured boxes represented different parties.

- Chhindwara in Madhya Pradesh is the only constituency in the Hindi belt which has always returned the Congress candidate during the general elections.

- Atal Bihari Vajpayee is the only politician who has won from six different constituencies: Balrampur-1957, 1967, Gwalior-1971, New Delhi-1977, 1980, Vidisha-1991, Gandhinagar-1956, Lucknow-1991, 1996, 1998, 2004. He is also the only parliamentarian to be elected from four different states-UP, Gujarat, MP and Delhi.

- BJP won Lok Sabha seats for the first time in the states of Tamil Nadu and West Bengal in 1998.

- Rajnandagaon in Madhya Pradesh has a unique feature-father, mother and son have represented this constituency at different times.

- The highest voting percentage in any general elections has been 62.2 per cent in 1957, the lowest was in 1967 when only 33 per cent citizens cast their vote. In the last general elections in 1999, 59.99 per cent citizens had cast their votes.

- The country's five biggest and smallest constituencies according to area (in sq. km) are as follows.

| Biggest Constituencies (km²) | Smallest Constituencies (km²) |
|---|---|
| Ladakh (J & K): 173266.37 | Delhi Sadar (NCT of Delhi): 28.09 |
| Banner (Rajasthan): 71601.24 | Mumbai South-Central (Maharashtra): 18.31 |
| Kuchch (Gujarat): 41644.55 | Mumbai South (Maharashtra): 13.73 |
| Arunachal West (AP): 40572.29 | Kolkata North-West (West Bengal): 13.23 |
| Arunachal East (AP): 39749.64 | Challdni Chowk (NCT of Delhi): 10.59 |

## General Elections of 2004 – Some Interesting Facts and Figures

- Total States & UTs - 35
- Total Parliamentary Constituencies - 543
- Total Electors - 6715210045
- Number of seats in the Lok Sabha - 545
- Total Number of Candidates - 5398
- Total Votes Polled - 387453223
- Number of polling stations - 7,00,000
- Lowest Number of Votes - 45 for Ashok Kumar, Independent Candidate from Chandni Chowk, Delhi.
- Highest Number of Votes - 855543 for Sajjan Kumar, Congress Candidate from Outer Delhi.
- Highest Number of Candidates from a Constituency - 35 from Madras (South).
- Lowest Number of Candidates from a Constituency - 2 from Cuttack in Orissa, Godhra in Gujarat and Tura in Meghalaya.
- Parliamentary constituency with largest number of electors – 3368399 (Outer Delhi); Parliamentary constituency with least number of electors – 39033 (Lakshadweep)
- Parliamentary constituency with largest area – Ladakh (Jammu & Kashmir) – 173266 sq. km.; Parliamentary constituency with smallest area – Chandni Chowk (Delhi) – 10.6 sq. km.
- Maximum contestants in a parliamentary constituency – Madras (South) – 35
- Maximum women contestants in a state – Uttar Pradesh – 61; Minimum women contestants in a state – Goa – 1
- Maximum women winners – Uttar Pradesh – 7

- Total Number of Parties - 220.
- Total Number of Independent Candidates - 2369
- Seats needed for majority - 272
- Total cost of the Election - Rs 100 Million Approx.
- Voter turnout about 56% or nearly 380 million people.
- Electronic Voting Machines (EVMs) used - 10.25 lakh

## General Elections of 2009 – Some Interesting Facts and Figures

- India's general elections staggered over five dates, April 16, 23 and 30 and May 8 and 13
- More than 714 million people formed the electorate, an increase of 43 million voters over the last elections in 2004.
- Voter turnout has ranged from 55 to 63 per cent since the first general elections in 1952.
- Of the 543 constituencies going to the polls, 79 and 41 seats are reserved for disadvantaged castes and designated tribes, respectively.
- The elections were accompanied by state assembly polls in the southern state of Andhra Pradesh, Orissa in the east and north-eastern Sikkim.

## MAJOR ISSUES

- Economic turmoil and the loss of millions of jobs
- National security in the wake of continuous terrorist attacks
- Communalism

## ORGANIZATION

- A total of 828,804 polling stations were supervised by 2.1 million security personnel.
- More than 1.1 million electronic voting machines were used. They were first introduced in 2004.
- The 2009 polls are the first in India to feature the use of photo electoral rolls in nearly the entire country. About 585 million photographs have reportedly been included in the rolls to prevent impersonation and bogus voting.
- The elections are being contested on redistricted constitutional boundaries based on the findings of the Delimitation Commission. Of the 543 constituencies, 499 have been redrawn.

## SYMBOLS

Parties have been given symbols by the Election Commission. Among the most widely-known election symbols are:

Hand - Congress Lotus - BJP Hammer and sickle - Communist Party of India (Marxist) Elephant - Bahujan Samaj Party Cycle - Samajwadi Party

## CANDIDATE AGE

The members of India's Parliament are primarily of advanced age. In 2004, the oldest candidate and winner was 94-year-old Ramchandra Veerappa from Karnataka in the south. Several 25-year-olds also ran in the election.

## LONE VOTER

One polling booth is to be set up in the Gir Forest in India's western state of Gujarat to enable a lone voter, a priest, to cast his vote.

## INDIA'S GLORY

### The National Flag

- Our National Flag, the first and foremost symbol of our national identity, was first adopted by the Constituent Assembly of India on July 22, 1947, and presented to India at the midnight session of the Assembly on August 14, 1947.
- The ratio of the length of the flag to its breadth is 3:2.
- All the three bands are of equal width with deep saffron at the top, white in the middle and dark green at the bottom. In the centre of the white band is a wheel in navy-blue colour.
- The diameter of the wheel (chakra) approximates the width of the white band and it has 24 spokes.

### The Flag Code of India 2002

- It was brought into effect from January 26, 2002 and superseding the previous one.
- As per its provision, there shall be no restriction on the display the National flag by members of general public, private organisations, educational institutions, etc. except to the extent provided in the Emblems and Names (Prevention of Improper Use) Act, 1950, and

the Prevention of Insults to National Honour Act 1971, and any other law enacted on the subject.

## The National Emblem

- The Government of India adopted a replica of the Capitol of Ashoka's Pillar at Sarnath as its National Emblem and Seal on the 26th of January 1950.
- In the original capitol of the stone pillar, there are four lions carved out standing back to back.
- In the emblem, however, only three lions are visible.
- The capitol is mounted on an abacus (base plate).
- There is a Dharma Chakra in the centre of the base plate, on the right of which there is a figure of a bull, and on the left, that of a horse.
- There is an inscription in Devanagari script which reads *Satyameva Jayate* which means that the 'Truth alone Triumphs'.

## The National Anthem (*Jana Gana Mana*)

- The Constituent Assembly of India adopted *Jana Gana Mana* as its National Anthem on January 24, 1950.
- This song was composed by Rabindranath Tagore in 1911
- It was first sung on December 27, 1911 at the Calcutta Session of the Indian National Congress.
- Its English translation was first rendered by Tagore himself in 1911 under the title of 'Morning Song of India'.
- This song takes about 52 seconds to play for the full version
- A shorter version comprising the first and the last lines has a playing time of 20 seconds and is played on ceremonial occasions.

## The National Song (*Vande Mataram*)

- The song *Vande Mataram* was adopted as the National Song of India on January 24,1950
- It was sung for the first time during the 1896 Session of the Indian National Congress.
- It originally occurs in Bankimchandra Chatteijee's famous novel 'Anand Math'(1882).
- Its English translation was rendered by Sri Aurobindo.

## The National Calendar (*Saka*)

- A unified Indian National Calendar was brought into practice since March 22, 1957 (Saka 1879).
- This was to be used for official purposes.
- It was based on the Saka era which began with vernal equinox of AD 78.
- Chaitra is the first month
- Phalguna is the last month of the Saka year
- Chaitra 1 falls on March 22 in a normal year
- It falls on March 21 in a leap year.

## The National Animal

- The tiger (*Panthera tigris*) has been adopted as the national animal since November 1972.
- It has been kept in the categories of protected animals.

## The National Bird

- Our National Bird is Peacock (*Pavo cristatus*).
- It is fully protected under the Indian Wildlife (Protection) Act, 1972.

## The National Flower

- Lotus (*Neluinbo nucifera*) is the National Flower of India.
- It has been an auspicious symbol of Indian culture since time immemorial.

## The National Days

| National Day | Date | Importance |
|---|---|---|
| Republic Day | 26th January | India was declared to be a Republic State on this day in 1950. |
| Martyr's Day | 30th January | Mahatma Gandhi was assassinated on this day in 1948. |
| Independence Day | 15th August | India got independence from its long slavery on this day in 1947. |
| Teacher's Day | 5th September | Birthday of Dr. S. Radhakrishnan, the first Vice-President of India |
| Gandhi Jayanti | 2nd October | Birthday of Mahatma Gandhi, the Father of the Nation. |
| Children's Day | 14th November | Birthday of Pt Jawaharlal Nehru, the first Prime Minister of India. |

# PART EIGHT

# INDIA ON THE TOP

## Our Crowning Glories

*Women*

| | | |
|---|---|---|
| 1. | First Prime Minister | Mrs Indira Gandhi |
| 2. | First Chief Minister of a State | Sucheta Kriplani (Uttar Pradesh) |
| 3. | First Cabinet Minister | Vijayalakshmi Pandit |
| 4. | First Central Minister | Rajkumari Amrit Kaur |
| 5. | First Speaker of Lok Sabha | Shanno Devi |
| 6. | First Governor of a State | Sarojini Naidu |
| 7. | First President of Indian National Congress | Annie Besant |
| 8. | First Indian President of Indian National Congress | Sarojini Naidu |
| 9. | First President of UN General Assembly | Vijayalakshmi Pandit |
| 10. | First Woman on the Throne of Delhi | Razia Sultan |
| 11. | First to swim across the English Channel | Arti Saha |
| 12. | First to climb Mount Everest | Bachhendri Pal |
| 13. | First to Circumnavigate (Sail round the world) | Ujwala Rai |
| 14. | First IAS Officer | Anna George Malhotra |
| 15. | First IPS Officer | Kiran Bedi |
| 16. | First Advocate | Camelia Sorabji |
| 17. | First Judge | Anna Chandi |
| 18. | First Judge of a High Court | Anna Chandi |
| 19. | First Judge of Supreme Court | M. Fathima Beevi |
| 20. | First Chief Justice of a High Court | Leila Seth |

| | | |
|---|---|---|
| 21. | First Doctor | Kadambini Ganguli |
| 22. | First to Pass MA | Chandra Mukhi Bose |
| 23. | First Chief Engineer | P. K. Thresia |
| 25. | First to receive a Sena Medal | Bimla Devi (CRPF) |
| 26. | Youngest to Climb Mount Everest | Dicky Dolma (19) |
| 27. | First Magistrate | Omana Kunjamma |
| 28. | First to be crowned 'Miss World' | Reita Faria |
| 29. | First to be crowned 'Miss Universe' | Sushmita Sen |
| 30. | First woman astronaut from India | Kalpana Chawla |
| 31. | First woman President of India | Pratibha Patil |
| 32. | First woman Speaker of the Lok Sabha | Ms Meira Kumar |

*Men*

| | | |
|---|---|---|
| 1. | First Indian to swim across the English Channel | Mihir Sen |
| 2. | First to Climb Mount Everest | Tenzing Norgay |
| 3. | First to climb Mount Everest without Oxygen | Phu Dorjee |
| 4. | First to climb Mount Everest twice | Nwang Gombu |
| 5. | First Indian to join ICS (now IAS) | Satyendra Nath Tagore |
| 6. | First Indian to receive a Nobel Prize | Rabindra Nath Tagore |
| 7. | First Indian in Space (first astronaut) | Sqn Ldr Rakesh Sharma |
| 8. | First and the last Indian Governor-General of Free India | C. Rajagopalachari |
| 9. | First President of India | Dr Rajendra Prasad |
| 10. | First Vice-President of India | Dr S. Radhakrishnan |
| 11. | First Muslim President of India | Dr Zakir Hussain |
| 12. | First Sikh President of India | Giani Zail Singh |
| 13. | First Prime Minister | Pt Jawaharlal Nehru |
| 14. | First Speaker of Lok Sabha | G. V. Mavlankar |
| 15. | First Chief Justice of India | Justice H. L. Kania |
| 16. | First President of Indian National Congress | W. C. Bannerjee |

17. First Indian to become member of         S. P. Sinha
    Viceroy's Executive Council
18. First Indian to become President of       Dr Nagendra Singh
    International Court of Justice (UN)
19. First Emperor of Mughal Dynasty           Babur
20. First Field Marshal        S. H. F. J. Manekshaw
21. First Indian Commander-in-Chief of India   Gen. K. M. Canappa
22. First Chief of the Army
    Staff (India)        Gen. Maharaja Rajendra Singhji
23. First Chief of the Naval Staff (Indian)   Vice-Admiral R. D. Katari
24. First Chief of the Air Staff (Indian)      Subroto Mukherjee
25. First Air Marshal            Arjan Singh
26. First Indian in British Parliament       Dadabhai Nauroji
27. First Indian to Circumnavigate        Lt Col K. S. Rao
28. First Indian High Court Judge      Justice Syed Mehmood
29. First Indian to make a solo air flight       J. R. D. Tata
30. First Indian leader to visit England     Raja Rammohun Roy
31. First Indian member of House of Lords (Britain) Lord S. P. Sinha
32. First Bar-at-Law            J. M. Tagore
33. First Chairman of Rajya Sabha     Dr S. Radhakrishnan
34. First Indian Test Cricketer        K. S. Ranjitsinghji
35. First Indian to reach the South Pole      Col J. K. Bajaj
36. First Indian recipient of Victoria Cross     Khudada Khan
    (highest award before Independence)
37. First judge to face impeachment in the Lok Sabha    Justice V.
    Ramaswami
38. First Indian tennis player to win a grand slam event   Mahesh
    Bhupathi
39. First Sikh Prime Minister of India     Dr Manmohan Singh

## Trade and Industry

1. Largest exporter of tea
2. Largest manufacturer of cycles
3. Largest exporter of cut-diamonds
4. India tops the world in film production
5. Reliance Group of Companies in India has the maximum number of shareholders in the world
6. Brooke Bond Lipton India Ltd is the world's largest tea manufacturing company
7. State Bank of India has the maximum number of branches
8. Indian Railways is the world's largest employer.

## Agriculture/Natural Resources

1. Largest Producer of millet in the world
2. Largest producer of tea
3. Leads the world in irrigated area
4. Leads the world in cattle population
5. Largest producer of Cardamom (Kerala produces 60% of the total world production)
6. Largest exporter of spices in the world
7. Largest turmeric production in the world
8. Largest ginger production in the world
9. Largest sugarcane producer in the world
10. Largest grower of pulses in the world
11. Highest yield of potato —46,797 kg/ha
12. Highest rice yield— 17,862 kg/ha
13. Highest productivity of grapes (22 tonnes/ha)

## Buildings/Roads/Bridges

1. Khardungla Road in Leh-Manali sector is the world's highest road (5602 m above sea level)
2. All India Radio Leh is the world's highest radio station

3.  Mahatma Gandhi Setu between Patna and Hajipur(over Ganga river) is the world's longest river bridge.

4.  Kharagpur Railway Platform in West Bengal is the world's longest railway platform (833 m)

5.  Farakka River Barrage (Kolkata) is the world's largest river barrage

6.  Yuva Bharati Stadium, Kolkata, is the world's largest covered stadium

**Individual Achievements**

1.  Mrs Shakuntla Devi holds the world record for fastest computing— faster than a computer.

2.  Dr Rajinder Singh of Himachal Pradesh holds the world record for accurate and fastest typing.

3.  Shambhoo Govind Aubhawane holds the world record for marathon typing (123 hours).

4.  Dr M. C. Modi holds the world record for performing maximum eye operations @ 40 operations per hour.

5.  Mihir Sen of Kolkata holds the world record for long distance swimming.

6.  Capt. Durga Bannerjee is the world's first woman air pilot holding the record for logging maximum flying hours

7.  Lata Mangeshkar holds the world record for maximum number of recordings

8.  Dicky Dolma from Manali holds the world record for being the youngest climber of Mount Everest at the age of 19 years

9.  Ms Santosh Yadav holds the record for climbing Mount Everest twice (among women)

**Miscellaneous**

1.  The Ganges and Brahmaputra Delta (Sunderbans) form the world's largest delta

2.  Indira Gandhi National Open University (IGNOU) has emerged as the world's largest Open University

3. India has the world's largest reserves of iron
4. India has the largest deposits of mica in the world
5. South Point High School, Kolkata, is the world's largest school
6. World's highest post office is at Spiti Valley in HP
7. First hospital on wheels in the world—Jeevan Rekha (Life Line) Express.

## INDIA'S SUPREME PRIDE

### Structures

| | |
|---|---|
| Highest Tower (Minaret) | Qutab Minar |
| Highest Gateway | Buland Darwaza |
| Highest Dam | Bhakra Darn |
| Highest Bridge | Chambal Bridge |
| Largest Residence | Rashtrapati Bhawan |
| Largest Cinema Hall | Thangarn (Madurai) |
| Largest Museum | Indian Museum, Kolkata |
| Largest Tunnel | Jawahar Tunnel, Srinagar |
| Largest River Barrage | Farakka Barrage |
| Longest Dam | Hirakud Dam |
| Largest Auditorium | Sri Shanmukhanda Hall (Mumbai) |
| Largest Zoo | Zoological Garden, Alipur (Kolkata) |
| Largest Cave Temple | Ellora |
| Largest Gurudwara | Golden Temple, Amritsar |
| Biggest Church | The St John's Cathedral, Goa |
| Largest Mosque | Jama Masjid. Delhi |
| Largest Dome | Gol Gumbaz (Karnataka) |
| Largest Cantilever Bridge | Howrah Bridge |
| Longest River Bridge | Mahatma Gandhi Setu, Patna |
| Longest Corridor | Rameshwaram Temple Corridor |
| Longest Platform (Railway) | Kharagpur |
| Longest Road Bridge | Sone Bridge, Bihar |

| | |
|---|---|
| Longest Road | G. T. Road |
| Biggest Fort | Red Fort, Delhi |
| Tallest Light House | Prongs Reef, Mumbai |
| Tallest Statue | Gomateshwar Statue, Mysore |
| Tallest Chimney | Thermal power station, Mumbai |
| Largest man-made Lake | Govind Sagar (Bhakra) |

**Natural**

| | |
|---|---|
| Highest Mountain Peak | Narga Parvat |
| Longest River | Ganges |
| Largest Desert | Thar (Rajasthan) |
| Largest Delta | Sunderbans (West Bengal) |
| Largest Lake | Wular Lake |

**States**

| | |
|---|---|
| Largest State | Rajasthan |
| Smallest State | Goa |
| Largest Union Territory | Andaman and Nicobar Islands |
| Smallest Union Territory | Lakshadweep |
| State having Maximum Number of Cities | Uttar Pradesh |
| Most Densely Populated State | West Bengal |
| Most Populous State | Uttar Pradesh |
| State with Maximum Forest Area | Madhya Pradesh |
| State with Highest Cattle Population | Uttar Pradesh |
| State having Highest Literacy Rate | Kerala |
| Union Territory having Highest Literacy Rate | Chandigarh |
| State with Highest Mineral Output | Jharkhand |
| State having Maximum Paper Mills | Uttar Pradesh |
| State producing Maximum Sugar | Uttar Pradesh |
| State producing Maximum Wheat | Uttar Pradesh |
| State producing Maximum Rice | West Bengal |
| State producing Maximum Tea | Assam |
| State producing Maximum Cotton | Gujarat |

State producing Maximum Sugarcane                    Uttar Pradesh

Dances of India

## Bharatanatyam

- Origin from the South Indian temples
- It is a solo dance based on Natya Shastra, written by Bharat Muni in around 4000 c.
- Highly traditional dance form comprising items such as alarippu, varnam, padam, thillana, etc.

## Odissi

- A dance form having its origin in Orissa during second century BC.
- It is based on the principles of Natya Shastra.

## Chakiarkoothu

- A highly orthodox dance form believed to have been introduced to Kerala by the earlier Aryan immigrants
- It is usually performed by the members of Chakiar caste inside the temples
- It is only witnessed by the Hindus of higher castes.

## Manipuri

- A dance form, mainly popular in the north-east
- It is highly lyrical and ritualistic dance
- It however lacks dramatic facial and gestural expressions.

## Kuchipudi

- A solo dance.
- It is popular in Andhra Pradesh
- It is based on the principles of Natya Shastra
- Traditionally it was performed by men attired like women.

## Kathak

- A popular dance of North India
- It originated in temples in the form of Radha and Krishna lilas
- It moved out of the temples to Mughal courts
- Lucknow, Jaipur and Varanasi became its centres.

## Kathakali

- A popular dance from Kerala
- This is more dramatic than narrative in form.
- This one of the most scientific dance forms.
- The body gestures, hand movement and eye/eyeball movements comprise its language.

## Mohiniattam

- A solo dance form from Kerala
- It is also the heir to Devdasi dance heritage similar to Bharatanatyam, Odissi and Kuchipudi.

## OTHER POPULAR DANCES

| Dance | Regions |
|---|---|
| Bhangra | Punjab and Haryana |
| Bidesia | Bihar |
| Bihu | Assam |
| Chakri | Jammu and Kashmir |
| Chamar Gindad | Rajasthan |
| Chau | West Bengal |
| Chiraw (Bamboo dance) | Mizoram |
| Dandiya Raas | Rajasthan |
| Danda Nata | Orissa |
| Dasi Attam | Kerala |
| Garba | Gujarat |
| Ganpati Bhajan | Gujarat |
| Gangore | Rajasthan |
| Gidda | Punjab and Haryana |
| Giddha / Parhaun | Himachal Pradesh |
| Gopiki Leela | Rajasthan |
| Jata Jatin | Bihar |
| Jatra | West Bengal |
| Jhumar | Rajasthan |
| Kajir | Uttar Pradesh |

| | |
|---|---|
| Kayanga Bakayanga | Himachal Pradesh |
| Karyala | Hiinachal Pradesh |
| Kammi | Tamil Nadu |
| Khayal | Rajasthan |
| Khel Gopal | Assam |
| Kolattam | Tamil Nadu |
| Koodiyattarn | Kerala |
| Kottam | Andhra Pradesh |
| Krishnavattam | Kerala |
| Lagui | Bihar |
| Lai Haroba | Manipur |
| Lota | Madhya Pradesh |
| Luddi Dance | Himachal Pradesh |
| Munzra | Himachal Pradesh |
| Nachari | Bihar |
| Nautanki | Uttar Pradesh |
| Pandavani | Madhya Pradesh |
| Raslila | Gujarat |
| Roof | Jammu & Kashmir |
| Swang | Haryana |
| Tamasha | Maharashtra |
| Therukkoothu | Tamil Nadu |
| Tobal Chougbi | Assam |
| Veeti Bhagavatam | Andhra Pradesh |
| Wangala Laho | Meghalaya |
| Yakshagana | Karnataka |

## TRANSPORT AND COMMUNICATION

### Postal Service

| | | |
|---|---|---|
| First postal service started in | — | 1837 |
| First postal stamp issued (provincial) | — | 1852 in Karachi |
| First all-India postal stamp issued | — | 1854 |
| Establishment of Postal Department | — | 1854 |

Money Order service started in — 1880
Airmail Service — 1911 (Allahabad to Nainital)
PIN Code started — 1972
Number of post offices in India — 1,55,516 (Rural Area: 16,396; Urban Area: 1,39,120)

## Telecommunication

First telephone line — 1851, between Kolkata and Diamond Harbour
First telephone service — 1881 Kolkata
First telephone exchange — 1881 Kolkata (50 lines only)
First International telephone line — 1870 between London and Mumbai
First Automatic Telephone Exchange — Simla, 1913 — 14 (Capacity-700 lines)

## Indian Railways

Important Facts — On April 16, 1853—Mumbai to Thane
First Train in India — The Bhopal Shatabdi Express
First Electric Train — Deccan Queen, 1929

## Some milestones of Indian Railways

- The Indian Railway system is the largest in Asia
- The third in the world after US and Canada.
- It is the biggest employer in the world
- This is the largest single undertaking in the country.
- It has the second biggest electrified system in the world after Russia.

## Rail Track Routes of Indian Railways

| Rail Tracks | Distance between Rails | Route (Km) | Running Track (Km) | Total Track (Km) |
|---|---|---|---|---|
| 1. Broad Gauge | 1,676 mm | 47,749 | 67,932 | 89,771 |
| 2. Metre Gauge | 1,000 mm | 12,662 | 13,271 | 15,684 |
| 3. Narrow Gauge | 762mm/610mm | 3054 | 3057 | 3350 |
| Total | 63221 | 63,465 | 84,260 | 1,08,805 |

## Railway Zones

Indian Railways have been divided into sixteen zones:

| Zones | Date of creation | Headquarters |
|---|---|---|
| 1. Southern | April 14, 1951 | Chennai |
| 2. Central | November 5, 1955 | Mumbai VT |
| 3. Western | November 5, 1951 | Mumbai |
| 4. Northern | April 14, 1951 | New Delhi |
| 5. North-Eastern | April 14, 1952 | Gorakhpur |
| 6. Eastern | August 1, 1955 | Kolkata |
| 7. South-Eastern | August 1, 1955 | Kolkata |
| 8. North-East-Frontier | January 15, 1958 | Maligaon-Guwahati |
| 9. South-Central | October, 2, 1966 | Secundrabad |
| 10. East Central | October 1, 2002 | Hajipur |
| 11. East Coast | April 1, 2003 | Bhubaneswar |
| 12. North Central | April 1, 2003 | Allahabad |
| 13. North Western | October 1, 2002 | Jaipur |
| 14. South East Central | April 1, 2003 | Bilaspur |
| 15. South Western | April 1, 2003 | Hubli |
| 16. West Central | April 1, 2003 | Jabalpur |

## Railway Manufacturing Unit

| Name | Location | Ested in | Items manufactured |
|---|---|---|---|
| 1. Chittaranjan Locomotive works | Chittaranjan | 1950 | Locomotives |
| 2. Diesel Locomotive Works | Varanasi | 1964 | Locomotives |
| 3. Integral Coach Factory | Perambur | 1955 | Coaches |
| 4. Rail Coach Factory | Kapurthala | 1988 | Coaches, Wagons and Special Containers |
| 5. Rail Wheel Factory | Bangalore | 2004 | Wheels and Axles |

## Jeevan Rekha

- Jeevan Rekha or Life Line Express, the world's first hospital on wheels
- Flagged off from Mumbai on July 16, 1991
- The Express will cater to the medical needs of people in rural areas.

## Major Shipyards

- Cochin Shipyard Ltd (CSL)

- Hindustan Shipyard Ltd (HSL)
- Hooghly Dock and Port Engineers Ltd. (HDPEL)

**Shipping**

- Shipping plays a significant role in the transport sector of India's economy.
- India's merchant shipping Heet ranks 17th in the world-Shipping Corporation of India (SCI)
- Established on October 2, 1961
- SCI became a Public Limited entity on September 18, 1992
- Conferred 'Mini Ratna' status on February 24, 2000
- SCI in India is a pioneer for:
- (a) STS operations for crude PDL and dry cargoes
- (b) Crifogenic Operations (LNG/LPG)
- (c) Joint Ventures and other type of collaborations in Shipping
- (d) Shipping Consultancy services.

**Major Ports of India**

| Sea Port | State | Sea | Coast Side |
|---|---|---|---|
| 1. Mumbai | Maharashtra | Arabian Sea | West |
| 2. Kolkata | West Bengal | Bay of Bengal | East |
| 3. Kochi | Kerala | Arabian Sea | West |
| 4. Kandla | Gujarat | Gulf of Kutch | West |
| 5. Chennai | Tamil Nadu | Bay of Bengal (Indian Sea) | East |
| 6. Monriugao | Goa | Arabian Sea | West |
| 7. Mangalore | Karnataka | Arabian Sea | West |
| 8. Tuticorin | Tamil Nadu | Indian Ocean | East |
| 9. Visakhapatnam | Andhra Pradesh | Bay of Bengal | East |
| 10. Paradeep | Orissa | Bay of Bengal | East |
| 11. Nhaca Sheva | Murnbai | Arabian Sea | West |
| 12. Ennore | Maharashtra | Arabian Sea | East |

**NOTE:**

- India with a coastline of 7500 km has 12 major ports which are directly under Government of India's administration.
- There are about 184 minor and intermediate ports in the country.

## Air Transport

First Solo Flight: J.R.D.Tata, from Mumbai to Karachi (now in Pakistan) in 1931.

### Air transport in India:

| AIRLINE | ICAO | IATA | CALLSIGN | COMMENCED OPERATIONS |
|---------|------|------|----------|----------------------|
| Air India | AIC | AI | AIR INDIA | October 1932 |
| Air-India Express | AXB | IX | EXPRESS INDIA | April 2005 |
| Air India Regional | LLR | CD | | September 2007 |
| Blue Dart Aviation | BDA | BZ | BLUE DART | May 1994 |
| Club One Air | | | | August 2005 |
| Kingfisher Red | DKN | DN | DECCAN | August 2003 |
| Deccan Aviation | DKN | DN | DECCAN | December 1997 |
| GoAir | GOW | G8 | GOAIR | June 2004 |
| IndiGo Airlines | IGO | 6E | IFLY | August 2006 |
| Jagson Airlines | JGN | JA | JAGSON | November 1991 |
| Jet Airways | JAI | 9W | JET AIRWAYS | May 1993 |
| Jet Lite | RSH | S2 | LITEJET | April 2007 |
| Kingfisher Airlines | KFR | IT | KINGFISHER | May 2005 |
| MDLR Airlines | | 9H | MDLR | March 2007 |
| Paramount Airways | PMW | I7 | PARAWAY | October 2005 |
| SpiceJet | SEJ | SG | SPICEJET | May 2005 |

**NOTE:** Recently Indian and some private airlines have been allowed to fly across some select international destinations.

## AIRPORTS

- There are 127 airports in the country
- 87 domestic airports
- 25 civil enclaves at defence airfields provide air traffic services over the entire Indian airspace and adjoining oceanic areas.
- Airlines currently utilize only 61 of these airports.

## The Indian Airports

1. *International Airports*: The airports are available for scheduled international operations by Indian and foreign carriers.

2. *Custom Airports*:

- Custom Airports have customs and immigration facilities for limited international operations by national carriers and for foreign tourist and cargo charter flights.

- These include the airports at Bangalore, Hyderabad, Ahmedabad, Kozhikode, Kochi, Goa, Varanasi, Patna, Agra, Jaipur, Amritsar and Tiruchirapalli.

3. *Model Airports*:

- Model Airports are domestic airports which have a minimum runway length of 7500 feet and adequate terminal capacity to handle Airbus A320 type of aircraft and can cater to limited international traffic, if required.

- These include the airports at Lucknow, Bhubaneswar, Guwahati, Nagpur, Vadodara, Coimbatore, Imphal and Indore.

4. *Other Domestic Airports*: All other airports are covered in this category.

5. *Civil Enclaves in Defence Airports*: There are 28 civil enclaves in Defence airfields.

## International Airports of India

1.  Amritsar International Airport (Rajasansi Airport)          Amritsar
2.  Indira Gandhi International Airport                         New Delhi
3.  Lokpriya Gopinath Bordolio International Airport            Guwahati
4.  Sardar Vallabhbhai Patel International Airport              Ahmedabad
5.  Netaji Subhash Chandra Bose International Airport           Kolkata
6.  Chhatrapati Shivaji International Airport                   Mumbai
7.  Hyderabad Airport                                          Hyderabad
8.  Goa Airport                                          Vasco da Gama
9.  Chennai International Airport                               Chennai
    (Meenambakkam Airport)
10. Bangalore International Airport                            Bangalore

11. Cochin International Airport              Kochi
12. Trivandrum International Airport

## DEFENCE AND SECURITY

### India's Defence Set-Up

| | | |
|---|---|---|
| Supreme Commander | — | President of India |
| Administrative Control | — | Ministry of Defence |

### Army

| | | |
|---|---|---|
| Headed by | — | Chief of Army Staff |
| Headquarters | — | New Delhi |

The Chief of the Army Staff is assisted by:

1. Vice-Chief of Army Staff 2. Seven Principal Staff Officers:

(a) Deputy Chief— 2        (b) Adjutant General

(c) Master General of Ordinance (d) Quarter-Master General

(e) Military Security           (f) Engineer-in-Chief

### Major Commands

| *Command* | *Headquarters* |
|---|---|
| Western Command | Chandimandir |
| Eastern Command | Kolkata |
| Northern Command | Udhampur |
| Southern Command | Pune |
| Central Command | Lucknow |
| Training Command (added in 1991) | Mhow |
| South-Western Command (added in 2005) | Jaipur |

*South-Western Command (added in 2005)*

Each command is under a General Officer Commanding-in-Chief. There is a Nuclear and Strategic force Command.

### India's Battle Tanks

1. Vijayanta battle tank
2. T-55, T-59 and T-72, MI Ajeya purchased from erstwhile USSR
3. Arjun Indigenously built Main Battle Tank (MBT) inducted in 1993

**Air Force**

Headed by      —      Chief of Air Staff

Headquarters  —      New Delhi

The Chief of the Air Staff is assisted by:

1. Vice-Chief of Air Staff   2. Deputy Chief of Air Staff
3. Central Air Command   4. Officer incharge, Maintenance
5. Inspector General. Flight Safety and Inspection

**Major Commands**

1. Western Air Command
2. South-Western Air Command
3. Central Air Command
4. Eastern Air Command
5. Southern Air Command

**Aircraft**

- MIG-29 aircrafts were acquired from erstwhile USSR
- They have been named Baaz
- There are now five types of aircraft—MIG-29, MIG-23, MIG-27, MIG 21 and Su-30
- Su-30 is being manufactured by Hindustan Aeronautics Limited (HAL) to serve as jet training aircraft.
- India also acquired the Mirage-2000 from France
- It is renamed Vajra.
- The Defence Research & Development Organisation (DRDO) has also developed a Pilotless Target Aircraft
- This has been named Lakshya.

**Navy**

Headed by      —      Chief of Naval Staff

Headquarters  —      New Delhi

The Chief of the Naval Staff is assisted by five Principal Staff Officers:

1. Vice-Chief of Naval Staff
2. Chief of Personnel
3. Chief of Material
4. Deputy Chief of Naval Staff
5. Controller of Logistic Support

## MajorCommands

| *Command* | *Headquarter* |
|---|---|
| Western Naval Command | Mumbai |
| Eastern Naval Command | Vishakhapatnam |
| Southern Naval Command | Kochi |

Each Command is headed by a Flag Officer Commanding-in-Chief.
Fleets: (i) Western Fleet; (ii) Eastern Fleet

The Pride of India's Naval Fleet

### Aircraft Carriers

1. INS Vikrant — India's first aircraft carrier (retired from Indian Navy in 1997)
2. INS Viraat — India's largest aircraft carrier (will serve India till 2010)
3. INS Vikramaditya (ex-Soviet Admiral Gorslikov) to enter Indian Navy by 2008.

| Submarines | Warships | Missile Boors |
|---|---|---|
| INS Chakra | INS Sa itri | INS Vibhuti |
| INS Shahkul | INS Delhi | INS Prahar |
| INS Shalki | INS Mysore | INS Prashant |
| INS Sindushastra | INS Brahamputra | INS Nashak |
| | INS Ghariyal | INS Vipul |
| | INS Kulish | |
| | INS Satpura | |
| | INS Talwar | |
| | INS Tillanchang | |

## LOCATION OF DEFENCE ESTABLISHMENTS

### Army

| | |
|---|---|
| Indian Military Academy | Dehradun |
| Army Officers' Training School | Pune and Chennai |
| The Armoured Corps Centre and School | Ahmednagar |
| The College of Military Engineering | Kirkee |
| The School of Signals | Mhow |
| The School of Artillery | Deolali |

| | |
|---|---|
| The Infantry School | Mhow |
| The Army Ordnance Corps School | Jabalpur |
| The Army Education Corps and Training Centre | Pachmarhi |
| The Service Corps School | Bareilly |
| The Remount, Veterinary and Farms | Corps |
| Centre and School | Meerut |
| The School of Physical Training | Pune |
| The School of Mechanical Transport | Bangalore |
| The Corps Military Police Centre and School | Faizabad |
| The Military School of Music | Pachmarhi |
| The Electrical & Mechanical Engineering School | Trimulghery and Secundrabad |

**Navy**

| | |
|---|---|
| Indian Naval Academy | Kochi |
| INS Venduruthy Academy | Kochi |
| Naval Air Station | Kochi |
| INS Shivaji | Lonavla |
| INS Valsura | Jamnagar |
| INS Circars | Vishakhapatnam |
| INS Hamla | Mumbai |
| INS Agrani | Coimbatore |
| INS Gomantak | Mormugao |
| INS Jarawa | Port Blair |
| Naval Gunnery School | Kochi |
| Torpedo/Anti-Submarine School | Kochi |
| Navigation Direction School | Mormugao |

**Air Force**

| | |
|---|---|
| Pilot Training Establishment | Allahabad |
| Air Force Administrative College | Coimbatore |
| School of Aviation Medicine | Bangalore |
| Air Force Technical Training College | Jalahali |
| Air Force School | Jalahali |
| Air Force School | Tambaram |
| Paratrooper's Training School | Agra |

**Inter-Services Institutes**

| | |
|---|---|
| National Defence Academy | Khadakvasla |
| National Defence College | New Delhi |
| Defence Services Staff College | Wellington |
| School of Land/ Air Warfare | Secundrabad |
| School of Foreign Language | New Delhi |
| Rashtriya Indian Military College | Dehradun |
| Armed Forces Medical College | Pune |
| Himalayan Mountaineering Institute | Darjeeling |

**Defence Production Undertakings**

1. Hindustan Aeronautics Limited (HAL) at Bangalore (five factories):
   - Koraput
   - Nashik
   - Karwa
   - Kanpur
   - Lucknow
   - Barrackpur
   - Hyderabad.

2. Bharat Electronics Limited (BEL) at Bangalore, Ghaziabad, Pune, Machilipatnam, Taloja, Panchkula, Kotdwara, Hyderabad and Cheimai.

3. Bharat Earth Movers Limited (BEML) at Bangalore, Mysore and Kolar Gold Fields. Hyderabad.

4. Ship Building Factories: (i) Mazagaon Dock Limited (MDL), Mumbai; (ii) Garden Reach Shipbuilders and Engineering Ltd (GRSE), Kolkata; (iii) Goa Shipyards Limited (GSL), Goa.

# PART NINE

# INDIA'S ACHIEVEMENTS IN SCIENCE

## India's Space Programme

- India is a fast growing nation especially in field of space exploration
- The primary aim of Indian Space Programme is to establish operational space services
- It aims to do so in a self reliant manner.
- The satellite-based resources survey and management & environmental monitoring are its aim
- Also satellite-based communication for various applications
- meteorological applications
- development and operation of indigenous satellites
- launch vehicles and associated ground regiment
- To provide these space-based services it has made indigenous development of application satellites, their payload and capability to launch and operate these satellites, are integral
- ISRO activities are oriented predominantly towards the design and development of application satellites for communications, remote sensing, television broadcasting and meteorology
- To design and development of satellite launch vehicles to place these application satellites into required orbits
- To establish and operate ground station facilities.

## Indian Space Research Organisation (ISRO)\

- This Organisation was setup in 1969
- Aim was to provide the overall guidance and direction to the scientific, technical and managerial tasks
- It has different programme offices functioning for different specialised tasks:

## 1. Vikram Sarabhai Space Centre (VSSC).

- Its office is at Thiruvananthapuram
- It undertakes the responsibilities for development of rocket launch vehicles.

## 2. SHAR Centre

- Its office is at Sriharikota
- Its function is to launch complex and production centre of propellants.

## 3. ISRO Satellite Centre (SAC)

- Located at Bangalore (renamed as Bengaluru)
- Responsible for spacecraft mainframe development.

## 4. Space Application Centre (SAC)

- Located at Ahmedabad
- It works as the main centre for space application and development of spacecraft's payloads.

## 5. Auxiliary Propulsion System Unit (APSU)

- Located at Bangalore & Thiruvananthapuram
- Responsible for the development of propulsion control packages for launch vehicles and spacecrafts.

## 6. Development and Educational Communication Unit (DECU)

- Headquarters is at Ahmedabad
- Produces development and educational television programmes.

## 7. ISRO Telemetry, Tracking & Command Network (ISTRAC)

- Consists of five ground stations located at:
- Sriharikota
- Kovalpur
- Thiruvananthapuram
- Nicobar
- Ahmedabad
- Headquarters at Bangalore i.e. Bengaluru
- Its Satellite Control Centre (SCC) is located at Bangalore.

## 8. National Remote Sensing Agency (NASA)

- Located at Hyderabad
- It is a grants-in-aid autonomous registered society
- Registered under the Department of Space for utilising the potential of remote sensing, mainly in the context of natural resources survey.

## 9. Indian National Satellite Space Segment Project Office (INSAT-INSSPO)

- Responsible for implementation and operation of the space segment for INSAT
- INSAT is India's multi-purpose domestic satellite system
- The Master Control Facility (MCF) for INSAT spacecraft is located at Hassan in Karnataka.

## 10. Physical Research Laboratory (PRL)

- Located at Ahmedabad
- It is a grants-in-aid institution of the Department of Space
- Responsibility is to carry out research in space science.

# INDIA'S MISSIONS IN SPACE

## 1. Aryabhata

- India's first experimental satellite ARYABHATA
- Aim was to indigenously design and fabricate a space-worthy satellite system
- India launched its weighing 360kg, with the help of a Soviet Intercosmos rocket, on April 19, 1975 from a Soviet cosmodrome.

## 2. Bhaskara-I

- The 436 kg India's second satellite
- Launched on June 7, 1979
- Project was to collect information on India's land, water, forest and ocean resources.
- NOTE: A slightly improved version of Bhaskara-I, **Bhaskara-II** was launched on November 20, 1981.

## 3. Rohini

- The Rohini series of satellites were designed and built for Indian scientific programs

- Four satellites were launched in the Rohini series; Rohini- I A, I B, II and III.
- The Rohini-I B was also the first Indian satellite launched by an Indian rocket.

## Rohini I B:

- Launched on July 18, 1980 from Sriharikota aboard the SLV-III
- India's first successful launch
- This experimental satellite followed the failure of the Rohini-I A launched on August 10, 1979
- Re-entered the orbit on May 20, 1981.

## Rohini II

- Launched on May 31, 1981 by SLV-III from Sriharikota.

## Rohini III

- Launched on April 17, 1983 from Sriharikota aboard the SLV-III
- C carried two cameras and L-band beacon
- Satellite returned with around 5000 earth images before being de-activated on September 24, 1984
- It re-entered orbit on April 19, 1990.

## 4. APPLE (Ariane Passenger Payload Experiment)

- India's first experimental, geostationary satellite
- Weighed 673 kg
- Launched on June 19, 1981.

## 5. SLY Mission (Satellite Launch Vehicle)

- India's first satellite launch vehicle SLV-III
- Successfully launched on July 18, 1980 from Sriharikota.

- Rohini-II (RS-D2) was put into orbit on April 17, 1983 using SLV-III, and this completed the planned developmental flights of the SLV-III.

## 7. IRS Mission (Indian Remote Sensing Satellite)

- IRS-IA India's first IRS was launched on March 17, 1988
- Used for monitoring and management of natural resources.
- NOTE: IRS-1B India's second remote sensing satellite was launched on August 29, 1991 to replace IRS-IA which was nearing the end of its life.

- The IRS system has been further enhanced by IRS-IC, IRS-P3, IRS-ID and IRS-P4, the last three having been launched on December 28, 1995 by a Russian rocket and IRS-ID launched by PSLV on September 29, 1997.
- IRS-P3 was launched by the third developmental flight of PSLV-D3 on March 21, 1996.
- Another satellite IRS-P4 (OCEANSAT) was launched by PSLV on May 26, 1999.

NOTE: Two more satellites, IRS-PS and IRS-P6 for cartography and agricultural resources survey respectively are planned for launch in next three years.

## 8. ASLV Mission (Augmented Satellite Launch Vehicle)

- ASLV is designed to augment indigenous satellite launching capability
- To put 150 kg class satellite into low earth orbit.

## 9. SROSS (Stretched Rohini Satellite Series)

- SROSS-III
- 105 kg satellite
- Successfully placed in a 450 km high orbit via the launching of ASLV-D3, on May 20, 1992
- The lifespan of the satellite was only 55 days.
- NOTE: this was after failure of two ASLV launches,
- The fourth developmental flight was made on May 4, 1994
- SROSS-C4 was successfully placed into the earth orbit from Sriharikota.

## ASLV

- The forerunner of the more powerful Polar Satellite Launch Vehicle (PSLV) and the Geosynchronous Launch Vehicle (GSLV).
- The first developmental flight of the PSLV was called PSLV-Dl
- On September 20, 1993 failed
- However, according to ISRO it was a partial success which established India's capabilities in liquid propulsion system.

## 10. INSAT Mission (Indian National Satellite System)

- Established in 1983
- , INSAT is one of the largest domestic communication satellite systems in the Asia Pacific Region
- Has nine satellites in operation—INSAT-2E, INSAT-3A, INSAT-3B, INSAT 3C, 1NSAT-3E, KALPANA-1, GSAT-2, EDUSAT and INSAT-4A
- The latest, INSAT-4A, which was launched successfully from Kourou in French Guyana on December 22, 2005
- Has given further boost to 1NSAT capability, especially, for Direct-To-Home (DTH) television broadcast.
- The Indian National Satellite (INSAT) system is a joint venture of the Department of Space, Department of Telecommunications, Indian Meteorological Department, All India Radio and Doordarshan
- The overall coordination and management of INSAT system rests with the Secretary-level INSAT Coordination Committee
- Launch of INSAT-4C was unsuccessful on July 10, 2006.
- List INSAT launches:
- INSAT-IA
- launched on April 10, 1982
- Failed prematurely.

### INSAT-IB

- launched on August 30, 1983
- This was successful.

### INSAT-IC

- launched on July 22, 1988
- Became redundant in 1989.

### INSAT-I

- launched on July 17, 1990
- Successful
- Completed the mission INSAT-II Project.

## INSAT-IIA

- India's first indigenously built second generation satellite
- Launched on July 10, 1992
- Equipped with 50 per cent more capacity than the INSAT-I series.

## INSAT-IIB

- India's second indigenously built satellite
- Launched by the European Space Agency from Kourou, French Guinea on July 23, 1993.
- INSAT-IIB took place of INSAT- IB whose functioning ended following the completion of its ten-year life.
- NOTE: At present the system is served by ISRO-built satellites, INSAT-IIC, INSAT-IIE, INSAT-IIIB and INSAT-IIDT procured from ARABSAT in October 1997.
- Five Satellites, INSAT-IIIA to INSAT-IIIE were planned to be launched in 1999— 2002 time frame.
- INSAT-IIIB was launched in March 2000
- Carried 12 extended C-band transponders, 3 ku-band transponders and CxS mobile satellite service transponders
- NOTE: Press Trust of India (PTI) has implemented a system to provide its news and information services at high speed and increased volume by utilising broadcast facilities of INSAT satellite.
- With the availability of INSAT-IIC, INSAT-IIE and INSAT-IIIB business communication in ku-band and mobile satellite service are being tried out.
- INSAT has enabled a vast expansion in the television services with over 1079 TV transmitters linked through INSAT.
- The fourth developmental flight of ASLV-4 was made on May 4, 1994 and the SROSS-C4 was successfully placed into the near earth orbit from Sriharikota.
- NOTE: Today, India has realised the operational launch vehicle, PSLV, capable of launching 1200 kg IRS class of remote sensing satellite into polar sun synchronous orbit.
- The first successful developmental launch (PLSV-D2) took place on October 15, 1994 when it placed the IRS-P2 remote sensing

satellite into polar orbit.

- The second and final developmental test (PSLV-D3) was conducted on March 21, 1996 when IRS-P3 was placed into the intended polar orbit.
- The first operational flight, PSLV-C 1 placed IRS-I D in orbit. PSLV-C2 places IRS-P4 (OCEANSAT), a Korean satellite KITSAT-3 and a German satellite TUBSAT into 727 km polar sun synchronous orbit on May26, 1996.
- PSLV-C3 is planned to launch IRS-P5 and Belgium satellite PROBA
- The development of Geosynchronous Satellite Launch Vehicle (GSLV), incorporating a cryogenic stage, which will be capable of placing 2000 kg INSAT class of satellites in geosynchronous transfer orbit, is at first developmental test stage.
- PSLV C-7 carries four satellites—the 680 kg Indian Remote Sensing Satellite CARTOSAT-2, the 550 kg Space Capsule Recovery Equipment, indonesia's LAPAN-TUBSAT and Argentina's 6 kg nanosatellite, PEHUENSAT-1.

India has developed following space launch vehicles:

- SLV - Satellite Launch Vehicle
- ASLV - Augmented Satellite Launch Vehicle
- PSLV - Polar Satellite Launch Vehicle
- GSLV - Geosynchronous Satellite Launch Vehicle

India is also developing following space launch vehicles:

- GSLV Mk
- GSLV Mk-11
- GSLV Mk-HI

**NOTE:**

- The launcher and propulsion represents the ISRO's largest single development area
- The launcher program has seen a gradual evolution (from the all-solid SLV-3 to solid, liquid and cryogenic fuelled stages currently used in PSLV series (Delta class launcher) and GSLV (Ariane-class)

## Chandrayaan -I

- Chandrayaan-I is an unmanned lunar exploration mission by the Indian Space Research Organisation (ISRO), India's national space agency

- The mission includes a lunar orbiter and an impactor

- Spacecraft was launched by a modified version of the PSLV XL on 22 October 2008 from Satish Dhawan Space Centre, Sriharikota, Andhra Pradesh.

- NOTE: The remote sensing satellite weighs 1,308 kilograms (2,884 lb) (590 kilograms (1,301 lb) initial orbit mass and 504 kilograms (1,111 lb) dry mass) and carries high resolution remote sensing equipment for visible, near infrared, soft and hard X-ray frequencies

- Over a two-year period, it is intended to survey the lunar surface to produce a complete map of its chemical characteristics and 3-dimensional topography.

- The polar regions are of special interest, as they might contain ice

- The spacecraft was successfully launched on 22 October 2008 at 06:23 IST (00:52 UTC)

- After the spacecraft reaches its lunar transfer orbit, it will take 5.5 days to reach the Moon

- Estimated cost for the project is Rs. 3.86 billion (US$ 80 million)

- Two scientists considered largely responsible for the success of the project are Mylswamy Annadurai, the project director, and S. K. Shivkumar, considered the "father" of India's deep space network.

- NOTE: The mission includes five ISRO payloads and six payloads from other international space agencies including NASA, ESA, and the Bulgarian Aerospace Agency, which are being carried free of cost.

Some Personalities of Eminence

- *Rakesh Sharma* (born January 13, 1949), a Squadron Leader in the Indian Air Force, was the first Indian and 138th person to travel in space

- Retired from the Air force as Wing Commander.

- Rakesh Sharma, then squadron leader and pilot with the Indian Air Force embarked on the historic mission in 1984 as part of a joint space program between the Indian Space Research Organisation and the Soviet Intercosmos space program and spent eight days in space aboard the Salyut 7 space station.
- Launched along with two other Soviet cosmonauts aboard Soyuz T-11 on the 2 April 1984, was 35-year-old Rakesh Sharma
- During the flight, Squadron Leader Sharma conducted multi-spectral photography of northern India in anticipation of the construction of hydroelectric power stations in the Himalayas
- In a famous conversation, he was asked by the then Prime Minister Indira Gandhi how India looked from the space and he replied, *Saare Jahan Se Achcha*
- He was conferred with the honour of 'Hero of Soviet Union' upon his return from space
- The Government of India conferred its highest gallantry award(during peace time), the Ashoka Chakra on him and the other two Russian members of his mission.
- Squadron Leader Sharma and his backup, Wing Commander Ravish Malhotra, also prepared an elaborate series of zero-gravity Yoga exercises which the former had practised aboard the Salyut 7
- Retired with the rank of Wing Commander, Rakesh Sharma joined Hindustan Aeronautics Limited (HAL) as a test pilot
- He was based at the National Flight Test Center (NFTC) in Bangalore and worked on the indigenous Light Combat Aircraft program.
- Rakesh Sharma has now retired from active employment and is currently the Chairman of The Board for Automated Workflow.
- In November 2006 he took part in India's top scientists gathering organized by ISRO which gave the green light to an Indian manned space mission.

*Kalpana Chawla* (July 1, 1961- February 1, 2003)

- An Indian-born American astronaut and space shuttle mission specialist
- Was one of seven crew members who died aboard Space Shuttle Columbia during mission STS-107 when the shuttle disintegrated

upon re entry into the Earth's atmosphere on February 1, 2003.

- On February 5, 2003, India's Prime Minister announced that the meteorological series of satellites, "METSAT", will be named as "KALPANA"
- The first satellite of the series, "METSAT-1 ", launched by India on September 12, 2002 will be now known as "KALPANA- 1"
- Asteroid 51826 Kalpana Chawla is named for her.
- She died a hero and a role model for many young women
- Her hometown- Karnal
- *Sunita L. Williams* (born on September 19, 1965)
- Awarded the Navy Commendation Medal (2), Navy and Marine Corps Achievement Medal, Humanitarian Service Medal and various other service awards
- Williams was commissioned as an Ensign in the United States Navy from the United States Naval Academy in May 1987
- Was designated as a Naval Aviator in July 1989
- She has logged over 2770 flight hours in more than 30 different aircraft.
- Was selected by NASA in June 1998
- She reported for training in August 1998
- Williams has worked in Moscow with the Russian Space Agency on the Russian contribution to the International Space Station (ISS) and with the first Expedition Crew to the ISS
- After the return of Expedition-1, Williams worked within the Robotics branch on the ISS Robotic Arm and the follow on Special Purpose Dexterous Manipulator
- As a NEEMO2 crew member she lived underwater for 9 days in the Aquarius habitat
- Sunita Williams currently lives and works aboard the International Space Station
- She launched with the crew of STS-116 on December 9, 2006, docking with the station on December 11, 2006
- Williams joined Expedition- 14 in progress and served as a flight engineer during her 195 days tour of duty aboard the ISS.

India's Missile Programme

- India's Integrated Missile Development Programme (IGMDP) was started in 1982- 83
- It was started by the Defence Research and Development Organization (DRDO) under the Chairmanship of Dr A. P. J. Abdul Kalam
- Agni, Prithvi, Trishul, Akash, Nag and Astra also form part of the IGMDP,
- DRDO is working on development of specialized missiles such as Brahmos, Sagarika etc.

## 1. Agni

- The Agni missile family is envisaged to be the mainstay of the Indian missile-based strategic nuclear deterrence
- The Agni family will continue to grow its stable, providing a breadth of payload and range capabilities
- The Agni-I is a short range ballistic missile (SRBM) with a single stage engine
- The Agni-II is an intermediate range ballistic missile (IRBM) with two solid fuel stages and a Post Boost Vehicle (PBV) integrated into the missile's Re-entry Vehicle (RV).

*Variants*

- Agni-TD: Two stage, solid booster and liquid fuelled second stage. IRBM Technology Demonstrator.
- Agni-I (A-l): Single stage, solid fuel, road and rail mobile, short-range ballistic missile (SRBM).
- Agni-II (A-2): Two stage, solid fuel, road and rail mobile, Intermediate Range Ballistic Missile (IRBM).
- Agni-IIAT (A-2AT): Improved A-2 variant using more advanced and lighter material. Two stage, solid fuel, road & rail mobile IRBM.
- Agni-III: Two stage, solid fuel, submarine, road and rail mobile, IRBM/ ICBM.
- Agni-IV: Three stage, solid fuel, road and rail mobile, ICBM. (launch failed in July 2006)

## 2. Brahmos

- It is a Supersonic Cruise Missile
- Can be launched from submarine, ship, aircraft and land based Mobile Autonomous Launchers (MAL)
- The missile is launched from a Transport. Launch Canister (TLC), which also acts as storage and transportation container
- Primarily Brahmos is an anti-ship missile.

## VARIANTS

## BRAHMOS D01:

- The first flight-test of the BRAHMOS missile was conducted on 12 June 2001 at the interim Test Range, in Orissa state of India.

## BRAHMOS D02:

- The second flight test (D02) of the BRAHMOS supersonic cruise missile was conducted successfully from Interim Test Range in Orissa, on 25 April 2002.

## BRAHMOS D03:

- The BRAHMOS (D03) missile was successfully flight tested on 12 February, 2003 from one of the warships off the eastern coast.

## 3. Prithvi

- India launched the Integrated Guided Missile Development Program (IGMDP) in 1983 to concurrently develop and produce a wide range of missiles for surface-to-surface and surface-to-air roles
- Prithvi was the first missile developed as part of IGMDP.

## Variants

- SS- 1 50/Prithvi-I
- A battlefield support system for the army (range 150 km, 1000 kg payload)
- It is a single stage, dual engine, liquid fuel, road- mobile, short-range surface-to-surface missile.
- SS-250/Prithvi-II
- Dedicated to the Indian Air Force (range 250 km, 500 - 750 kg payload)

- It is a single stage, dual engine, liquid fuel, road- mobile, short-range surface-to-surface missile
- DRDO has decided to increase the payload capability of the SS-250/Prithvi-II variant to 1000 kg by using boosted liquid propellant to generate higher thrust-to- weight ratio.
- SS-350/Prithvi-III
- This is a solid fuelled version with a 350 km range and a 1000 kg payload
- It is a two stage, solid fuel, road-mobile, short-range, surface-to-surface missile.
- NOTE: Sagarika and Prithvi-III are two different acronyms for the same missile
- A related program, known as Project K 15, is in development and will enable the missile to be launched from a submerged submarine.
- Dhanush (in Sanskrit/Hindi means Bow) is a system consisting of a stabilization platform (Bow) and the Missile (Arrow)
- The system can fire either the SS-250 or the SS-350 variants
- There may likely be certain customizations in missile configuration to certify it for sea worthiness.

## 4. Akash

- It is a medium-range, theatre defence, surface-to-air missile
- The Akash's first flight occurred in 1990, with development flights up to March 1997
- Operates in conjunction with the Rajendra surveillance & engagement radar
- This system will replace the SA-6/Straight Flush in Indian service
- Also also expected to be integrated with the S-300V (SA-10 Grumble) low-to-high altitude SAM in an integrated air defence system to counter SRBM/IRBM threats along the Pakistani and Chinese borders.

## 5. Trishul

- A short range, quick reaction, all weather surface-to-air missile designed to counter a low-level attack
- Has been flight tested in the sea-skimming role and also against moving targets
- Range of 9 km

- Fitted with a 5.5 kg HE-fragmented warhead
- It's detection of target to missile launch is around 6 seconds.

## 6. Nag

- It is a third generation, all weather, top-attack, fire-and-forget anti-tank guided missile
- One of five missile systems developed by the Defence Research & Development Organization (DRDO) under the Integrated Guided Missile Development Program (IGMDP)
- Design work on the missile started in 1988 and the first tests were carried out in November 1990.

## 7. Astra

- Astra is a state-of-the-art beyond visual range air to air missile (BVRAAM) designed for a range of over 80 km in head-on mode and 20 km in tail-chase mode
- Its first test flights were conducted in May 2003. Astra can engage highly manoeuvring targets.

## INDIA'S ATOMIC RESEARCH

### First Nuclear Explosion

- The First Nuclear Explosion of India was carried out on May 18, 1974 at Pokharan in Rajasthan (Thar) desert
- Main objective was the use of atomic energy for peaceful purposes, such as, digging canals, reservoirs, oil exploration, as well as to study rock dynamics.
- This successful explosion made India the sixth nuclear nation in the world.
- **Atomic Energy Commission**
- Established in 1948, with Dr H. J. Bhabha as its first Chairman
- Its main responsibility was to look after India's atomic energy programmes.

### Department of Atomic Energy (DAE)

- Set up in August 1954 for implementation of atomic energy programmes
- It has been put under control of the Prime Minister of India

- Has five research Centers:
1. Bhabha Atomic Research Centre (BARC). Established in 1957, it is located in Trombay (Maharashta) and is India's largest atomic research centre.
2. Indira Gandhi Centre for Atomic Research. Established in 1971, it is located at Kalpakkam (Tamil Nadu).
3. Centre for Advanced Technology (CAT). Established in 1984, it is located at Indore.
4. Variable Energy Cyclotron Centre (VECC), Kolkata.
5. Atomic Minerals Directorate for Exploration Research (AMD), Hyderabad.

**Public Sector Undertakings:**
1. Nuclear Power Corporation of India Limited (NPCIL), Mumbai.
2. Uranium Corporation of India Limited (UCIL), Jaduguda (Jharkhand).
3. Indian Rare Earth Limited (IREL), Mumbai.
4. Electronic Corporation of India Limited (ECIL), Hyderabad.

**Service Organisations**

Directorate of Purchase and Stores (DPS), Mumbai.

Construction, Services and Estate management Group, Mumbai

General Services Organization (GSO), Kalpakkam (Tamil Nadu).

Atomic Energy Education Society (AEES), Mumbai.

DAE also financially supports seven autonomous national institutes:
1. Tata Institute of Fundamental Research (TIFR), Mumbai.
2. Tata memorial Centre (TMC), Mumbai
3. Saha Institute of Nuclear Physics (SINP), Kolkata
4. Institute of Physics (IOP), Bhubaneswar
5. Harish - Chandra Research Institute (HRI), Allahabad
6. Institute of Mathematical Studies (IMS), Chennai.
7. Institute of Plasma Research (IPR), Ahmedabad

The Board of Research in Nuclear Sciences (BRNS) and the National Board for Higher Mathematics (NBHM) promote research in nuclear and allied fields, and mathematics respectively.

**Nuclear Power Project**

The Nuclear Power Corporation of India Ltd. (NPCIL)
- Set up in 1987

- Responsible for the design, construction and operation of nuclear power plants in the country
- It is envisaged that by the year 2000, India's atomic power generation would be in the vicinity of 10,000 MW.

## Atomic Power Plants

| Name | Location |
|---|---|
| 1. Tarapur Atomic Power Station (TAPS) | Tarapur (Maharashtra) |
| 2. Madras Atomic Power Station (MAPS) | Kalpakkam (Tamil Nadu) |
| 3. Rajasthan Atomic Power Station (RAPS) | Rawatbhata |
| 4. Narora Atomic Power Station (NAPS) | Narora (Uttar Pradesh) |
| 5. Karkrapar Atomic Power Project (KAPP) | Karkrapar (Gujarat) |
| 6. Kudankulam Nuclear Power Project (KNPP) | Kudankulam (Tamil Nadu) |
| 7. Kaiga Power Project (KPP) | Kaiga (Karnataka) |

## Robotics and Automation

- Robotics is one of the major thrust area of R&D programme both at BARC and IGCAR.
- The Bilateral Master Slave Servo Manipulators, manufactured under collaboration between BARC and HMT-Bangalore, have undergone field trials.
- A five-degree of freedom robot for deployment in radioactive chemical laboratories, and a six-degree of freedom robot and a mobile robot have been depolyed at Trombay.
- At IGCAR, for automation and non-destructive evaluation, Mobile Scanner (MOB SCAN), a Remotely Operated Power Manipulator (ROPMAN) and a robot for capping and decapping bottles, have been developed.

## Pokhran Tests

- On May 18, 1974 India conducted a peaceful underground nuclear experiment at Pokhran in Rajasthan desert.
- India successfully conducted five nuclear tests on 11th and 13th May, 1998 at Pokhran.
- These included a thermonuclear device, a fission device and a three sub-kiloton nuclear device.
- Analysis of the measurements carried out at the time of tests confirmed the initially declared yields and other design parameters for all the devices.

# PART TEN

# QUANTITATIVE ABILITY

## MULTIPLICATION

### SQUARE OF A NUMBER ENDING WITH 5

**Example:** 25 × 25 is equal to…

**Solution:** The digit other than 5 is 2 and the digit next to 2 is 3.

The product of 2 and 3 is 6. Annex 25 after the product. Hence the required answer is 625.

### PRODUCT OF NUMBERS ENDING WITH 5 AND DIFFERENCE 10

**Example:** 25 × 35 is equal to…

**Solution:** The digits other than 5 in the two numbers are 2 and 3. The greater of the two numbers is 3. Square the greater number and substract 1 and annex 75 on the right side. The square of 3 is 9 and 1 less than 9 is 8 and after annexing 75 the required answer is 875.

### MULTIPLICATION BY NUMBERS NEARING THOUSANDS

**Example:** 7832 × 999 is equal to…

**Solution:** 999 times means 1 time less than a thousand times. A thousand times of a number can be obtained by annexing three zeroes on the right hand side from the thousand times of the number if the number itself is subtracted, 999 times of the number can be obtained.

In the above example a thousand times of the number is:

$$\begin{array}{r} 7832000 \\ -\ 7832 \\ \hline 7824168 \end{array}$$

Hence the answer is 7824168.

## MULTIPLICATION BY 5, 25, 125, 625 ETC

To multiply by 5, annex a zero to the right of the number and divide by 2. Annexing a zero means the number becomes 10 times and half of 10 times is 5 times. Similarly to multiply by 25, annex two zeroes to the number and divide by 4 ($\therefore$ 100 $\div$ 4 = 25). To multiply by 125, annex three zeroes and divide by 16.

**Example:** 6397 $\times$ 5 is equal to ...

**Solution:** As explained above, a zero should be annexed to the number 6397 and then divide by 2.

Hence the answer is $= \dfrac{63970}{2} = 31985$

## PERCENTAGE

Per cent means for every hundred. When we say a man made a profit of 20 percent, we mean to say that he gained Rs. 20 for every hundred rupees he invested in business, i.e. $\dfrac{20}{100}$ for each rupee and so on.

Percentage therefore is a fraction, the denominator of which is 100.

Abbreviation of per cent is P.C. and it is generally denoted by the symbol %.

Many questions on percentage can be handled more easily by converting the percentage into a fraction

5% means $\dfrac{1}{20}$ th                    10% means $\dfrac{1}{10}$ th

$20\%$ means $\frac{1}{5}$ th                    $5\%$ means $\frac{1}{20}$ th

$30\%$ means $\frac{3}{10}$ th                  $40\%$ means $\frac{2}{5}$ th

$60\%$ means $\frac{3}{5}$ th                   $70\%$ means $\frac{7}{10}$ th

$80\%$ means $\frac{4}{5}$ th                   $90\%$ means $\frac{9}{10}$ th

$6\frac{1}{4}\%$ means $\frac{1}{16}$ th        $12\frac{1}{2}\%$ means $\frac{1}{8}$ th

$37\frac{1}{2}\%$ means $\frac{3}{8}$ th        $50\%$ means $\frac{1}{2}$ nd

$6\frac{1}{2}\%$ means $\frac{5}{8}$ th

And so on...

## SQUARE ROOT

Square of 4 means $4 \times 4$ i.e. 16. Thus the square root of 16 is 4. Similarly square of 5 is 25 and thus the square root of 25 is 5.

The square root of a decimal fraction should have as many places of decimal as the number of pairs in the decimal fraction i.e. the number of decimal laces in the answer should be half of the number of decimal places in the question.

Thus it is concluded that if the number of decimal places of the fraction is even, the number of decimal places in the answer should be half of the number of decimal places in the question.

**Example:** $\sqrt{.00016}$ is equal to...

**Solution:** There are four places of decimal in the number hence the square root of the fraction should have half of four i.e. two places of decimal. The square root of 16 is 4 and to have two places of decimal the answer should be .04.

## RATIO AND PROPORTION

In ratio we compare two quantities of the same kind and consider what multiple, part or parts one is of the other. In comparison 8 with 4 observe that it is 2 times 4. This comparison can be represented as

$8 \div 4$ or $\dfrac{8}{4}$ .

Hence ratio is that relation between two numbers which is expressed by the fraction, the numerator of which is the measure of the quantity and denominator irs the measure of the second quantity.

The expression $\dfrac{8}{4}$ is otherwise read as the ratio of 8 to 4 and is usually expressed by the notation 8 : 4.

The two numbers which form the ratio are called terms. The first number is called the antecedent and the second number the consequent. When both the terms of a ration are prime to each other, the ratio is called imple ration.

If terms of a ratio be multiplied or divided by the same quantity, the value of the ratio remains unaltered.

Study the following notation and try to understand it.

$$x : y :: a : b$$

The above notation means that the ratio between x and y is the same as the ratio between a and b. The above notation can also be expresses as:

$$\frac{x}{y} = \frac{a}{b}$$

In the notation $x : y :: a : b$, x and b are termed as extremes whereas y and a are termed as means. The basic rule is that the product of the extremes is equal to the product of the means.

If $x : y :: a : b$

Then $x \times b = y \times a$

Or   If $\dfrac{x}{y} = \dfrac{a}{b}$

Then $x \times b = y \times a$

# HIGHEST COMMON FACTOR AND LEAST COMMON MULTIPLE

## GREATEST COMMON MEASURE (G.C.M) OR HIGHEST COMMON FACTOR (H.C.F)

Consider the two numbers 36 and 54.

(i)   $36 = 2 \times 2 \times 3 \times 3$

∴   Possible factor of 36 are 2, 3, 4, 6, 9, 12 and 18.

(ii)   $54 = 2 \times 3 \times 3 \times 3$

∴   Possible factors of 54 are 2, 3, 6, 9, 18 and 27.

Of these 2, 3, 6, 9 and 18 are the factors common to both and are, therefore, called common factors of 36 and 54. Of all these common factors 18 is the highest and is, therefore, the highest common factor (H.C.F) or the greatest common measure (G.C.M) of 36 and 54.

Hence the highest common factor of two or more numbers is the greatest number that can divide them exactly.

## LEAST COMMON MULTIPLE (L.C.M.)

The least common multiple of two or more numbers is the least number which is exactly divisible by them all:

(i)   Consider the two numbers 6 and 8.

We easily comprehend that 24, 48, 72 or any multiple of 24 can be exactly divided by both 6 and 8. But 24 is the least of them all; and we do not find any number smaller than 24, which can be exactly divisible by 6 and 8 and hence 24 is the Least Common Multiple (L.C.M.) of 6 and 8.

(ii) Similarly, 30, 60, 90 .........can be exactly divided by (or are multiple of) 6, 10 and 15. But 30 is the least.

∴   30 is the L.C.M. of 6, 10 and 15.